DEAR AMERICA

KARL HESS

DEAR AMERICA

WILLIAM MORROW & COMPANY, INC., NEW YORK   1975

Library of Congress Cataloging in Publication Data

Hess, Karl (date)
  Dear America.

  1. Decentralization in government—United States.
2. Community power. 3. Right and left (Political
science) 4. Hess, Karl (date) I. Title.
JS341.H47   320.9′73′092   74-28286
ISBN 0-688-02898-5

Book design by Helen Roberts

TO MY NEIGHBORS

DEAR AMERICA

1

RIGHT AND LEFT

I served capitalism very faithfully for very many years. And now, like most servants, I know a good deal about it in both its dress clothes and work clothes, and even without any clothes at all.

I have studied socialism closely for as many years, critically at first and then quite sympathetically.

What I have learned about corporate capitalism, roughly, is that it is an act of theft, by and large, through which a very few live very high off the work, invention, and creativity of very many others. It is the Grand Larceny of our particular time in history, the Grand Larceny in which a future of freedom which could have followed the collapse of feudalism was stolen from under our noses by a new bunch of bosses doing the same old things.

What I have learned about state socialism, roughly, is that it is an act of betrayal through which aspirations for a humane and cooperative way of living together and in peace are sacrificed to or stolen by bureaucrats who have contrived a new synthesis of capitalism's obsessive bookkeeping with feudalism's top-down, absolute authority. It seems the worst of all possible worlds, a mirror image of corporate capitalism, reflecting the same ultimate purpose: to produce a social order in which docile, carefully taught people follow, without whimper or shout, the commands of a ruling class.

Through it all I have been a patient part of the American two-party system. A conscientious payer of taxes. A volunteer in wartime. A persistent Dreamer of the American Dream. A persistent pathfinder along the American Way. A devoted employee. A loyal worker. A player on the team. A player of the game. A pillar of the church. A maker of substantial salaries. A hunter of witches. And Reds. A dweller in the better neighborhoods. A dresser in the right styles. A laugher at the right jokes. A prompt payer of bills and conscientious seeker of new debt into which, with proper capitalist zeal, I could plunge for God, the Rockefellers, and, great glory almighty, that all-American, pasteurized, deodorized, sanitized, improved, sanctified, holiest of all ghosts: PROGRESS.

I don't believe in those things now.

It's not because of some book I read or some speech I heard, or some fad that passed with a lilting song and a snappy step. I don't believe in those things because they are bad for your health, bad for your head, and because they are tunes played by someone else's piper, for someone else's payment. They are things we do because we are taught to or told to. They simply do not make sense, common sense for common people. They make sense for a very few people. They make dollars and cents for those people. Billions of dollars. They make those billions for those people who do the least, not the most, work; who add the least, not the most, to the common store of knowledge, beauty, science, and invention.

There are almost no superrich creative people. The superrich are served by creative people, made richer by them; their histories are written by them, their myths are fashioned by them. I did some of that work. I never will again. I feel free now from service to the superrich and to the praise-shouting, order-taking politicians who do their bidding in a supposedly democratic government which, almost from its outset, has served the long-term interests of the rich against the interests of the people who do the work.

In turning from the religion of capitalism, it might be tempting to seek a new Rome, to trade Wall Street for Moscow —but no. I may have lost my faith in capitalism. I know I have lost my faith in capitalism. But I haven't lost my mind. I would not trade service to the cashiers for service to the commissars. A servant is a servant still, even if the masters are swapped.

No. I have found something a good deal better, I think, than faith now. I have found hard and good work, good and fast friends, the pleasures of neighborhood life, the treasures of cooperative living, and the measure of human meaning by the facts of human action and human love.

In the process, I feel fine. But there are some other considerations—publicly at any rate. I am a tax resister.

I refuse to support a predatory government which wastes the work of the citizens on welfare programs which debase, harass, and regiment the poor into a special political constituency—without even scratching the surface of a solution to poverty, a solution which, common sense tells us, is to be found in work.

Conservatives often say that they *want* welfare recipients to work. But what they want is merely menial service, people willing to be the servants of the well-to-do. They do not want work to mean the sort of independence that will be discussed throughout this book: the work of self-managing people. Liberals, on the other hand, don't want welfare recipients to work. They want them to be clients of their liberal programs, programs which depend upon retaining a constituency of dependent poor rather than upon encouraging independent and therefore quite probably anti-liberal, self-managing workers. State socialists want the poor mainly as cannon fodder for their supposedly revolutionary movements; movements which are more in the nature of palace coups than real revolutions, deposing one ruler, installing another.

I refuse to support a government which wastes the work and lives of citizens in war programs which do not defend the citizens, which make some rich and others dead, which reflect dreams of empire rather than the good works of democratic life.

If everyone took that attitude, I have been told, democracy would fall.

The rulers say that. The rich men say that. The women in the social clubs say that. The professors say that. The labor bosses say that. The factory bosses say that. The professional patriots say that.

Common sense says something else. If everyone took the attitude of refusing to support government which offends them, which transgresses their own good sense and morality, we *would have* democratic life in the fullest, most participatory sense. Government which could not find the loyal support of people would fall. Government which could find the support of only some people would have to move with modified respect to those who would not support it. And everyone would be absolutely responsible themselves for what government did not do and did do. Perhaps it is true that government of the absolutist, winner-take-all kind we have today would fall. But in its place would rise a system of governance rooted firmly and absolutely in the will of the people and not in the whims of their representatives.

I have heard so-called conservatives preach mightily for government which is absolutely subservient to the people, to the citizens, government which is merely a reflection of actions which people want to take in a concerted fashion. Then I have heard those selfsame conservatives denounce as lawbreakers any who defy the will of the state, the rules of the government. They cry for self-reliance and conscience on the one hand, they scream for its abandonment on the other. There can be no rationalization of that in the weary cry of permitting the will of the majority to rule supreme. That was the German plea. It was the law of the land that sent the millions to their barbarous, incinerated deaths. Well, most people, again, in common sense, have come to know that the so-called will of the majority must never be an excuse for a lapse of conscience by any person. Conservatives who betray their conscience when the majority speaks are the truest collectivists, believing only in an arithmetical mass majority, a set of numbers that rules their lives, sets the rules, overwhelms their conscience.

Collectivists of the supposedly opposite stripe—liberals and state socialists—say the same thing. They are conservative collectivists too. But they are more frank. They know that the will of the majority is filtered always through the whims of the rulers. And they accept, they applaud, they wheel into line behind the pronouncement of ruling elites, like well-drilled soldiers they hup-two-three, proud that ideology thinks for them, glorying in the figures they follow, wallowing in self-abasement, eager to be the most obedient, ravenous to chew to pieces the deviant or the questioner.

The conservatives call it law and order; liberals and the state socialists call it democratic centralism. Conservatives refer to traditions and mean the privileges which affect them. The liberals and state socialists refer to the people and mean the leaders.

There are other so-called conservatives and other socialists who really do believe in liberty and in the ability of people to manage their own lives. There is a common theme in what they say and what they do.

I have worked with both the liberty-loving conservatives and the life-loving socialists and the differences between them have seemed smaller and smaller over the years. Common sense says that. Not the rulebooks.

And so I resist. I resist this capitalist nation-state and I resist the one that the liberals and state socialists want to replace it with.

One result of resistance is that I cannot own property (aside from clothes and tools) and I do not. It is a lesson which, although it seemed harsh for a time, is in fact wonderfully useful and gently strengthening. With property removed as a major consideration, at least the sort of property for which we are taught to strive, for which we are prepared to kill others or ourselves—with that sort of property legally denied me, I have attended more carefully than ever to other sorts of things: to friendships and to skills, to self-reliance and to active performance rather than obsessive accumulation.

The thugs and bullies of the Internal Revenue Service, as properly befits their disposition, consider the tax rebels, the tax resisters, the worst of all criminals. They are prepared to wheel and deal, of course, with any gangster or any millionaire, any ordinary felon who wants to make a deal. Presidents who stray, politicians who connive, businessmen who chisel, can all, without exception, make deals, settle for so much on the dollar, hire great attorneys, even have the laws rewritten. Ordinary people cannot. The marauders of the Internal Revenue Service, with strict quotas for how much they have to squeeze from taxpayers, descend on ordinary working people like locusts and plague them even unto death. But they treat the rich with kid gloves and they deal, deal, deal. But tax resisters! That is something else. Millions are spent to recover the piddling war tax on phone bills which so many war opponents have refused to pay. And with full-fledged resisters, the "revenooers" have virtual seizures of fury, go blind with rage, and sow the whirlwind. In my case, in the half-dozen years I have resisted them, they have applied a 100 percent lien to everything they can get their hands on. I cannot own a car, have a bank account, receive a salary.

But the lesson learned is better than the angers aroused. I am a competent commercial welder. I can work for people on a barter basis, taking an exchange for my work on the spot. I tell the "revenooers" how much of that I do, for I understand that not to tell them would give them a grand chance to clap me in jail for an ordinary crime. I know, of course, that they must be planning to try to get me there anyway, but if they do it will be simply because of principled resistance to their power and to the corporate system it represents.

This is not an ordinary crime. It is a resistance, precisely the same sort of resistance that some of my ancestors mounted against the power of the British Crown and the corporate colonizers who were treating Americans as nothing more than work animals, to be flogged for all they were worth and bled for all they could stand. So are the citizens generally today regarded by the spenders and the wheelers and the dealers in Washington and, in particular, by their most bullying agents, the tax collectors. They need to be resisted. And they need to know that in that resistance is the same spirit that overthrew the bureaucrats once before. Something needs to haunt those people. Certainly their consciences never haunt them. Well enough. Let the traditions of this country, this country of re-sisters and rebels, haunt them. I hope the same spirit eventually will do more than haunt them.

And there is the other spirit that resistance engenders, that they cannot jail and cannot stifle; a spirit of work that arises from your own mind and muscles, and not from kowtowing to a boss. It is the good feeling of knowing that you can do some-thing which in the ordinary world, among your ordinary neigh-bors, is regarded as useful. And it is, further, the feeling that comes when human association and the wonders of everyday life replace the rat-race maneuverings of corporate life and the sideshow salesmanship of corporate or state political life. That too is what this book is about.

An opposite feeling, one of subtle fear, seemed pervasive in the other sort of life, the standard upward-mobile life which

I have shared richly with so many Americans, with the perhaps 20 percent of Americans for whom "the system" works wonderfully well.

With those for whom the system does work I also shared a grand delusion: that I was part of the ruling class, the elite that got things done, the bright-eyed and bushy-tailed race of doers. It is true that people like me did and do a lot. But we are no rulers—not even of our lives. Beneath the level of the great owners of wealth and the great owners of political power, we are all peasants or proletarians in this most lopsided of class societies. I would have hated the very thought when I was riding high in the system, but it seems absolutely clear to me today that the working class in America, as distinct from the ruling class, starts right up at the level of the supposedly privileged professionals—the engineers, scientists, entertainers, managers—and that they have more in common with toolmakers and grocery clerks and farm workers than they do with the directors of big banks, the Joint Chiefs of Staff, the leaders of the two parties, and the owners of great corporate conglomerates.

So long as you live mainly from work, and not mainly from the ownership of property, you share the problems of most workers. Even for those who eke out an existence by owning some small property, the petty landlords and so forth, there is a share in a concern common to all working people: that the interests of the great owners and the great politicians are to accumulate property and power, not to share it. The wholesale extinction of small businesses by large corporations is an example. And the tendency of some small businessmen to identify themselves with the interests of the great corporate owners, and even against the interests of, say, unionized workers, is a tragedy similar in nature to the false identification of any other working American with the fate, future, or finances of the supercapitalists. Our only link is to be a part of the machine that serves their purposes overall and our purposes only co-incidentally, sometimes. One outstanding example: The absorption of the transportation market by the three great auto-makers is sometimes said to serve us all, giving us wheels. Actually, the monopoly of transportation has served first of all to give such great owning families as the Fords preeminent personal fortunes. Secondarily it has given us the largest consumer debt in the world as transportation is turned into fashion, with new cars being built with planned obsolescence, with repairability declining every model year, and so forth. We do get wheels, but at an incredible price. (Before the big three grabbed just about everything in sight, it might be recalled, automobiles were a highly localized product, incredibly long lived, and available in a staggering array, with most large towns having at least one carmaker right in the city limits. Of course, such independent carmakers might not be able to build millions of cars a year, but then who would need those millions of cars if the ones we already had would last and last?)

While serving as a paid hand for major capitalist interests, I used to cling to the notion that the bigness of the automakers was all good, all sacred, all American. And not once did I bother to think of how that directly contradicted my other notions, as a conservative, about the virtues of controlling your own life, of being self-reliant, and of locating political and economic power close to home and not in remote areas.

Most Americans today, quite clearly, are considered, and consider themselves to be, conservative. It has taken several generations of so-called liberal failure to convince the majority of Americans that conservative is not a dirty word. But they are now convinced. Ironically, they are convinced of it at exactly the time when those qualities of life which they value, and call conservative, are being systematically destroyed by the politicians who are supposed to represent this conservative majority, and when those same values, almost exactly, are being represented most strenuously—even stridently—by the people the conservatives are supposed most to hate: the far left. At least it may be comforting for conservatives to know that this far left has nothing whatsoever to do with liberalism, in the modern American sense. Maybe, as some have said, this New Left is *so* far left that it has swung all around the political circle and ended up just where the right used to be or where some like to think it still is.

My own notion of politics is that it follows a straight line rather than a circle. The straight line stretches from the far right where (historically) we find monarchy, absolute dictatorships, and other forms of absolutely authoritarian rule. On the far right, law and order means the law of the ruler and the order that serves the interest of that ruler, usually the orderliness of drone workers, submissive students, elders either totally cowed into loyalty or totally indoctrinated and trained into that loyalty. Both Joseph Stalin and Adolf Hitler operated right-wing regimes, politically, despite the trappings of socialism with which both adorned their regimes. Huey Long, when governor-boss of Louisiana, was moving toward a truly right-wing regime, also adorned with many trappings of socialism (particularly public works and welfare) but held together not by social benefits but by a strong police force and a steady flow of money to subsidize and befriend businessmen.

An American President could be said to move toward the right to the extent that he tended to make absolutely unilateral political decisions, with no reference to Congress, for instance, or to the people generally, and when the legitimacy of the regime was supported or made real more by sheer force, say of police power, than by voluntary allegiance from the people generally. Such a regime, also, would be likely to suppress or to swallow up potentially competing centers of power such as trade unions. Major financial interests, however, if Adolf Hitler's relations with industry, for example, can be considered instructive, would be bought off, rather than fought off, with fat contracts and a continuing opportunity to enrich their owners. Joseph Stalin, of course, had no problem with anything such as independent trade unions or business, since both had been killed off earlier.

The *overall* characteristic of a right-wing regime, no matter the details of difference between this one and that one, is that it reflects the concentration of power in the fewest practical hands.

Power, concentrated in few hands, is the dominant historic characteristic of what most people, in most times, have considered the political and economic right wing.

The far left, as far as you can get away from the right, would logically represent the opposite tendency and, in fact, has done just that throughout history. The left has been the side of politics and economics that opposes the concentration of power and wealth and, instead, advocates and works toward the distribution of power into the maximum number of hands.

Just as the scale along this line would show gradations of the right, so would it show gradations of the left.

Before getting to a far-right monarchy or dictatorship, there are many intermediate right-wing positions. Some are called conservative.

Somewhere along the line, for instance, a certain concentration of power, particularly economic power, would be acceptable in the name of tradition. The children of the rich, characteristically, are accorded very special places in the regimes of the right, or of conservatives. Also, there is great deference to stability and a preference for it rather than change—all other things being equal. Caution might be the watchword toward the center of this right-wing scale, simply a go-slow attitude. That is, admittedly, a long way from the far right and dictatorship, but it is a way that can and should be measured on a straight line. The natural preference for law and order that seems such a worthwhile and innocent conservative preference is from a political tradition that came to us from kings and emperors, not from ancient democracy.

This hardly means that every conservative, if pressed, will go farther and farther right until embracing absolute dictatorship or monarchy. Far from it. It does mean to suggest only that the ghosts of royal power whisper in the conservative tradition.

The left shows similar gradations. The farthest left you can go, historically at any rate, is anarchism—the total opposition to *any* institutionalized power, a state of completely voluntary social organization in which people would establish their ways of life in small, consenting groups, and cooperate with others as they see fit.

The attitude on that farthest left toward law and order was summed up by an early French anarchist, Proudhon, who said that "order is the daughter of and not the mother of liberty." Let people be absolutely free, says this farthest of the far, far left (the left that Communism regularly denounces as *too* left; Lenin called it "infantile left"). If they are free they will be decent, but they never can be decent until they are free. Concentrated power, bureaucracy, et cetera, will doom that decency. A bit further along the left line there might be some agreement or at least sympathy with this left libertarianism but, it would be said, there are practical and immediate reasons for putting off that sort of liberty. People just aren't quite ready for it. Roughly, that's the position of the Communist Party today— except in China, where there still seems to be insistence that people *are* ready for it, no matter how many bureaucratic ambitions have to suffer in the process. But even there it is obvious that some Chinese do constitute themselves as a ruling class, and so there is the rather divided picture of a country which seems to be working on being very far to the left out in the countryside while still being much more to the right in the seats of power.

It is this prevalence of contradictions in all nations, as a matter of fact, that makes it absolutely impossible to attach any hard and fast labels to *any* political situation in the entire world. All are mixed bags. The important factor, for now at least, might be more to take special note of the direction in which the people are moving, and whether the people are moving in one direction while the rulers move in another.

At any rate, at some point on the spectrum there is the great modern American liberal position. Through a series of unfortunate but certainly understandable distortions of political terminology, the liberal position has come to be known as a left-wing position. Actually, it lies right alongside the conservative tradition, down toward the middle of the line, but decidedly, I think, to the right of its center. Liberals believe in concentrated power—in the hands of liberals, the supposedly educated and genteel elite. They believe in concentrating that power as heavily and effectively as possible. They believe in great size of enterprise, whether corporate or political, and have a great and profound disdain for the homely and the local. They think nationally but they also think globally and now even intergalactically. Actually, because they believe in far more authoritarian rule than a lot of conservatives, it probably would be best to say that liberals lie next to but actually to the *right* of many conservatives.

The values of the conservatism in which I was most deeply involved for most of my life, but which today are values expressed almost exclusively on the so-called New Left—or, better, let us say the values to be found *in action* on the New Left—begin with a profound sense of the importance of individual people, as opposed to the importance of leaders and the insignificance of almost everyone else.

Common sense, not great leaders, could save our lives, our sanity, and our country.

Great leaders, say the great leaders, lead us to greatness. It is their ambition that they, and we, shall be Number One. The Winners. Give leaders power and they will give us direction and our destiny. And that is exactly what we have done. The leaders have power. We are said to be Number One. We are the Winners. We have gobbled the earth and gulped even the moon. And if that is enough, no more need be said. Nor should it be. Nor would it be. But other things do seem to need saying. Common sense keeps whispering heresy to us. Common sense sees that some emperors are, indeed, naked. Common sense wonders why, if we are winners, there is a sense of loss; loss of control over our lives, loss of open dealing between neighbors, loss of a sense that the ground we are on is really stable and not likely to be quicksand.

And the great leaders continue to say "follow." In circles. Through places we have been before.

Common sense might say "wait." Let's not follow quite so soon or quite so unquestioningly. Common sense might ask some questions about things we hear.

We hear that the reason we cannot control our own lives is that "society" is just too big and too complex for that. It must be "run." *We* can't do it. That's why we are given identifying numbers by the government—numbers which have more profound meaning to our freedom and future than the names given by our parents. The state actually is our parent; society is too big and too complex; we, the children of the state, cannot handle it.

Common sense could view it this way: If, indeed, society is too big and too complex for people generally to control it, or to allow us even a name rather than a number, then maybe it *is* too big and too complex.

The commonsense alternative would be: Make it smaller. Make it less complex. Return to people, in the process, the practical possibility of controlling their own lives, being responsible citizens rather than responsive numbers. Make it simpler, either actually, or, by another commonsense alternative, make it more understandable to more people. Complexity, common sense tells us, is often a result of lack of information which makes a situation appear complex; a lack of information which permits others, with information, to convince us that it is too complex for us; a lack of information which makes arrangements confusing and thus easily called complex.

Today, the idea of elected leadership is to static, oppressive, and inexorably centralizing coercive power just what the divine right of kings concept was to the hereditary bums of old, the bosses who got to their thrones not by hoaxes and handshakes but by the far less tiring route of being born.

To examine this concept of leadership usefully, examine a leader such as Richard M. Nixon, the serious little boy from a small town in California who grew up to save us from being a pitiful giant. Since this same person was elected by so many of us, his role in relation to us, personally, must be scanned. Recall for instance that his wife became the First Lady. If you are a woman, that puts you in your place with one of the most egregious examples of male chauvinism imaginable. But, woman or man, the position of Richard M. Nixon as "the nation's leader" should mean that he actually must be better than you, more competent, more *something*—or else why was he the leader and you the follower? Forget Watergate. The Nixon of the crimes was the same Nixon of the "national mandate."

Therefore it seems logically to follow that Richard Nixon, or Gerald Ford, the leader, must have had some ability which you could not match, some wisdom which you could not possess. He led, therefore he was, let's face it, your boss and your better.

There may have been some arcadian time when the dewy-eyed could cop out of this critique by saying, "But he was not better, he was simply the one among equals we chose to administer affairs of state."

Bunk.

American political leaders have, actually, no peers except among the ranks of the great money owners or money managers. The two groups are so often interchangeable, or one controlled by the other, that the statement can stand: American leaders have no peers, they are leaders indeed. Would a merely elected *equal* have been treated as, say, Teddy Kennedy was treated after the incident at the bridge? Would the fortunes of merely elected *equals* rise, zooming into the millions, while they "served" the people? Would merely elected *equals* go before the people and say that "a vote for ME is all that stands between you and disaster?" No. These things are characteristics not of merely elected equals but of bona fide leaders, special people playing special roles, not elected equals but elected elites.

You can also cop out of this by claiming that you are one of the actual numerical majority of Americans who did not vote for Richard Nixon to be your leader. But then you must in all fairness apply our little test probe of leadership to George Wallace, Hubert Humphrey, George McGovern, or whomever you did vote for. The results figure to be the same.

Now consider *whichever* President you want.

Could he do *your* job, whatever it is, better than you?

Remember, he may never have been gainfully employed in the usual sense, or most honorable sense, of doing work for people and receiving a reward in return. His "jobs" might have involved not productive or creative work but political advantage and political manipulation.

No, most leaders produce no poems, no product, no inventions, no pleasuring performance, no song, no solace, no crop, no cure. They certainly save no lives, since war is their grandest exercise.

This is not to say, of course, that they do nothing. They rise to power.

Could a leader make decisions in regard to your personal

life, or family life, better than you? And should a leader do that? Excepting cases under medical advice, you, the person, probably are closer to the data concerning your life than any leader, right?

Well, then. Can the leader make better decisions than you and your neighbors in regard to your neighborhood? Is the leader, along with being Commander in Chief, also Neighbor in Chief? Of course not. In all likelihood your neighborhood has never even wondered what the leader would do when it came time to make a neighborhood decision. The leader is not your neighbor nor is the leader competent to make decisions for your neighborhood. The quality of leadership, then, does not include leading your neighborhood. It must be that the elusive quality of leadership lies elsewhere. But where?

You do not need or probably want a leader to tell you what meals to plan, what hobbies to pursue, what outlook on life to maintain, how to relate to your friends, what books to read, what dreams to dream. You certainly don't feel that the leader could cure your common cold or set a broken bone. Would you want the leader to lead the handling of your personal finances?

Why *is* a leader needed?

The answer does not lie close to home. The leader is not needed to live your life, or run it. The leader is not needed to set your sights. The leader is not needed to operate your job. The leader is not needed to teach you anything. The leader is not needed to lead your neighborhood. A city is composed of these neighborhoods. If people in their neighborhoods can lead their own lives then the composite of that skill adds up to running the city—again, no need for a leader. The nation, in turn, is but an amalgam of those neighborhoods, formed into those cities, and so forth. If they can handle their affairs—and they must, just to survive—then they can interconnect and communicate with other communities also, effectively joining the energies of the neighbors there, and so on, up and up a ladder of cooperation that nowhere seems to require One Special Leader to claim credit for it all, much less actually run it.

The practical purpose of the kind of leadership represented by any great, global-type leader lies in relating, lo and behold, to other Great Leaders. The curious mind will immediately detect a soft spot in that practicality. If there were no other Great Leaders, no other Heads of State—none of whom actually *do* anything for *their* citizenry (any more than Richard Nixon did for his)—then there would be no practical purpose for *any* such function.

In this discussion, however, we are not dealing with anything as obvious as the outmoded nature of the nation-state. We are dealing with the roots of the problem and the roots are entwined in the leadership concept, not in any particular national or specific example of it.

Richard Nixon, to take the most soul-trying example, may be counted a leader who got to be a leader not because of his ability or efficacy in "leading," but because of his efficiency in playing the political game, a game in which success is measured solely by a plebiscite—with major personalities in all American political parties admitting the fact that in the game of politics, instances of good works must be accounted not to any special greatness of soul, or great leadership, but, in the coldest of terms, to how many votes they produce. And getting one vote more than the opponent gets is quite enough. Or, in short, no matter how badly 49 percent of the people, or possibly even a majority—very possibly always a majority of all citizens, ignoring the artificial characteristic of actually going to the polls —no matter how badly great numbers of persons are treated, if a sufficient number of other persons vote for the candidate he is counted a success. There is absolutely no other measure of leadership in American politics. Losers are not leaders and that is all there is to it. American political leadership consists in leading people toward the "proper" ballot, and where is the political expert who has not, in confidential memos or public confessions, confirmed this? They all do.

Is *political* leadership, then, the leadership problem and concept with which we must be concerned? No. It is leadership itself, excepting only that leadership which can be called exemplary or technical. Exemplary leaders inspire men and women forward because they *do* inspiring things. Technical leaders take a role in affairs dealing with material objects because they *know* something special or can *do* something special in the physical world.

Other kinds of leaders may be called administrative leaders. Political leaders are in that category. Those leaders do not manipulate technologies. They do not manipulate ideas and deeds which simply inspire other men and women. They manipulate, directly, men and women. What is meant by leader is summed up better in the word boss—a person with power, whether or not earned or deserved; a person *over* you.

The bosses are far from being all political. Men who work in factories know that there are bosses, administrative bosses, who do nothing in a specifically productive sense. They do not enhance the product. They do not make it or design it, or even sell it. They have two functions: to maximize profits—by any means possible—and to manipulate people, as one way of doing that other, primary job, but also as a way, simply, to justify their own existence.

Recent and ongoing industrial experience has shown, however, that bosses are not only nonproductive but actually may be counterproductive. Certain factories have turned the job of scheduling shifts and performance over to the logical persons, the ones involved. The result has been better work all around. Leaders, bosses, simply are not needed to tell people how to do things that they, the people, are obviously competent to do because they are the ones who must perform in those things.

Various left-wing countries, a definition which specifically excludes the state-capitalist Soviet Union, have experimented with even greater systems of worker control, student control, neighborhood control, to their reported delight. In the actual left-wing world, as a matter of fact, it is precisely the concept of leadership that is most under discussion, with results ranging from the decentralization of authority, even during the war, in the Democratic Republic of Vietnam, to Fidel Castro's ongoing exhortation that the leaders of the revolution have got to get out and *do* things and not just draw up blueprints, to Yugoslavia's worker-run factories, and so forth.

It is ironic, bitterly so, that in an era when an American leader, Richard Nixon, could so personify boundless leadership as to claim the immunities of a king, there are places in Eastern Europe, in Latin America and in Asia where *communists* are questioning the very concept of leadership itself and moving, by different paths and at different paces, toward the end of administrative leadership, which is the beginning of participatory freedom.

Administrative personnel, in all fairness, should be judged as part of the general service staff if they are needed at all. They perform housekeeping chores—chores which could be performed, in a true community, by other members on a part-time basis, just as custodial services might also be so performed to remove that ever-present, odious notion that somehow contemplative work is more worthy, rather than just different from, active work.

The overwhelming fact of leadership seems to be that most people do not question it even when they question its results. In factories, until very recently, there were few who questioned the role of leadership. Rather, they questioned its results. Some managers were said to be efficient, some not. Whatever was meant, it was distinctly not meant that the manager was *doing* productive work. At very best it meant that the manager was permitting others to do work for which, of course, the manager would take credit.

Actually, working and skilled or energetic people design and make all of the things which we regard as material "progress." Those cloying abundances which are neither progress nor needed but are simply churned out because idle machines must make profits, no matter *what* they produce, are the results of the "work" of administrative leaders. It is their special work. Would working people generally *prefer* to make junk? Common sense says no. People generally would prefer work of which they could be proud.

Economic leadership often is honored simply because a person possesses power and not because the leadership accomplishes anything. All of the great fortunes in America are the results of accumulation and not of innovation. Technical and exemplary leaders, the men and women who invent and produce, have not been able to equal those fortunes.

There are well-to-do inventors and innovators, of course. Some are even called rich. They may indeed have a lot of money. But it is still the older, greater fortunes that control and hold the power, that eventually come to absorb the work of the inventive and creative. For the hereditary rich it is only necessary that they "have" in order to be honored and followed.

The Great Leaders have countenanced the near-fatal pollution of the planet itself, often doing it in the name of progress (which is a term characteristically defined *by* the leaders and not by the people generally, who should, but do not, have a word in the definition). The goal of leaders is to secure their own positions.

People generally, on the other hand, most often have the goals of peaceful cooperation, of getting along together, of living interesting lives, loving lives. These goals are abandoned when leadership becomes a goal. These goals are abandoned when leaders, preaching what they define as progress or security, reduce people to a cipher in their grand schemes, ordering them into battle or to boredom by the millions with no more emotion than an accountant stacking figures.

The world as we see it, sick in its own wastes, wasted by its wars, is not so because of the failure of people generally to live and let live. The world as we see it and as we are either saddened or sickened or frightened or, at least, frustrated by it is the result of the failures of leaders.

More, it is the result of the failure of leadership as an elite concept.

It is a failure that can be ended only by the beginning of a world in which people at last, *all* the people, become their own leaders, exercising their own power, forming their own great community of humankind, owing no allegiance to any crown, to any elite, to any wealth.

The leaders have failed. Before that failure becomes fatal, it could be erased by the new age of fully participatory social organization, of control of production by those who produce, of mutual aid, of one stateless world, of privilege ended and responsibility begun, of order founded upon freedom (and not vice versa), of self-management.

Utopia? No. Necessity.

The practical person today is the person who dreams of such change. The impractical are those who would seek the solutions of a threatened tomorrow with the discredited processes of the past.

The leaders have failed. Leadership has failed.

Now it is our turn.

2

BEING AND DOING

The way I have lived explains the way I think. Out of what I was came what I am. It seems to me this is generally true for all of us. Even in those moments where the opposite seems true, in those crashing moments where some single human seems to have, by an act of mind, shattered history and flung loose from the past, there is, in fact, nothing but the flowering of the moment before—a direct line through what the person had been doing to what the person suddenly does and which appears to watchers suddenly to have changed the world. And, indeed, it may change the world. My point is that it does not change or transform the person, but simply develops out of everything that person has done, out of every experience, out of every interpretation of that experience, internally, by the person.

Newton, suddenly knowing the awesome presence of invisible but real forces; Einstein, suddenly knowing the awesome changes of those forces as they enlarge to galactic scale; Cézanne, suddenly realizing that there is a mood, an impression, to shape, color, and texture, as well as formal form—all of those moments were in fact not moments at all, but process-parts of the lives of whole, constantly developing human beings; human beings who led everyday as well as special lives, who lived in the world generally, although apart from it in the special emphasis of their obsessions.

This hardly means that we are just inert lumps, shoved around by history or circumstance. The shoving is both ways. Circumstance shoves us, we shove back—or at least some shove back. And things change because of that shoving. And they change because the minds of particular human beings reacting to particular circumstances and opportunities make particular connections, make particular concepts, make particular decisions.

But each of those actions comes from the entire life, and not just the separated mind of the human being.

It does not seem sensible to say that Newton's genius, for instance, would have burst forth no matter what and no matter where Newton had been. The language taught to him by the people of his childhood included certain absolutely vital conceptual ingredients—for a mechanistic examination of invisible forces—altogether lacking in other languages. And so it started: the long interaction of Newton and the neighborhoods of his existence, and the information filtered into those neighborhoods by certain books and by certain experiences and certain other people.

It's true for us all.

It's true in everyday life as well as in the special life of so-called great discoveries.

My own everyday life began, as did yours, with parents. There is no easy way to overcome that fact. Parents may be hated. They may be ignored. They may be rebuffed or they may even be loved. But all of that is long after the fact of the first impact. Once born, parental environment is certainly significant, possibly formative, depending upon its intensity or lack of intensity. The child virtually abandoned in a household, hardly ever touched, never loved, not spoken to, with little visual or aural stimulation and with little or no oxygen-to-brain nutrition, is a battered child even without visible bruises. Its mind, according to all the research I've seen, is irreparably damaged and dulled.

It may be possible to say that society did it by saying that the social circumstances made of the parents uncaring people. But the immediate and inescapable facts are that certain parents did it to the child, that not all parents under exactly similar circumstances do the same, and that the differences between the way people react to social circumstance is never more dramatic or, probably, meaningful than at that first moment of creation, the beginning of life, the earliest childhood.

It might even be possible to say that decent parents would assure a decent world. Fortunately, it is not possible to say that the lack of decent parents makes a decent world impossible. In most cases, except those of total early deprivation, children can and children do build up an independent capacity to challenge parents if necessary.

My own parents separated so soon after my birth that for all practical purposes I had only a mother. Fortunately, however, she was an immensely attractive person and there always were men around to relate to also. The balance seems to me to have been important.

But, balance or not, I cannot conceive of anyone being brought up by my mother who would not have got into considerable trouble, and been wonderfully happy, throughout life. History may be visions to one person, frontiers to another, crowns and sables to another, machines and numbers to another, and so forth. Probably it is all of those things. But surely it also is parents. Certainly the human person, growing taller and longer-lived throughout history, is also evolving in the head as well—and how can that evolution be totally divorced from the entire parental process? Who we are depends to some extent on who they are. What we do depends to some extent on what they do and, again, most particularly on what they do before we have any choices in the matter; while our heads and our bodies are beginning to fashion the basis of their own future from the bits and pieces of attention given by the living things that shape our earliest environment. Those living things are our parents or surrogates for them.

First there seems to me to be the matter of touching, of sensory stimulation. My mother, like some American Indians, believed in constant contact. Where she went, while I was an infant, I went. She sang constantly, talked constantly to me. And when she didn't do those things, someone else did. Her marriage was to a very rich man in the Philippines and there was a nursemaid to do the carrying and crooning as well.

The fact that the marriage could not survive the sort of attention that my mother apparently wanted to lavish on me in distinct conflict with the attention my father apparently wanted lavished on him has always seemed to me a good comment on how really fragmented many marriages are at the very outset. They often do not take place in the context of the sort of extended family that can provide surrogates for parents when they do things, as they certainly should, other than cart around the infant children. Also, the role of the mother as totally attached to the child while the father is totally attached to the World is a fatal fragmentation. There is a modern variation proposed by some young counter-culturists today which seems as fatal: deny special attachment to the child by anyone and let it be raised by everyone, rather like a stray animal; in fact, specifically like a stray animal, since this attitude also seems to be attached to a notion that humans are, after all, simply animals. My feeling is that children are like rivers in an important respect. If you say that the river belongs to everyone, then no one will take responsibility for it. This is so today, where rivers are said to belong to everyone, and are as a result polluted by people who treat them simply as sewers. Same with children. To say that they must be cared for by everyone is to lapse into sheerest fantasy. "Everyone" is too vast a concept for a tiny child. Everyone, even the small number of everyones in a small community will have other matters to attend to. The tiny, demanding child will relate to or be related to by a number quite smaller than everyone in practical circumstances.

To deny that there can be or should be special attachments between particular grown-ups and particular children, perhaps but not necessarily their own, is like denying that there are such special attachments between grown people. We *know* there are and all of the mystical 'we all are one" or mystical-political "there is only the collective, there are no individuals" theorizing has not and, I will bet, will not change the situation.

Further, the notion of particular attachments does not strike me as undesirable. Rather it seems to me to be quite in keeping with that most desirable of natural manifestations, diversity. Nature is a process. It is lush where diverse, austere where ground down to single attributes.

The notion of difference and diversity was certainly central in my childhood. But it was a diversity founded upon unity. My mother had an incessant lesson for me after the sensory age of love and sound and sight was replaced by the reasoning age of talk, laughter, and companionship. The lesson was that everyone is different in many, perhaps most, ways, but that we are all the same in requiring and deserving recognition *as distinct human beings*. She put it in many ways. You have the right to your opinion—and so does everyone else. Just because somebody else does something doesn't make it right—or wrong. You've got to make up your own mind. People should help each other but they shouldn't try to run each other's lives. Just because you disagree with a person is no reason to be mean to them. We are all different but we are all human.

The idea of difference was not just an idea. It was a constant practice. My mother did not encourage silly idiosyncrasy but she certainly never demanded conformity—even with her own ideas.

First of all there was the matter of information. She really regarded very highly the proposition that if you knew what was going on in a particular situation you not only could, but definitely should, make up your own mind about the way you would relate to it. One practical effect of this notion was that she taught me how to read before I entered school. She was able to do this because of her own decision and not because of any subsidiary aid. She was not rich, having left my father and also having refused to take any alimony from him. She was working as a switchboard operator in an apartment house in Washington, D.C., supporting not only me but her own mother, and helping out a younger brother besides.

After the reading came the questions. I had a million. She had one answer: Look it up. We talked about general things, went to the zoo together, walked a lot, and I even stayed with her many days while she operated the switchboard. But on matters of very specific information she would always insist that I look it up. That, in turn, meant spending a lot of time in a public library. The only books we had at home were some romantic novels (Dumas, Sabatini), some poems, H. G. Wells' *Outline of History*—and a dictionary. I have always thought that it was simply and incredibly fortunate that we had the dictionary instead of a Bible. Later, when I read the Bible, I had at least a fighting chance to understand it rather than simply believe it. I think that the dictionary helped.

School was another matter of information. Since I could read before I got there, it seemed more frustrating than enlightening. There were so many children eager to learn, to talk, to work, to build, and so little room in the bureaucratic scheme of things to let them do it, whether it might be reading a book for sheer pleasure or building some useful item in shop class rather than the sort of chintzy stuff (napkin holders, cigaret boxes, etc.) that the course prescribed. The fact that boys couldn't study cooking and girls couldn't study carpentry was another odd and bureaucratic decision which, around my house, would never have been seen as anything but busybody nonsense. My mother's feeling would be that if a girl (she would say young lady) wanted to study carpentry that was nobody's business but the young lady's. The same went for a boy who wanted to study cooking.

At any rate, school didn't last long. Mother made it quite clear that when I was ready to leave, I *should* leave; but not just to mope around the house or hang out at the drugstore. I decided to leave at fifteen, in the middle of high school. Already, I had been out of school just about as much as in it. (My truancy also was assisted by a scheme that I worked out in what must have been an early recognition of the nature of bureaucracy and its incompetence when overloaded. By transferring from several schools and then several more, building up, in short, a tangled trail of red tape, I was able to be actually lost in the system for a while, with no single school really aware that I was supposed to be on hand.) Mother had a standing deal with me. If I didn't want to go to school on any particular day, she would write me an excuse if, instead, I went to the library and read a book. She also had, in all the years before that, another standing deal—never compromised. If ever I wanted a toy, I would have to read a book first. The toys got less tempting as the books got more interesting. (Also, it was hardly *just* books. By puberty I had had my nose broken several times in fights and sandlot football; had been in a gang; had done the usual stealing and vandalism which seems to be a necessity of city life in which most children are offered damn near nothing else to do with their time and energy. Also, I had the usual young obsession with sex, chasing and lusting after the pictures in everything from the Sears Roebuck catalog to *National Geographic*, sex playing with everybody else in the neighborhood, and starching enough sheets to keep a laundry going. By fifteen I had also met a young lady nymphomaniac who traumatized the entire neighborhood when it was discovered that she had gonorrhea—fortunately half the kids missed it—and also knew a useful and, I presume, customary share of nasty old men, fiery older women, and peer group acquaintances with so many theories on masturbation as to make Masters and Johnson look to their laurels. When it comes to sex, and until told otherwise, kids are totally healthy, it seems to me. If you are lucky you never forget it—or stop it, whatever it was you were doing.)

At any rate, school ended at fifteen. I went to work for the Mutual Broadcasting Company in Washington, D.C., thanks to a remarkable news commentator named Walter Compton, who lived in the apartment house where my mother worked, and where she was by then resident manager. He never bothered to ask my age. I wrote newscasts, did research for several network question-and-answer shows, and now and then got to perform in radio skits.

That stint ended when, having borrowed a car to pick up some important guest for an interview show, I was stopped by the police, discovered to be not old enough for a driver's license, and arrested. I was also fired.

Next stop, the *Alexandria Gazette* in nearby Virginia. There, working with a newsman who became a lifelong friend, Thomas Moore McBride, I learned some of the craft of newspapering and, also, developed a very strong regard for the declarative sentence. Then the *Times-Herald* in Washington and then the New York *Daily News.* I got from the one to the other in what was a lasting lesson about the sensibilities of administrators. There was, on the *Times-Herald*, a city editor chosen strictly for his administrative ability. He could keep track of things. A friend of mine who left his gloves in the city room one day recovered them the next by looking in the G section of the city editor's file drawer. He was also pompous. It seemed a natural act of re-bellion, therefore, to attack the pomposity. The nightclub col-umn, which was alternated among members of the staff, was a suitable place to do it. Whenever I got the column to write, I would report at its conclusion that the city editor had been observed swapping witticisms with friends at one of the raunchier hangouts in Washington. He never objected to it on any human grounds, such as that it was causing him embarrassment. He simply made it an issue of authority, ordering me to stop. When I didn't, he fired me. Well enough. Rebels can only be dealt with rationally (I would have stopped immediately for any decent reason) or violently. Ever since then I have come to expect that administrators almost always will choose the path of violence. Lacking any skills but those of manipulation and command, it is a natural choice for them.

I was fired also from the *Daily News,* where I had become assistant city editor. I was twenty-two years old, married for a year, and politically opposed to the then current regime of Franklin Delano Roosevelt. When he died I refused an order to work on the obituary stories extolling his Presidency. I regarded his regime as social fascism then and I still do.

My next job was with McGraw-Hill, as news editor and then copy editor of their aviation magazine. It was enjoyable. I had learned to fly somewhere along the line, loved the skill and loved the equipment. In fact the physical sciences always had appealed to me. When I left school I was really torn between taking the job in broadcasting, which I did take, and going to the Massachusetts Institute of Technology to study chemical engineering. A chemistry teacher in high school had even been good enough to suggest that I might get in without graduating from high school, if that would keep me in science and out of other mischief.

Now there was a great turning point which, I dare say, like most great turning points in most of our lives, was taken on the most flimsy of pressures, really just on the basis of convenience. Can most of us really say that the crucial turns in our lives have come about through more profound circumstances? Of course some do, but not all, and surely not all of the small choices which, when summed, make the fullness of our lives.

I know that this thought can be carried too far and that there is danger in it of seeming to feel that life is nothing but chance and convenience and that Whimsy is the ruler of it all. I don't believe that. I know that many choices are made after long inner struggle and against vast exterior pressures. But there is also a danger in overromanticizing every choice that, in the past, moved our life one way or the other. From such romanticizing come the fantasies of the so-called self-made people who, as they recall turns in their life, make those turns sound like Great Moments in History. The oil billionaire who lucked into a lease, the young lawyer who just happens to begin practice in an area where a soft Congressional seat comes up for grabs, the novelist who gets to the publisher just when the business office has decided on a blockbuster ad expenditure for the next book of a certain sort to come in, and so forth.

The most pernicious effect of making it appear that every such turn was the result of nothing but hard work is to make it appear that endless opportunity is ahead of all of us and to make us forget that fortunate circumstances are still involved, circumstances with which we collide rather than which we control. On the other hand, a fixation that says there is nothing *but* circumstance can lead to an unhealthy preoccupation with sheer gambling and with a sort of resigned paralysis in which a person does nothing because nothing matters, only chance. The point is this: Circumstance is important, but so is the nature of the person faced with the circumstance. The person who lucks into the lease at least is presumed to be moving in oily circles. The lawyer does have a degree to go along with ambition, and lawyers often are favored for political posts by political pros. And the novelist, of course, had to at least write the book—the monster ad campaign would not be given to blank pages.

Perhaps the worst impression of all that can be gained from so-called models of success, however, derives from the successes of the rich. When a rich person achieves something, that person and many of those watching are likely to say or suggest that the rich have natural qualities of leadership or accomplishment. Working people, in particular, are likely to draw false conclusions from all this. They may be led to believe that people of wealth are in fact people of quality—a dreadful mistake.

David Rockefeller is a howling success as the head of Chase Manhattan Bank. Banks deal with money. The Rockefellers alone own a significant amount of all the money in North America, even in the world. It should not be surprising that David Rockefeller is a success. It would be shocking if he were not. That would be impressive and require explanation. His success really doesn't. He is rich, so rich that banking is as natural a path to success for him as football would be for a 250-pound man who can run like a sprinter, loves body contact, and is superbly coordinated.

Another example that comes to mind is that of William F. Buckley, Jr., with whom I worked for a while. He is brilliant, of course. That is, he speaks beautifully, is wonderfully well-educated and certainly possessed of a quick mind, able to assimilate information quickly, make connections accurately. He has been trained to think precisely at a time when few are trained to think at all. This training is not an accident of birth but a perquisite of birth. He too is rich, not altogether by ability but by birth. He is, to be sure, richer today by ability than he would have been if he had done nothing but spend his patrimony, but the birthright cannot be overlooked. It certainly shouldn't be. The wonder is that so many who are born rich are so miserably brought up that they, unlike Buckley, do nothing but spend their inheritance and seem to be possessed of little wit to do anything more.

The thought that the rich are somehow less than normally

well-endowed with creative ability might strike a commonsense person as every bit as reasonable a proposition as that they are endowed with any special quality at all.

The truth probably is that, by and large, the rich are a bit smarter than people generally if only because many of them have doting servants to bring them up, with plenty of good, loving contact, with plenty of sensory stimulation and, of course, with a diet quite high in those proteins and other food chemicals without which the brain, no matter how hopeful, languishes and turns to a sort of unfortunate mush.

Again, the mistake is to think of life in terms of mystery, in terms of wonders worked for and by the rich, wonders denied to the poor who may unhappily conclude that they are born to be poor. Do not forget that the rich were not born to be rich. Most were simply born rich. And those who were born poor and got rich got that way by means not so mysterious, not so romantic as to defy commonsense analysis.

My mother was the most natural, complete democrat I've ever known, and lived as though all people were exactly equal in terms of being human and deserving of respect as humans, no matter their other accomplishments or failures. She was also a member of the Republican Party throughout her life, a fact which was not to her, or to me for a long time, any sort of contradiction at all. At any rate, Mother's attitude toward the rich was exactly the same as her attitude toward anyone else and at one point she taught me a memorable lesson exactly along those lines.

Because we used to walk about the city a good deal together, we would end up in odd places, often in need of a rest room, or a soda pop. One of those times found us in the lobby of one of the most exclusive hotels in Washington. I was neatly but rather plainly dressed. Switchboard operators who buy books for their kids do not have much left over for fancy clothes, for the kids or themselves. So, to be quite fair about it, you might say that

I was dressed in a way which the rich of that particular hotel lobby must have considered shabby. In fact it became quite apparent to me, aged then about six or seven, that they did indeed regard me as something pretty odd and probably undesirable. The fashionable and rich have a fine casual way of insulting working people and poor people with a glance. It is a second nature to them and one of their few natural talents although even there I suspect that it is not so much a talent as an acquired skill.

Noting the glances, I must have said something humble or defensive to my mother. Zap. She stopped, right in the middle of the lobby, and proceeded quietly but firmly to discuss with me the sad plight of people who have so little of importance to do that they bother sneering at small children, and the necessity of never being appalled by what others think of you in such trivial and cosmetic matters as your clothes. Cleanliness, she suggested, was an entirely separate matter, but style and fashion she considered to be so far beneath the contempt of serious people as to be merest fluff. And, finally, she made it very clear that if you spend all of your time worrying about what other people think about you, you will never have any time to develop your own self. Your opinion of yourself, she said, is more important than anyone else's. Self-respect is the foundation of any other respect that is worth having.

I have forgotten many lessons taught in classrooms. I have never forgotten that lesson, taught in a hotel lobby. Perhaps it is because that lesson was so clearly and immediately involved with the real world and with real people.

I have been exposed to considerable sophisticated thought since then, including philosophical positions that say the same thing but in complex phrases or that deny it in even more complex phrases. I am convinced, after it all, that there is a general human wisdom and general human common sense which, generation after generation, rediscovers fundamental humanistic positions. It is good that philosophers discourse and elaborate upon those positions. It is marvelous that the positions persist, agelessly it seems, in people's everyday lives.

Perhaps it is fortunate that I did not go to school but, instead, learned practical philosophical lessons from my mother and theoretical ones from books. The books did not overpower the practical as they might have if they had been accompanied by the authority of a professorial presence in a classroom. To be awed by the sheer authority of a teacher may well be the first step toward intellectual colonization taken by many people. They become colonized by accepting outer authority, denying inner doubts. Books, on the other hand, may be judged in a sense of discovery rather than awe. To be sure, being with a learned person can be delightful. But to be at the command of a learned person, in the top-down authoritarian structure of so many classrooms, is simply to be bossed in the head just as a machine operator is bossed in body by the foreman.

It was not just escape from the authority of teachers that my mother's insistence on self-respect and self-reliance made possible. It made possible also an escape from the preachers. She had been raised and, indeed, raised me as a fairly strict Roman Catholic. But one Sunday, at mass, in Washington, I saw an old, poorly dressed woman refused a seat in the church—it was in a fashionable neighborhood, near the apartment where my mother worked. The lesson of the lobby, the contradictions between what the church preached and what it practiced, got to me very strongly. All of that, coupled with a growing interest in science and growing doubts about the supernatural, led to long talks with Mother and, within just a few months, to my leaving the church and rather quietly discovering that I was an atheist. Mother has always attended church, though not obsessively, but has never expressed shock or stern disapproval of my own anti-religious position. Rather, I think she would be shocked and disapproving if, having lost faith, I had persisted in pretending to have it.

Lately, when recounting this, Mother has reminded me that there was another factor involved with the rejected lady. She was black. Not to give too grand an emphasis to a point which probably was totally unselfconscious, but it could be said that this was an early and natural introduction to a class analysis of social conflict, as distinguished from a racial one. But, more probably, it was simply a point of ordinary perception. To be poor and white might naturally make you attend to matters of class, which you share with such a person as the lady in the church, rather than to ethnicity, which you do not share and, unlike class, cannot share.

There has, as a result of all this, never been a serious doubt in my mind that my own reaction to social circumstances has been conditioned almost absolutely by my parent. Nor can I believe that if I had lived apart from both my parents that sheer genetic inertia would have made me Me. Rather, it was a living, actual influence, a person, not just genes and society, that impinged upon me, nudged and formed that general person which became that particular person.

In a good and free society it would seem to me crucial that young people have constant and close relationships with older people—parents or not—in such a way that, in effect, the younger people are apprentices, discussing, loving, walking, talking, playing, making the amazing transition from infant dependency to self-motion, self-respect, and self-reliance, all of the self-realizing factors which are the only firm base for that other great human capacity, cooperation.

There is in this the central core of an entire social philosophy. It holds that social action, human action, proceeds from the acts of people, specific people taking specific actions. No one of those actions, however, is taken in isolation and all interact with each other, like ripples in a pond intersecting to form turbulence in some cases, waves in others. With the source of society being people (not mysterious forces such as "history") and the relation of people to material things such as the land, their tools, their neighbors and so forth, the nature of a society will depend at root on the natures or dispositions of the people involved. If each person has a well-developed sense of self, of self-identification, then there is a good chance that the society will be one of cooperative interaction. I suggest cooperative rather than competitive because, in truth, societies as they have developed—beyond the arenas of court society, royal society and, in recent years, corporate society—have developed with practices of cooperation, not competition.

If a person has some inner sense of worth, in other words, it may not be so urgent to acquire values from the outside, as in a competitive society, or to feel inner worth on the basis of, say, outer conquests, or to derive a sense of self-importance by dominating others (making *them* less important).

These seem to me the sorts of issues that arise naturally in a warm relationship between a young person and an older person. Questions of personal value arise in ever so many practical ways, day after day.

If, on the other hand, the notion of society is that correct practices arise from definite discipline and from vested authority, then monarchy, state socialism, state capitalism would seem inevitable. People or institutions. The fundamental choices, or at least emphasis, are limited.

My own perception, of course, was in favor of the more optimistic view of human beings: that they develop most pleasingly from the relations they have among themselves and from the self-identification that proceeds from inner sources and not altogether from outer compulsion.

For reasons which may now seem bizarre, that was why I was first, in politics, a member of the Socialist Party, at age sixteen or seventeen, and then later a Republican.

Socialism was appealing because it seemed to reject the idea that the world was fashioned for an elect or elite, with the many destined to serve the few by divine ordination according to many preachers or by social imperative according to many sociologists.

It became less appealing when, as a member of its then leading political entity in America—the party of Norman Thomas— it became apparent that socialism was, in fact, just New Deal liberalism. Its programs, as Norman Thomas later pointed out with pride, were mainly designed to transfer authority from the corporations to the government, installing a set of social planners in place of the profit planners of private industry. In truth, the New Deal effected a compromise between those views, transferring to the government the power to regiment more and more people socially while preserving the right of the corporations to regiment them economically. Also, the government took on the chore of handling the human waste of capitalism—the unemployed, the underemployed, the maimed and some of the sick. The bills for all this were paid by the middle class and the working poor.

Nowhere in the program of the Socialist Party as I knew it were there even dreams of abolishing authority and of restoring a society of people rather than a government of institutions. The Democrats were simply socialists in terms of government programs and capitalists in terms of corporate programs—the worst of all worlds for the people generally, and the best of both for the political and economic elite.

That left the Republicans.

Republican policy opposed the extension of government power. I focused on that. Some Republicans also opposed the growth of corporate power. I liked that. And all Republicans, it seemed to me, opposed Franklin Roosevelt, many characterizing him as a would-be king. That too seemed sound.

It was, then, with Republican politics that I pursued a professional career that became, itself, more and more political. But, since I will discuss the politics in detail, the career alone will be sketched here. And that is done mainly for this reason: I am harshly critical of institutions of power. That criticism is not the result of jealousy, of longing for power and resenting not having it. There is criticism of that sort readily at hand for all who enjoy or feel they benefit by it. My criticism is based upon knowledge of, not jealousy of, major institutions of power. I have been there. I have had the choice of whether to stay there. I left. After leaving, and now, the criticism grew and so did my gratitude that I had made the choice to move from institutions and from power to neighborhood and to unmediated human relationships.

After McGraw-Hill, I worked for an amazing publication called *Pathfinder,* a weekly magazine aimed at rural audiences with a circulation, back in the forties, of more than a million, making it the second largest newsmagazine in the land, behind *Time* but ahead of the newcomer *Newsweek.* There I wrote about everything, but particularly about religion (atheists, if not bitter, can do a more objective job than most on that subject, in newsmagazine terms), about Communism and about national defense (partly as a hangover credential from having edited an aviation magazine, aviation being the most crucial mechanical side of national defense).

Also there is visible in that set of interests the exact metaphor that came to stand for America throughout the period of the Cold War: religious mission, anti-Communism, and the absolute identification of nation and defense with military hardware.

After the defeat of Tom Dewey in the 1948 election, the Republican National Committee was either desperate enough or adventurous enough to try new people on its speech-writing staff. I got one of the jobs, seeing it as a chance to make history rather than just write about it—a temptation fatal to the careers of many journalists. After only a few months on the job, however, one of the committee's officials, in close touch with *Newsweek* magazine, recommended me for an associate editorship there. Moving to New York, and to residence in a Westchester County suburb, I worked at *Newsweek* for five years, serving mainly as editor-writer of the Press section.

There was an interlude during my *Newsweek* period that was interesting and significant if only to make a particular point. I have always felt that to be whole, a person should keep as small a distance as possible between beliefs and actions. Politics is the way you live your life. The point arose emphatically one day when an old friend, a political writer, came to see me to discuss Cuba. That was when Fulgencio Batista was running and ruining the island. It was well before the time of Fidel Castro and the liberation from Batista. My friend said that among the factions trying to depose Batista there were people particularly friendly to the United States and thus, in the assumption of the time, above reproach. They needed guns and napalm—a strong suggestion that they did, indeed, appreciate Yankee ingenuity. I was approached, I gather, because of a longtime interest in firearms, a license as a professional gunsmith, and wide acquaintance in the field. So, for a few months, I became a full-time gunrunner. I recall with at least visual pleasure the garage of my suburban home, housing the tricycle of my young son and, at one time, about fifty semiautomatic military rifles and barrels of the chemical base for napalm explosives. I took a picture of it, the contrast between child's toy and grown-up toys being so striking. Contrast or similarity, I would ask now. But not then.

At any rate, the work went well and I made just enough money to survive the time, not understanding, as I did later that gunrunning is supposed to be immensely lucrative. So much for an ideologue in a capitalist's world.

There was, however, in the process of my Cuban caper, obvious and considerable official forebearance. Friends of mine in the intelligence community, including the FBI, knew exactly what trips I had made to Florida for money, what guns I had bought, and to whom I delivered them. I was never bothered by even a threat of official interference with what was clearly an illegal activity—an activity for which many are severely punished. I conclude, of course, that the punishment is for those who are guilty, not of the act, but of committing the act on behalf of any faction not in favor with the intelligence community itself. Looking back, I also conclude that there was one reason above all others why help to certain factions fighting Batista would be winked at while others would not—aid to Castro, for instance. The difference between the "liberator" I was helping—Dr. Carlos Hevia, a former president of Cuba and a staunch ally of American business interests—and Castro did not turn on any subtle ideological focus but on a purely practical one. Castro was and is an intensely pro-Cuban politician. The people of Cuba have obviously come first for him rather than service to a particular ideology. This is not to say that Marxism is not his touchstone. It seems to be. But it does mean that the ordinary people of Cuba, and not a particular political faction, have benefited most from the Castro period. His eager pursuit of a peaceful relationship with the United States, despite the Bay of Pigs invasion, despite revelations of CIA plots on his life and, most particularly, despite the vast amounts of Soviet aid poured into the country, certainly indicates that Castro is thinking first of his country, rather than first of any sort of ideological crusade in which the people would be mere and expendable pawns.

On the other hand, the loyalty of the people I was helping was to business and to money. They and many others argue that it's all the same thing. Help business and bring in money and the people will be helped. Better to work for an American corporation, they say, than be a worker in a Communist Cuba. In the very short term there might well be advantages to being an American corporate employee rather than a Cuban Communist citizen. But certainly not in the long run. In the long run, the liberation of every country like Cuba is going to depend upon the self-reliance of the people themselves. As Communists, working toward their own local self-sufficiency, developing skills, husbanding resources for their own use and not for foreign profiteering, educating children to think for themselves and not to think as corporate employees (not that they couldn't end up being employees of a corporate state run by Communist functionaries), as Cubans doing those things for themselves, they should face a better future, even though a harder-working one, than as the totally dependent labor pool of American corporate ambitions. And, finally, the hope that one can have for Cuba rests on an almost esthetic difference between Castro and the people I helped. Although Dr. Hevia was a splendid gentleman and, I believe, a man of considerable honesty, he was part of a class and a style removed from the people generally, an already existing business aristocracy, with allegiance not to the land, the people, and the spirit of Cuba, but to the international ledger sheet, the global profit system. Communism seems to breed nationalists and patriots. Capitalism breeds the true internationalists, loyal to no neighbors, to no land, loyal only to the collective abstraction of profit and profitable growth. Castro, piddling around in his Jeep through the Cuban boondocks, playing baseball in public parks, endlessly talking with farmers, factory workers, teachers, kids, is a far different sort, a Cuban at home with his neighbors. I find that, now, so much more trustworthy a sort of personality than the aloof, admittedly charming commercial nobility for whom, at that special time, I did an armorer's work.

Finally, there is the difference that Castro fought in the hills. The guns he obtained were the guns he used. My friends fought from paneled rooms, remotely, austerely, like antique barons sending the peasants off to war while they hung new banners of glory on the castle keep.

I have always kept that difference in mind. Lately it has been so sharp. There is that difference in common between people who are called rightists or conservatists and people who are called leftists. (I exclude Stalinist bureaucrats, of course, from even being in the "left" category.) On the right there is a marked tendency to deploy other people in the service of your ideology. On the left there is the tendency to live the ideology personally as well as profess it publicly.

Perhaps I should have begun earlier than I did to realize which side I would end up on—I might have observed, for instance, that in the Cuban gunrunning situation, there were many friends who sympathized with the cause. But the guns were in my garage.

More than anything else, however, the experience at *Newsweek* was an experience with suburbia. It is an experience too widely shared to require much description.

First of all, there is the incredible separation from the natural world—despite the professed desire of suburbanites to get away from the city and, presumably, closer to nature. Actually they withdraw almost totally from nature.

The separation is caused mainly by the many fractures in your life when you live in the suburbs and work in the city. Your major attention is focused on the job in the city. From it come the major fears and fantasies of the day, the tensions or rewards that color completely the time at home. The idea of the suburbs as a refuge from the city seems to me quite false. The city's imperatives distort every moment in the suburbs. It is not a place to flee from the city so much as a place of deceptive calm in which the demands of the city may be viewed at greater length, and thus more obsessive length, than during the rush of the city day.

If, say, gardening is chosen as a refuge from the city work, it is gardening that depends totally upon the city in that the typical suburbanite buys voraciously from the local hardware and garden store—using the very money from the city job from which the person is supposed to find refuge by gardening. Every bloom is a part of the indebtedness to the city job.

But the attempts to separate from the city job do not stop with the suburban premises, they soar to the extravagant heights of the great hunting and fishing escape. Fishing, in particular, is a rewarding way to spend time or, at least, a wonderfully relaxed way to do it. It also produces food. Hunting does the same for many Americans. For the suburbanite it is supposed to produce something else. For male suburbanites it produces a sense of strength, of familiar "manliness" of the sort that is never permitted at the city job where courage would be rewarded with instant dismissal for rocking some boat or another. And so the slaughter of the innocents proceeds, to fuel up the sagging egos of suburban men who can be craven in their work during every week but pretend to mock heroics and swaggering strength by buying an expensive shotgun, fancy hunting clothes, and blowing the brains out of a charging bunny rabbit or a rampaging deer or, for that matter, another hunter. For female suburbanites who hunt or fish, there is the instant production of the image of special womanhood, the mouth-watering Good Sport.

For both sorts of suburbanite, however, the main product of the Great Escape is sheer action, motion seemingly unattached to job or home. But of course that is simply an illusion. The hunters with their fancy guns, the anglers with their fancy reels, are for the most part just getting a bit deeper in debt to their city service by trying to escape it in this manner.

One undeniable bonus, however, is at cocktail time. This is, if there is one, the truly sacred moment in suburbia. I cannot recall Christians approaching the mysteries of their devotion with any more insistent zeal than suburbanites approaching the cocktail hour. It is inviolate. It is the moment around which all socializing revolves. It is the moment around which most families revolve. And it is during the cocktail hour that the great bonus from hunting and fishing can become clear. Men who hunt and fish in the suburban mode—as distinguished from rural people to whom every relationship with nature is fairly unselfconscious—tend to clump together at cocktail time, near the top of a sort of pecking order in which other suburban pursuits may be seen as relatively effeminate. These are the great studs of the cocktail time, the talkers about calibers and catches, the gray-flanneled, pink-shirted cavemen.

I used to do that sort of thing at cocktail time, weaving a magic barricade of sheer bully bravado beyond which to place, with polite sneers, the pantywaists who merely played tennis or grew flowers.

Suburban people, by and large, must identify with labels and things they can get in stores or out of cans because their own lives, totally dependent upon remote work, totally devoted to an endless grind of debt and consumption and social one-upping, simply aren't their own. Their lives belong to remote board rooms and remote plans controlled by other and more powerful suburbanites. They compete endlessly against each other because there is no other measure of accomplishment for them, no community in which to be cooperative, only what they always call "the rat race."

Suburban marriages do not last well. Mine didn't. Most don't. The women are debased in the relationship despite their seemingly pampered positions and leisure. But so are most women in most marriages where there is a presumption of roles regardless of individual capacity, where everything from sex to dreams emerges from the work role of the male.

The measure of many women in the suburbs is whether they are good, indifferent, or magnificent hostesses. They are the geishas of America, programmed and paid to be entertaining and, like geishas, to hide their human faces altogether behind the thick makeup of their hostess faces.

Soon, the perfect hostess becomes a machine luxury in the house, like a good stereo system. Soon, the suburban rituals, driven by incessant drinking, turn to wives becoming objects of pride while other wives become the objects of passion. Next to drinking, promiscuity is the favorite mixed social recreation of the suburbs. I do not think this is an unkind observation, either. Of course there may be suburbs where there is a sturdy sense of community, where men and women in loving equality are regarded for their virtues as human beings (energy, talents, compassion, capacity to love, capacity to cooperate, and so forth). I just don't happen ever to have lived in one or to have heard anyone else describe one.

The suburbs I know, and for which I, like all of my neighbors, for so long mortgaged my mind and dreams, are the suburbs of harsh consumerist competition, of shifty, fanny-pinching, quickie-sex promiscuity, of constant drinking, of boasting, of new cars treated like symbols of actual personal worth, of kids shoved into joyless Little Leagues for the vicarious pleasure of nearly impotent fathers, of endless shopping by women who are reduced to being mere extensions of cash registers, the way their mates are reduced to being mere extensions of machines or corporate plans.

The suburbs of New York were like that. The suburbs of Washington were like that. And so were the suburbs of even Hamilton, Ohio, where, after leaving *Newsweek,* and after a very successful several years as a free-lance writer specializing in anti-Communist articles, I worked as, first, editor of an outdoors magazine and then as assistant to the president of Champion Papers and Fibre Co., a major corporation now merged with U.S. Plywood.

The Champion experience was crucial for me. It took me inside a major corporation. I learned these things:

Corporate life is largely mindless. The purposes of the people living in it have little to do with creative, passionate, loving life. Corporate life is like a pool of sharks. The object is survival and the food is whatever gets in the way. It is not the work or accomplishment that drives people in most corporate areas. It is fear and the fearful conviction that unless you are winning, which means getting up on top of someone else, then you are losing. Losing, to corporate people, means not losing in the sense of failing to accomplish. It means losing in the sense of being beaten out, of having someone else get the credit, the bonus, the position, the title. The rewards in corporate life are wholly monetary. They are numbers. Numbers of people you can boss, numbers of dollars you get. I have never met a corporate person whose passion was for the work or the product or for some personal pleasure. This hardly means that there are none. It means I never met any.

A sure indication of the mindlessness of corporate life is the fact, which I observed at impressive length, that the main contribution people make to it is sheer time on the job—at least at the so-called managerial level.

The actual work of management (keeping track of production processes and personnel, deploying resources, kicking the salesmen and so forth) takes not too much talent and not much effort. It takes time. In a craft that is essentially uncomplicated but which, because it is so highly paid, must be made to appear complicated, the desired result may be achieved by endless activity. The activity itself is the game. Those who can appear to be active are better corporate people than those who can simply do work.

Personnel departments are a prime example, and, for a time, the president to whom I was assistant was preoccupied with personnel matters. Production matters, as a matter of fact, *always* seemed to be secondary. Management, I heard time after time, was the skill of manipulating people, not machines. Actually, it means manipulating people as though they were machines, putting them into charted spots, assessing their output, varying their input.

Personnel departments have long ago learned that simply hiring people and then firing them if they don't work out is too primitive, does not justify large budgets and does not fit into the modern concepts of management skills, in which people who study management theory try to act as though they are engaged in as precise a science as the drudges in the research and development laboratories; the drudges, incidentally, upon whom the very existence of the business almost always depends, but who are given the bottom end of every single stick in the corporate game.

If simply doing a simple job isn't enough, the corporate mind teaches you to devise a complication which will enable the appearance of more activity and thus justify the consumption of more power, prestige, and money.

This meant, during the time I was in business, the devising of endless tests and methods of placement, of endless training programs and morale boostings. I believe that fashion has passed and I don't have any idea of what the current vogue is, but I am sure that corporate life remains solidly on course in the fundamental sense of rewarding sheer energy rather than actual creativity, of cherishing sheer devotion to the company rather than dedication to any other excellence. I am also sure that, as when I was in business, the products are absolutely secondary to the profits, the profits are the reason for being in business and if they could be had by selling bubonic plague, the plague would be Number One on the agenda at the next sales meeting and woe to the meathead so dull as to question the decimation of the customers. The high marks would go to the toady who, after applauding the president, would produce a statistic to prove that even after the customers died from the plague, the current birthrate and age of children would assure a new market within a reasonable time.

The people who spend their time selling tooth-rotting soft drinks, lung-rotting cigarettes, and mind-rotting whiskey would be obvious cases in point, but then what business is different?

Again, I am sure some are. They just aren't heard from, are they?

The *product* policy of any successful corporation may be summed up simply as: the least for the most—the cheapest product for the most price. No matter how the corporations attempt to pretty the picture, that, at root, is the policy.

The *personnel* policy of any successful corporation may be summed up as: more work for less pay. And no matter how you try to pretty it up with recreation programs, good relations with the union and time off for good behavior, that is the policy.

The purpose of a corporation is to make money and to make money, in particular, for the major stockholders or owners who control the patronage (management jobs). Every other activity of the corporation is secondary to that purpose. To expect otherwise is to expect shrimp to whistle. It is simply not in the nature of the beast.

If the employees themselves owned the company and if the people who used the products had more than a consumer voice (a voice usually limited by marketing systems which are anything but free and open), then the situation might be different. But, so long as a class of owners controls industry, whether that class is the moneyed plutocracy of America or the political oligarchy in the Soviet Union, then the people generally will be extensions of the machines, extensions of the ledger, and not truly human at all in the eyes of the owners. Serfs, good natured peasants, loyal followers—but not fully developed, self-managing and responsible human beings.

My own disgust with corporate life did not come from any high-blown theoretical analysis, however. It came from disgust with myself. I found, after several years in corporate life, that one of the things I had begun to do was to go to the office very early in the morning, just to be there. Many others did the same. We were not there to accomplish anything concrete. We were there to impress one another and, particularly, to impress our bosses. We had nothing to offer in the way of real accomplishment except our physical presence. And that we offered up like altar sacrifices, with much boasting about who spent the least time at home, who neglected children the most—and had to spend extravagant amounts on schools and shrinks to compensate for it—all for the greater glory of the company.

The Company. When loyalty to it becomes a full substitute for loyalty to your own self, then the time for self-disgust has come. It came for me—and I didn't even know what to do about it, except feel worse and worse, dirtier and dirtier, and get worse and worse to be with, I am sure, at home, in bed, everywhere.

Somewhat before the time of absolute disillusionment with corporate life, however, I got a good chance to play another sort of corporate game. Politics.

The president of the company, Reuben Robertson, Jr., was a prominent Republican in Ohio and nationally, formerly a Deputy Secretary of Defense and a close associate of then President Dwight Eisenhower.

Three times, while working at Champion, I was given extended time off, with pay, of course, to work for the Republicans. First there was a stint at the White House working on a plan to provide new machinery for the support of Republican Congressional candidates—the forgotten people, as a matter of fact, in many campaign schemes. Then I was released for a time, technically on vacation, I believe, to work with the House Republican Policy Committee in preparing a huge report on American Strength and Strategy, a formative statement of Republican foreign policy, purely interventionist in nature, and based upon armed superiority over and brute strength diplomacy against the Soviet Union. (It was not until John Kennedy's Administration that the foreign policy of every faction, Democrat and Republican, shifted from opposition to the Soviet

Union, to simply opposition to revolutionary change in either the disputed areas of the Third World or in the periphery of the American Empire.)

Finally, I was released for another period to serve as chief writer for the 1960 Republican platform. This form of corporate service to political parties is, of course, bipartisan. My company also released people to work with the Democrats. Who wins is important to the extent that corporation presidents have partisan preferences. But who wins is not nearly so important in the long run as making sure that the corporation is represented in high places no matter who wins. It is not ideology that drives this. It is simply practicality. The government is a golden goose to the corporations, to be plucked as much as possible. To pluck it you've got to have your pluckers on the scene. Simple. Very patriotic. It is called public service in the corporate manuals.

3

CONTRADICTIONS
OF A CONSERVATIVE

One powerful middle-class myth is that hard work and individual acts of thrift, ambition, and skill are the determining
factors in the life of an upward-mobile, successful person.
Individual salvation is the credo of the executive. The lonely
competitor—the pitcher on the mound, the manager with his
briefcase of papers, bleary-eyed in the night, oblivious on the
holiday—those are the images of success in the hustling middle
class. There is ever-present guilt if you don't work hard enough.
Someone else may. There is ever-present fear if your hard work
isn't known, seen, praised, recorded. Someone else's may be.
The attitude is emulated pretty much throughout the business-
industrial world. It is an attitude which, among other things,
marks people off from unionization or from any other form of
organization on their own behalf.

Out of the myth comes the notion that to be truly successful,
even to have the potential for success (whatever that means),
a person must stand alone, competing against rather than cooperating with fellow workers. It is a powerful means to
render powerless an entire class or caste of people, the entire
nonowning, nonunionized group of working people; very possibly a majority of American working men and women.

No myth plays more importantly into the hands of the owners
of business and industry. If they could foster the same attitude
in everyone there wouldn't be any fear, ever, under any cir-

cumstance, of aroused working people thinking of their welfare as a group. There would be, as there is, a largely fractured, isolated, compartmentalized work force, each person of which is convinced that not only success but sheer survival depends on independent action.

Some come to see the myth as hollow and detrimental through good, common sense, through knowing that the world of work is a social world and that the acts of all are, inevitably, linked to the welfare of either all, or just a few—and *if* just a few, then common sense also would say that the few who benefit most are bound to be not the workers but the owners.

It is possible to see it as hollow and destructive also through the fact that it is simply a lie. Hard work and hard worrying may help, no doubt, to place a person advantageously for some next rung up the ladder. But the lever of actual fate is the boss, some boss, somewhere, and the special needs of the special boss. The old truism "It's not what you know but who you know" is a tribute in ordinary perception to that fact.

I guess I always knew the right people.

One of the right people was associated with the American Enterprise Institute for Public Policy Research which, no matter the flashier performance and more prominent position of others, seems to me to be the strongest intellectual-effort bastion of conservative thinking in all America. The Chamber of Commerce may make more noise. The National Association of Manufacturers may make more enemies. *National Review* may make more conversation. The Brookings Institution may make use of government positive policy to effect conservative ends —the continued dominance of economic growth as national policy—and *Commentary* magazine may make more use of cultural elitism to support the national security state—another cherished conservative position. But month by month, Administration by Administration, the American Enterprise Institute, through solid research, reliance on studies by the most respected authorities, and the most cautious, low-profile approach in all political influence—by all these ways, the American Enterprise Institute presses the conservative cause more effectively and persistently than any group in America and perhaps in the entire world.

As an example: AEI has been a major support for conservative scholars in American universities. They have tried to balance, by quite marvelous selectivity and insistence on excellence, the otherwise lopsided support of scholars who take the liberal approach of "rationalizing" business and industry through the increased use of state policy. The conservative way is to support "progress" in business and industry by lowering taxes and ending regulations, particularly those of the current environmental nature. Liberal policies, in another area of difference, seek to control labor unions by making them a part of the business-industrial complex (labor statesmen). Conservative policy aims at simply reducing the power of the unions. But both liberals and conservatives agree basically on national security, the conservatives tending to emphasize the armaments industry as the key to it, while the liberals emphasize the *arms-using* bureaucracy, the national security bureaucracy, as the key to it.

Just a few other examples of AEI's role, to indicate its effectiveness and to indicate also why having a friend there is just about as good as having a friend at Chase Manhattan: At one point in the Nixon Administration, when it was fairly conservative, the reason might have been that the Secretary of Defense, Mel Laird, was an old line AEI supporter and now in charge of a substantial two million dollar AEI program to study the energy situation; one of his deputies, G. Warren Nutter, of the economics department of the University of Virginia, is a foremost AEI-supported scholar; Milton Friedman, the famed free-market economist, was a key adviser to the President and also a longtime AEI associate; the chairman of the President's Council of Economic Advisers, Paul Mc-

Cracken, was and is an AEI official; and sown throughout the Administration were at least a score of other AEI stalwarts. Now a scholarly and well received description of the American Revolution as one in support of things just as they are is being conducted for the Bicentennial by AEI.

I had come to AEI's attention while working, on leave from Champion, on the Congressional report on Strength and Strategy, a definitive statement of Cold War policy which has held in effect for most Republicans without change no matter how the world itself has changed. My writing ability and speed would be the accepted and obvious reasons for catching their eye. It would be the middle-class myth in action. I'm afraid, in looking back, there was another reason. I was reasonable, not a prima donna, not given to insisting on hard ideological points or even ego trips about beloved phrases and personal inclinations in crafting political statements. I was a good craftsman, a tractable hired hand, a team player—and that, middle-class myth or no, is what, it seems to me, really counts. Of course you must be willing to work long hours and all that—but that really isn't so much in order to produce things as it is to produce a properly humble state of mind and to endlessly prove that your loyalty, more than to family, to self, or to ideals, is to the Company, whatever it may be.

With AEI's encouragement, I moved back to Washington, D.C. For a short time, I worked on an experimental newspaper, the *Washington World*, which was of brief interest to conservatives because of an ingenious but unimplemented idea of sharply contrasting the results of private versus government action. After that, I went to work on AEI's staff, as director of special projects. What that meant was answering special requests from Congressmen, regardless of partisan bias, who wanted studies on . . . you name it. The guiding rule at AEI was to be scrupulously accurate and fair in handling these requests— a rule that was never breached while I was there—on the assumption that even if the report included substantial "liberal" material, the fact that it would include also basically conservative material would be a solid plus.

Most particularly, however, my job was to be a speech writer and phrasemaker. There were scholars aplenty at the beck and call of AEI. That was the product. My job was packaging.

It does not take long for a professional ghostwriter for professional politicians to discern that the way things are said is considered to be approximately as important as what is said. Nor does it take long to understand that most professional politicians are actors reading scripts, rather than philosophers thinking and considering, conceiving and contemplating.

Rarely does any politician present a position which the politician has both formed and then phrased. The supposedly most-gifted politicians have a knack for timing, for understanding when a position on a certain matter will be most effective, and they have also a feel for the sort of position generally that will be the most effective. But effective means just one thing: enhancement of the possibility of reelection.

In my personal experience I have known only three politicians who have defined effective as something else, as, for instance, support of a principle. The three are Barry Goldwater, Mark Hatfield, and Fred Harris. By observation, I suspect there are a few others—people like William Proxmire, Wright Patman, Steven Symms, John Conyers, Robert Kastenmeier, H. R. Gross, and Shirley Chisholm. And, of course, there must be many more. But, by and large, and based upon quite a few years' work with the cream of the Republican Party and closely observing the entirety of the Democrats (we sometimes know the enemy better than our friends), I would stick to the point: politicians are creatures of their own showmanship and their own staffs, not of their own conscience and conceptions.

The three great exceptions to that, Goldwater (at least when I knew him well), Hatfield, and Harris, have all taken stands, based obviously on belief, that have threatened their political careers. Barry Goldwater's 1964 campaign for the Presidency, in which I served as chief speech writer, was an unbroken series of Goldwater decisions to say unpopular things simply because he thought they needed saying. Mark Hatfield, running scared for reelection to the Senate during the war in Indochina, risked his standing in the polls, dipped close to defeat and just squeaked through when he attacked the war policies of the government—simply because his conscience would not permit any other course. Fred Harris, of course, broke one of the most enduring rules of modern politics by being (1) from Oklahoma and (2) not subservient to the great oil interests there. As a result he couldn't raise any money for campaigning for the Democratic nomination for President or even to stay in the Senate. He quit elected politics and now, on money he painfully raises, runs an institute devoted to reviving the populist politics of an American past in which people dared openly to challenge great corporate institutions, not to reform them, but to remake them.

At any rate, it was working at AEI that put me in touch with elected politicians on a wide basis and let me ply, for some years, the ghostwriting trade, being a carpenter for other people's political platforms, a paid set of fingers on the keyboard. Had typewriter. Did travel.

Among the people for whom I wrote during the AEI years, as best I can remember, were Senator Hubert Humphrey, Mel Laird, Rep. John Rhodes (R–Ariz., current House minority leader). Gerald Ford, Richard Nixon (a *Saturday Evening Post* article), Sen. Carl Curtis (R–Neb.), Sen. Peter Dominick (R–Colo.), Rep. Omar Burleson (D–Tex.), former Rep. Tom Curtis (R–Mo.), Rep. Peter Frelinghuysen (R–N.J.), Sen. Strom Thurmond (R–S.C.), Sen. William Roth (R–Del.), Sen. James B. Pearson (R–Kans.), former Sen. Thruston Morton

(R–Ky.), Sen. Roman Hruska (R–Neb.), Sen. Robert Taft, Jr. (R–Ohio), Sen. Hugh Scott (R–Pa.), Sen. John Tower (R–Tex.), Sen. Wallace Bennett (R–Utah), Rep. Bob Wilson (R–Calif.), and some others.

The process of being a ghost is not too complicated, particularly with the absolutely competent research backing of a group like AEI. Interestingly enough, I don't know of anything similar on the left—a regular service for legislators, objective enough to be useful to all parties but still a source of solid viewpoints for those who can use them. The trade unions maintain very effective research organizations, although none with the intellectual depth of AEI, and they, of course, prepare reams of material for legislators. But the material is more narrow, reflecting union interests, and the favors are done more as a form of lobbying than as an ongoing, available-to-everyone service. AEI's great contribution is that, in fact, it *does* objective research and will do it for anyone. Its daily news summary, for instance, is probably used by more Congressmen, Republican and Democrat, than any other bipartisan outside service. That AEI's objective research includes conservative material is, in their eyes and, I must say, mine, only fair. A left research group could do the same, dedicating itself to simply assisting Congressmen, tending to help some more than others, perhaps, and presenting left analysis in solid settings of fair comparison with right-wing analysis. Curiously enough, as will be discussed later, some of the most radical positions on both sides would seem to coincide. But, overall, the sort of left analysis which is so different from squishy liberalism could be seen in a sensible, matter-of-fact way rather than bombastically. Liberals, of course, have such groups as the Brookings Institution and the majority of universities as well as government agencies to do their research for them—the research that always supports corporate power with government regulation and establishes new programmatic ways to regiment the population, and particularly the poor, into totally dependent federal constituencies.

But AEI was effective in other ways than just the presentation of its scholarship. It was, as Champion Papers had been earlier, an effective focus of loyalty, morality, self-identification, and ethics, a substitute for self which is apparently the internal personnel goal of every corporate institution. Total loyalty to the corporate institution is demanded and, for those who stay, given.

The outward and visible sign of the loyalty is always the clock. To work late and long is seen as desirable. Last minute crises are cherished because they so dramatically separate the eager from the others. I am absolutely convinced that in most corporate groups there is a tendency to do and redo work right up to the last minute, through long hours, over weekends and (the annual Great Test) through Christmas or any other holiday—not because this improves or is even in the final analysis intended to improve the quality of the work, but because it tests the loyalty of the corporate employees, their willingness to subjugate and sacrifice themselves. And, to the outside world, it is a busy, busy sign of hard work, a sign that is more easily assessed by the obtuse than if they had actually to judge the quality of the work. I have seen too many speeches done and redone because of innocuous changes, for instance, to feel that sheer quality was involved. No, the command principle is involved. A boss must command or not seem a boss. One way to command is to change and change and change again.

The corporate group also becomes the center of every facet of your life. Home is clearly secondary. Wives are functionaries for corporate entertainments. Children are conversation pieces for corporate chit chat. They are sometimes heard of but seldom seen.

There is no limit to the lengths to which corporate loyalty will drag individual conscience. Personal habits are, of course, at the absolute disposal of the corporate procedure and image. At AEI the top people even lived close together. For a time we used the same tailor.

But it is not just that. Conscience too soon starts to bend to the corporate mold. This is not to say that people join a corporate body like AEI, or General Motors, without any internal equipment at all, that they are simply clean slates for the corporation to write on. No. Each person carries into the corporate life some disposition to favor the particular corporation or at least a willingness to be bought at whatever cost the corporation demands. Corporate creatures are volunteers, after all, even though heavily conditioned by the entire environment of American education and culture to believe that corporate loyalty is the perfectly proper substitute in a complicated world for individual self-reliance and self-realization. It is also seen as a substitute for the traditional communities of natural association in which most people have lived throughout most of history.

My dispositions were all just right for the AEI life. I was a rather reflexive anti-Communist, reflexive in that I had really no interest in understanding the Communist philosophical view but had an interest only in attacking it as it is manifested through Soviet state policy. I was conservative particularly in my dislike of liberal politics and programs. And I was absolutely unquestioning of the role of the major corporations in American life, a role which I later came to see as identical to that of the liberal dream for the role of the federal establishment, a role of monopoly and unlimited power over people generally.

There was one way in which I did not fit the conservative mold—I was not religious. But AEI was, or at least its principal powers were and so were many of its power principles—to turn an old speech writer's phrase.

There is, for example, a strand of conservatism that sees Communism as evil principally because it is atheist. Poverty is seen as having divine sanction, as is wealth. God's hand is everywhere in the politics of many conservatives. I have found, for instance, that many conservatives, when engaged in a long discussion of communism and when shown how Soviet and American state policy is more similar than different in favoring heavy industry over local business, or in using the welfare state to regiment as well as to aid, or in using the terror of national security as an excuse for obliterating liberties—that when many conservatives go through such an exercise they are left at the headshaking end of it all with the simple declaration, "Well, I don't care what else there is, Communism denies God and says that human beings can work out their own salvation here on earth. We don't believe that and that's why we hate Communism and why there can be no coexistence with it."

There is an immensely confusing point that could arise here. The same conservatives who see God as central to their foreign policy evict him altogether from important parts of their domestic policy. The Communists are hated because they say that the relationship of humans to humans is central, rather than the relationship of humans to God. Yet the American corporations say, by their actions, that the relationship of humans to the corporate entity is basic. Certainly religious faith plays no important role in mediating that relationship. The escape clause is a version of the separation of church and state. American religionists have been able to preach convincingly the notion that business is one thing and religion another, with little connection. Business connects not to religious morality but to legal morality alone. Conservatives have added to that separation by longstanding opposition to what they regard as social gospels, any religious position that attempts to interfere with the "natural" working of the marketplace or, for that matter, of the state. Religion, then, can become a strictly Sunday affair with God. The rest of the week belongs to lesser bosses.

AEI's leading religious tendency, the religion of its leading figures, was Roman Catholic. Having been born a Catholic, and never having mentioned that I was an atheist, was advantageous, therefore, to my going to work there.

But even though religion certainly didn't get in the way of workaday matters, there was Sunday. And on Sunday, a good many people at AEI went to mass. And they made convincing arguments for why they did it. They were learned people.

Before long, so deep had the habit of corporate loyalty become to me, I decided it would be wise to return to the Church. And I did, with a vengeance. It was up and out every Sunday, rain or shine, even before the frequent Sunday work sessions. My older son was dragged along. The younger son was too young. I can now recall no more profoundly dishonest and debased part of my life than this pretense to religion which grew from respect for the judgment of my bosses and the zeal of corporate loyalty—and from an utter lack of personal confidence, personal politics, or even a sense that those things were important.

It is, on a very personal level, the most meaningful criticism of conservative politics that they are, when all is said and done, corporate politics. In my long years of service to that politics it was conformity to corporate norms, whether of the corporate church or the corporate organization, that dominated, and not loyalty to—or even interest in—self in any deep sense. When there is no loyalty to or sense of self then there is only the most superficial loyalty to anyone else. And love is a meaningless concept. To love and be loved there must, it seems to me, be a person there, a self conscious of itself, possessed of an identity which can love and be loved.

If corporate loyalty comes before anything else, then the corporate person is just that—a corporate person, not an individual human person. The person's identity is that of the corporate group. The person's dreams, future, time, zeal, skills, everything, are shaped by and contained within the corporate body. Anything outside of that body is regarded as suspect, or frivolous. And nothing is seen as more frivolous than human love. The word itself is virtually outlawed in corporate life, including, of course, most political life, which is the life of the corporate body of the State.

Love, which is the total response, emotional, intellectual, ethical, and esthetic, of one person to another, a response that involves commitment, sharing, openness, is the exact antithesis of any corporate undertaking.

Corporate bodies, being hierarchical, emphasize dominance, obedience, secrecy, relationship to abstractions such as rules, and quantifiable rewards and accomplishment. Love cannot be handled well on ledger sheets.

I cite the lack of love in corporate matters mainly because it is possible that, for some, religion can be seen as a substitute. Love of God is harmless in corporate terms. It is not anticipated that religious people will rock any secular boats. And, indeed, for every rebellious religious person (such as Quakers generally, radical priests, a few Protestants, particularly fundamentalists who take their religion very seriously), for every one who acts on the basis of belief, there are dozens of others who are paralyzed by it, rendering unto Caesar anything Caesar wants and rendering unto God somewhat less on a Sunday than is rendered to the National Football League.

What religion meant to me in terms of corporate loyalty was, looking back, a nightmare. I recall actually going to church to pray to believe, for some enlightenment that would turn the chore of professing into the joy of believing. It never came, and for several years, church and churchly profession was just another profession not of love of God but of loyalty to and acceptance of the ethics of corporate life.

The total involvement with corporate life is corrosive of human life generally. My marriage, to a remarkably fine woman, became like most corporate marriages a sham. Loyalty, not love, is the name of the corporate game. Home, family, self, all disappear into corporate loyalty and corporate striving. Abstractions replace real life. There is no connection to nature. There is less and less connection to self and more and more absorption into the corporate body. It exists. You function. And just as labor of any sort is alienated by this relationship so is intellectual work. It becomes a craft function in and totally subordinate to corporate abstractions.

And the great weights of "responsibility" begin to accrue. Debt, fear of not rising in the corporate structure, fear of not possessing those things by which people are judged in the corporate suburbs, fear of having to deal with problems of everyday life which might interfere with corporate life—the fear that drives people into more and more extravagant addictions to time-consuming corporate work—all of those things wear away whatever is left of human life in corporate absorption. Soon there is nothing left but function. You are valuable because, like any other piece of corporate furniture, you function. You are function. Not person. Function.

I cannot imagine how people can remain married under corporate conditions. All of the purposes of mutual support and consideration which make marriage a decent relationship evaporate when corporate life dominates. There may be many specific causes cited for the rising tide of divorces in the country but it seems to me that everyone of them is at least exacerbated and in many cases prepared by the overall facts of life in corporate institutions.

My own marriage ended some time after my leaving AEI, but from the time I first entered corporate life seriously, back at Champion Papers in Ohio, the possibility of decent relationships with anyone or anything not related to corporate purpose vanished.

The AEI years did, however, serve as the instrument of my association with Barry Goldwater and it is one I have never regretted. It was warm and even loving. It served to plant anti-corporate seeds that finally, I now feel, brought me back to life.

I first worked for Goldwater during his fight against legislation to ban nuclear weapons testing in the atmosphere. I was geared up for this by my own belief, then, that in the fight against the Soviet Union victory would be decided by military hardware. It was a simple formula: If we maintained an edge we would dominate and that would be good. If they got the edge, they would dominate and that would be bad.

There is a simplicity to such an equation that drives every other consideration into the ground. It is an argument that simply overpowers common sense. For instance, it permits you to say, as I often did in speeches read by important people, that in the struggle against Communism we had to forego certain luxuries of freedom in order to preserve freedom. Later, when some soldier with his own version of the simple explanation said that, in Vietnam, a village had to be destroyed in order to save it, we could all begin to see the edge of madness on which the simple explanation of Us versus Them rests.

At any rate, Goldwater's crusade against the test ban was one that I viewed enthusiastically. (His major reason for opposing the ban on testing was that we would be seriously disadvantaged by never testing actual nuclear warheads and, particularly, would be disadvantaged by not testing, in the atmosphere, the various electromagnetic phenomena associated with airbursting nuclear weapons—phenomena which, to the slight extent already observed, can wipe out radio communications, perhaps even interfere with missile operations and aiming.)

The response to our collaboration was good. *The New York Times*, reprinting one of the speeches in full, said that it had raised the level of discussion well above the expected. Goldwater, an Air Force reserve general, an experienced pilot, and a man knowledgeable and technically capable in electronics, knew the technical issues personally and well.

But there was something else. Quite a bit, as a matter of

fact. Barry Goldwater has been criticized most violently for being a simplistic person, seeking and offering simple solutions. He is, personally, however, subtle and complex. Even while we worked on the test ban opposition, perpetuating the purely military side of the Cold War, the side where there can be no winners, Goldwater was discussing with me an amazingly perceptive insight: that in the natural development of federal power in this country there was a natural tendency toward totalitarianism. At the same time, he felt there were forces at work in the Soviet Union that would force that nation toward a free society. He suggested then a most amazing version of convergence theory. Usually convergence theory says that the two superpowers will simply become more alike until they reach a state of equilibrium, each having become enough like the other to make intense competition unnecessary. Goldwater's was a different theory. In it, the United States would move *continually* along the road to authoritarianism, mainly through the spread of federal power, while the Soviet moved to freedom —and the two of them, rather than reaching equilibrium, would simply pass one another going in different directions, the Russians toward an altogether free society, we toward dictatorship.

If that theory were advanced today by some academic authority, I am sure it would be given a good hearing. Goldwater never advanced it publicly then, because his staff took an absolutely negative view of it and he didn't think it important enough to buck them. But if he had advanced it then or now, there would be people who would oppose it simply because it came from him, a relatively ordinary person, and not from a foundation study group.

But there is a contradiction in the position which common sense quickly reveals. The main lever with which the federal government pries its way into more and more power is the national-security claim that it lays on virtually every one of its actions.

To advocate a strong national-security state, as Goldwater

always did, while at the same time facing the fact that one of its consequences—increased federal power—would accomplish in the long run just what an enemy invasion would, is to engage in a great contradiction. I certainly didn't see it at the time. Goldwater didn't seem to see it. It was never discussed. But it was the sort of contradiction which can haunt you for a long time. It did me—a long time later.

Actually, it was the many extraordinary contradictions raised by Barry Goldwater which finally shook me out of conservative politics altogether. For a time I thought they might do the same for him. They haven't seemed to—but I still keep hoping.

One of the contradictions is that of concentrated power. Most conservatives understand fully the dangers of concentrated power, politically. They do not discuss, understand, or even seem to care about the implications of concentrated economic power. Actually, Barry Goldwater did care about it and even discussed it, at least privately; and discussed it enough, apparently, so that in his 1964 run for the Presidency he did not get the support of major corporations. They threw their money to Johnson, with whom they knew they could wheel and deal without worry.

But that terrible contradiction of criticizing concentrated political power without worrying a bit about concentrated economic power—power that is concentrated in close collusion with state power at every step of the way—is a contradiction that absolutely haunts the entire conservative position.

There is another contradiction—one the Senator and I discussed many times. That is the contradiction between supporting concentrated power at the level of the fifty states while opposing it at the federal level. The reason for opposing it at the federal level is in large part because it represents power over people which the people cannot control. But the same thing is true when state governments extend their powers. It is power that is relatively far from the reach of people where they live. I always did think that conservatives were simply deluding themselves when they suggested by their policies that power at the state level is different from power at the federal level. It really isn't, for the people directly affected. The state police have, within the state, the sort of easily abused power that the FBI has within the nation or the CIA throughout the world. The state revenue officers are, to people in the state, as great a threat as the IRS is to taxpayers on the national level.

It seemed to me even in my darkest conservative days that no political power not directly within the reach of the people generally is safe or desirable.

Yet, so powerful is the yielding to corporate pressure, to the wisdom of the superior group, or to the boss, that I spent years willingly supporting the conservative side of all those contradictions without really caring very much and without thinking very much.

Perhaps the sharpest contradiction of all, with Senator Goldwater, came with the Indo-Chinese war. As it grew and as his support for it grew, it contrasted sharply with, for instance, his very first 1964 campaign pledge to repeal and end the draft. He said very often that if there was a war that people didn't want to fight, you probably shouldn't fight it at all. The Indo-Chinese war, begun as an executive action, expanded as an executive action, was fought with draftees. It was not a war that people even knew existed until too late. It was a war that contradicted every basic principle I had thought Senator Goldwater stood for. Yet he supported it and, while I was too busy being a successful political theorist to do any real thinking about it, so did I.

I have often wondered, however, what Barry Goldwater would have done, if elected President, about the war in Indochina. The popular conception is that he would have waged all-out war, gone for a quick victory and even used nuclear weapons if that seemed sensible to get it over on American terms. And, because I know full well that a lot of Republican warriors have no more profound analysis of any military action than wanting to win, that certainly is a possibility. But so is this: As President he would have had available the information which later caused Daniel Ellsberg to risk his future and freedom to bring to public light. That information shows beyond the shadow of a doubt that the American intervention into the Indo-Chinese war was for absolutely cold-blooded geopolitical reasons, fed by John Kennedy's rabid fear of Asian Communism. It was not an intervention to counter an exactly equal intervention by the troops of the north. The Pentagon Papers show with anguished clarity the deception that John Kennedy had to exercise to justify using troops because he could not, in fact, produce any evidence of massive northern interventions of the sort which *followed* the American military presence on the Indo-Chinese peninsula.

Given that information, Barry Goldwater might just have ordered the troops home and quite possibly even ordered an investigation of the civilian and military authorities who permitted that most gross of Constitutional breaches, the waging of war without declaration by the Congress.

Might he have stayed, however, just to save American face? Well, he often said that saving your face wasn't worth losing your ass. And, publicly, he said that saving face wasn't worth one life.

The importance of the observation of contradictions as a beginning of wisdom probably will appear a commonsense, commonplace sort of thing to most people. It should be. It's the way commonsense people test the truth of many ordinary situations. That contradictions should arouse so little interest at the highest levels of American politics where, at least, I had some close glimpses, is striking to me.

It says very clearly that politicians are not involved in any sort of search for truth. It says that politicians are not involved with ideology or with ideas. They are involved, instead, with political advantages and with political competition, not between ideas but between personalities and factions.

Commonsense Americans know that at least one thing George Wallace said is true; that when it comes to the politicians of the two major parties there isn't a dime's worth of difference between them. The same commonsense Americans, observing George Wallace and his own flitting from position to position, may understand that there isn't a dime's worth of difference there, either. (George Wallace once proudly claimed that the way he would assure liberty in the land would be to put a policeman on every corner. The grand contradiction there, of course, is that the police are the principal agents of the state itself, and, over time, except where they are closely controlled by the people, as in small towns, operate to support not liberty but state power. So here, in the case of George Wallace, you have that fully-fleshed-out contradiction of a politician saying on the one hand that government power is the end of freedom while, on the other hand, offering to place on every street corner that ultimate symbol of government power, the armed agent of the state. The question must be asked, "And how are the police paid, and how much freedom would you have left after paying to put one on every corner?" It is doubtful that any gangs of ordinary criminals could steal as much from you as the state can legally levy from you.)

By the time the 1964 Presidential campaign rolled around, I was completely comfortable with Senator Goldwater, completely comfortable with the fact that even if there were a lot of contradictions around him, there were many more around Johnson, and that, after all, I was doing quite well in my profession.

And then there was the Senator himself. He is a good friend, the sort of person with whom it is pleasant to spend time. He is not pretentious. does not seek or demand deference. He is genuinely interested in ideas, but not stuffy about them. Walking with him on the desert is a special pleasure. He loves that native land, knows it well, relates to it in the best ecological sense. At home in Arizona he feels very much a part of nature and not apart from it. Back in Washington, in that most unnatural environment where the exercise of power is the practice, he is not quite the same, often siding with those who view nature as merely a subsidiary concern, always secondary to sheer economic growth. I cannot fully explain and certainly would never apologize for the fact that I cannot imagine *not* being a friend of Barry Goldwater—although I sharply disagree with many of his latest positions.

Just as I received my education in the dynamics of corporate life at Champion and AEI, I received an education in raw power during the 1964 Presidential campaign. It is a fairly simple lesson with complex parts.

Power does corrupt. Knowing that as a theoretical proposition does not necessarily equip you at all to cope with the situation as a practical reality. In the first place, one of the great corruptions of power is the conviction by the power wielder that it doesn't corrupt but, in fact, ennobles. I cannot imagine any wielder of power thinking otherwise. It is automatic, a reflex. As impressive as it is to hear of the so-called humble rulers who walk among the people and share their simple fare, it is unimaginable that there is not the moment, somewhere, sometime, when the impatience of power clears the streets so that the great one may walk faster, where the responsibility of power doesn't, even with regret, roll roughshod over everyday life in order to get at eternity. (As I have said, seeing Fidel Castro go so freely among the people is a wonder to behold, but prudence always reminds us that he goes home to a place of power and not a worker's cottage. Gandhi comes to mind as the great exception—for Gandhi's struggle was against power itself.)

If every lesson I have learned in a long political life had to be distilled into a single one, it would be that when the people generally permit positions of power to exist, the people generally and in the long run suffer and become subjects. In a world of power there always are two classes: the powerful and the powerless, the owners and the dispossessed. And between these two classes there must always be a conflict of interest. The exercise of power becomes and is an end in itself. Life, love, work, and creativity have historically been sacrificed to the demands of power. For loving, working, and creative people to throw off the yoke of power it is necessary to abolish power itself, not merely make the yoke comfortable. Where some have power, others do not, and the two classes persist. A free society is where all have power—power over and responsibility for their own lives, power and reason to respect the lives of others. This is, also, a society without classes, a society of human beings, not rulers and the ruled.

The whiffs of power that I have had confirm me in my belief that it is power itself that is the mortal enemy of freedom.

During the 1964 Presidential campaign the whiffs were sharp, even if small, and very heady. The police escorts, for instance. You sit in the back of a limousine, with motorcycle policemen and wailing sirens like a mantle around you. You see the streets and the people on them like a tapestry on your fantasy castle wall. The little people, frozen by the strobe light of your screaming speed, immobilized in half-steps, heads turned and frozen as you roar past. They are a tableau. You are alive. You move. They stand and vanish. You persist.

I do not believe for a minute that this is a particular craziness on my part. Look at the people you see in the cars when next a motorcade passes. Can you really imagine that they are just folks? Are their heads not filled with the glory of being where they are and the secret, or not so secret, pride that they are there and you are where you are, each in their place, the high and the low, the mighty and the masses? Wouldn't it be crazier, on the other hand, to pretend there are no classes when such evidence of it careens before your eyes?

What sort of im̧pervious head would it take not to be turned when airlines hold planes for you (as they will with even a casual call from the White House or even some senators)? What sort of ironclad piety could prevent a person from understanding that when the private corporate jet and the liveried servants await your pleasure you are being served and the persons serving are servants? When the police lines open up and let you through and keep them out, what ivory-headed detachment could keep you from understanding that there is, in this world, a Them and an Us?

Early in the planning of the campaign, Senator Goldwater had seriously wanted to do his campaigning in a small plane which he would pilot, with just a few friends along. He hated the motorcycle escorts. But he couldn't win the argument so long as it was not an argument, across the board, against power itself. That argument peeped around the corners of his campaign but never fully emerged. It couldn't. It was overwhelmed, as were we all, finally, by power itself, the lure, the barbaric pleasure, the actually sadistic pride of it all. And how could it be otherwise? Well, there had been a slim chance. Goldwater could have campaigned, from his little plane, on the streets, on the corners, even over television and radio, against power, pledging not to sit in the White House and exercise it but to roam the length and breadth of government and abolish it regularly, steadily, to the extent that a President can. But maybe even that's an illusion, to use power to destroy power. It is also, in all probability, the most important political-philosophical question we will have to face in our lifetime.

Facing it, for me, by the end of the 1964 campaign, meant the beginning of a change not just in beliefs but in my life, a change toward a politics of living rather than making a living from politics.

4

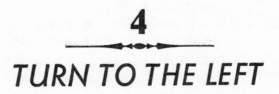

TURN TO THE LEFT

The day after the defeat of Barry Goldwater in the 1964 election, Senator Goldwater started building a color television set, at his home in Paradise Valley, on the edge of Phoenix. In about a week he was watching the news on it.

The day after the defeat, I started relaxing; taking a vacation and generally feeling that, having gone through a Presidential campaign at the very top level, I would scarcely have to worry about my future anyway. In about a year it turned out that I was right, but for none of the reasons that I could have predicted.

The year was spent, mainly, writing a book about the campaign, an endeavor well-financed by consultant jobs thrown my way through AEI. The book, entitled *In a Cause that Will Triumph*, was, should historians of that period be interested, a fair statement of the ideology of the campaign, fair and frank.

But, while writing the book, a sort of fate in its very strangest form entered and altered what I still thought was a settled pattern of my life. The private contradictions of the campaign nagged a bit but, by and large, it looked as though I could and would continue indefinitely a safe, well-heeled, upward-mobile, suburb-centered, country club career.

Then I bought a motorcycle.

It was just a little motorcycle but, to judge by the impact it had on friends, neighbors, and family it might as well have been a half-ton Harley chopper. And even though I wore proper suits and ties while riding the thing, I might just as well have been in the colors of the Hell's Angels.

Today, of course, it is fashionable to ride a motorcycle. There are excellent reasons. It is a big business, well advertised, and presented in four colors on TV and in the better magazines. When I started riding it was just a means of transportation and a sheer physical delight. Because it was just that, and not yet made respectable by being a big business, it was automatically disreputable. Not the thing to do. Odd. Weirdo. Proper people want new cars, not motorcycles. Proper people do not make decisions on the basis of how things feel. They make decisions on the basis of how things appear.

Not to make too much of my little motorcycle but, among other things, it started me thinking about how little the sensual and personal are permitted in modern middle-class lives.

On the one hand we are driven by the ethic that tells us we must compete against everyone, win, succeed, and do it in the vacuum of our own absolutely isolated effort. On the other we are surrounded by the ethos that teaches that the way we succeed is a marketing relationship with others, a relationship in which we sell exactly that image of ourselves which we feel the surrounding community wants and expects and which, in particular, we feel is wanted by the people in the society who actually control our lives, the owners and bosses. In the first instance we deny the personal because our entire life is stretched out, aimed might be the better word, at others, beating against them, using them, competing with them for rewards. We are identified as function, not as person. We hear wherever we go that we must not let our *personal* life interfere—with anything! And so we have less and less of the life of a person and more and more the life of a thing. And, in the second instance, we deny the sensual and the moral. We do not do things because of how they feel to us, or how they satisfy our conscience. Most of us do things because of how those things *appear*. Feeling is always subordinated to appearance. The car must look rich for us to seem rich—and we must seem rich because that is the best thing to be—not good, not wise, but rich. Wise can be arguable. Rich is numbers. You can't argue with figures, we hear and hear again. And so it goes.

The motorcycle felt good. Drinking never felt good. Sex, in the middle class and the very busy upward-mobile middle class particularly, isn't a feel-good thing either—so much as it is a do-good thing. Conquests are the way to count it. Sex is like any other form of entertaining. It serves a purpose to the upward bound and most of all, naturally, to the upward-bound man. I cannot recall, in any middle-class suburb, ever hearing men talk of sexuality of either their own selves or of women. They talked about sex. Conquest sex and oblivion drinking, those are the lives of the senses in the suburbs for most people there.

The motorcycle was an affront to all of that, I suppose. Even the little one. Then I got a larger one. And I rode it longer and farther and I began to meet other people riding longer and farther. How hateful the image must have seemed to the neighbors and, of course, to my wife. That great, roaring, nasty thing must seem like an erotic invader in the quiet suburbs. It trails fantasies of leather-jacketed violence, of crazy goings-on in wild groves and ramshackle houses. It is the vehicle of the barbarians in the sweet land of the safe and sanctified.

There is wisdom in that. So long as the pleasures of the suburbs are the pleasures of commerce, buying entertainment the way everything else must be bought, then the ethics of the suburbs may remain comfortably commercial as well, and the late night impulses of men and women to look at the ruins of their dreams and their families and their loves can be thrust back down into the mind as aberrant. The normal is the world in which buying a new hat is considered a therapy, in which buying a new car is considered masculine heroism, in which the broken dreams can be replaced by the packaged dreams, in which love is replaced by loyalties and in which, finally, feeling can be steadily denied as too personal and appearance substituted totally as being merely objective and absolutely safe.

There is a popular literature that ascribes to the middle class the one thing for which I cannot believe it should be blamed. That thing is the invention of its own condition. I do not feel that middle-class Americans, whether in the suburbs of little boxes or in the lattices of urban high rises, invented their own alienation from self, senses, nature, and work. The conditions arose from the needs of their employers. To devote an industrial nation to production for production's sake, to endless growth and soaring numbers without human meaning or scale, then people must be separated from their own sense of self, their own dreams, their own personalities, and from any solidarity with others within which to forge the bonds back to themselves.

The gleaming sameness of the supermarkets, glutted with differing brands that offer only the illusions of difference, requires people as both customers and employees who themselves will be content with illusions and who will confuse freedom of choice among mere numbers with the freedom to choose ways of life, meanings, and relationships.

Too, when quantity and not quality is the rule of production, it must be the rule of living as well—or else discontent and rebellion would shatter the idyll.

If people were to identify with work as a measure of their own meaning, and demand that it mean something in personal terms of satisfaction, then how could they work as robots on production lines or as machines in offices? To work like machines, people must be trained to live as machines, totally immersing their identities with the identities of their material possessions which, as the process progresses, actually become them. (Recall the signs you often see, advertising a mass-produced fashion item with the slogan, "Wear this because you've got to be you.")

The process of turning people into such partners of a commercial process is complex—advertising, schools, drama, music, all the means of acculturation are involved. Dominating them is the ethic of progress and growth—about which more separately and later.

The point is that millions of good and honest Americans cannot be blamed for being what they are and certainly cannot be called to task for permitting the system that makes them that way to dominate the earth and sometimes ravage it. Many of those who do call the millions to task and bitterly attack them as though they authored their own self-destructive lifestyles are people who cannot find it proper to blame all Russians for Stalin. Neither the Russians nor the Americans should be blamed as peoples for the culture and colonization that follows from the needs of their ruling classes. Far better than blame is the patience to work with those who want to change, wait for those who can't yet see the need, and struggle constantly, however and wherever and whenever you can against the rulers and most particularly the rulers *where you are.* To struggle against rulers by just having opinions about them is no struggle at all. To struggle against leaders about whom you can *only* have opinions, such as those remote in time or place, is also to substitute the structure of sentences for the substance of struggle.

But why struggle at all? Is it really necessary? Of course not. It only becomes necessary if the way you lead your life makes it necessary. There are few who make changes simply for abstract reasons or through abstract reasoning. Most often the changes in your head—one of which may be the desirability of working hard for hard changes—closely follow but do not precede changes in your life.

Once begun, the ride on the motorcycle was like that. It

was a ride away from the suburbs, for sure. And a ride toward that most heretical of questions that can be asked in the middle class, the question of whether one should do things because of the way they feel rather than the way they look. And for the first time in a long time, understanding that the sheer pleasure of the motorcycle was drawing the sheer displeasure of so many people, including those upon whom my living depended, I recalled the long walks with my mother and her advice. You mustn't care what it looks like to others, you must be sure of how it feels to you!

And I was really beginning to feel sure. I was meeting new people, understanding new interests, and beginning to feel something very strange. I was beginning to feel very much alive not as a function, not as a force of history, not as a servant to power, but simply as a person.

Seen from a certain angle I am sure it all seemed like the most arrogant selfishness, the craziest playing, a sort of second childhood. I can certainly understand that, because that is certainly the way I used to see everything.

In fairly rapid order all of this resulted in a divorce and the stark realization that I was completely beyond the pale of regular politics as well. Having worked for Barry Goldwater was, in a way, bad enough. The regular Republican Party treated ex-Goldwaterites, for a time, as total outcasts. Nimble ones, of course, escaped that fate easily, shifting from Goldwaterism to, for instance, Nixonism, with grace and alacrity. The diehards simply died.

In the midst of it all, the personal changes, the shifting ground of career and everything, I ran into the person who, more than any other, I really feel helped me survive it all and make sense out of it. This was Marcus Raskin, co-director of the Institute for Policy Studies in Washington, D.C. a onetime Kennedy Security Council functionary, a political scientist who was almost a concert pianist and a person whose great talent, in the very wise words of our friend Gary Wills, is for affection.

It was Marc who, of all the people I had considered liberal or leftist, after a seminar at the Institute seemed most appreciative of the notion that the Goldwater campaign had been, if nothing else, one of the great and dramatic confrontations between modes of political power; that Goldwater had, in fact, represented a real tendency toward Congressional government while Johnson epitomized Executive government. Marc understood that there *was* a crucial difference. It had not been nearly so clear to the people even in our campaign. Marc also understood, and elaborated on, the notion of Goldwater as a rather old-fashioned liberal, not a conservative. But Marc, more wisely than Goldwater himself, who often said he was a liberal, identified him as a Manchester liberal, a crusader against state power for a particular and not a general reason—the particular reason of industrial expansion. Above all, Marc seemed immediately to know, on each of the several times I saw him during the post-election period, that I would inevitably face a crisis of my own conscience over the contradictions of the conservative position in regard to freedom and the national-security state, and the contradictions between freedom and the power of giant corporations. He was kind enough never to push, wise enough always to know just a bit more about my concerns than even I did at the time. Above all, he was and is a constant friend and a constant struggler himself with the ambiguities and contradictions of the twilight time between where we are and where we want to be.

With Marc, also, I met people like Milton Kotler, also at the Institute. He brought me face to face with a very particular contradiction. For years my political writing had included an emphasis on accomplishing things at the lowest possible level of government, using the federal only where needed, usually just for defense and safeguarding the money supply, using the state for most other things, including welfare. Somehow or another there had been in all that writing only polite gestures toward actually local forms of social organization. It was mentioned in many speeches, but always in the same way that politicians mention God—not because of belief, but because of manners.

Kotler, on the other hand, was involved with entire neighborhoods where people were saying, in effect, let us govern ourselves fully. Localism was alive and thriving as a way of living where Kotler was working. It had been mere window dressing where I had been working.

And there was Richard Barnet, then working on a book which eventually caused me to make a public display of a private change in conviction. It was his work in particular, that brought me to that hardest of all confrontations, the confrontation with the contradiction between a free society and an all-consuming passion for security.

And so the changes in my head began. But, without a wrenching change of another sort, it might have all stayed there, just in my head.

The really big change involved work—the first I had ever done in my life, if work is defined the way most Americans are forced to define it: hard work, manual work, work in which mind and body are in immediate contact with material reality. Not the work of a mandarin, but the work of men and women.

Oddly enough, even the work came in a way from the motorcycle, that small stone which was the first hard object to shatter the soft clinging resistance of old habits and hopes. I had begun to race motorcycles in competition, not well, but enthusiastically enough to wreck them with some regularity.

Because of that I decided to study welding, to help put the cycles back together again. A shrewder judge of my riding ability would have suggested that I study orthopedic surgery, to put me back together again. But welding can be studied, free, at public night schools. Surgery, alas, cannot, so far.

I not only studied welding, becoming proficient with both oxyacetylene and submerged-arc techniques and at least familiar with inert gas welding, but I went to work as a welder. With Don Bried, a fellow student, I invested the last of my savings from the high life, got some equipment and went to work repairing heavy equipment, at night, when there was a maximum demand but a minimum of available welders. We worked on bulldozers, mainly rebuilding blades, building board-holders for big dump trucks, hard-facing teeth on big shovels, repairing lo-boy trailers and every other sort of weldment common to construction work and trucking.

It was there, under trucks, inside buckets, working hard, that I faced the final contradictions, the ones that ended any hope of anything in my life ever being quite the same again, that began the hope that the way I was beginning to think would be also the way I would live and that, at last, heart, hands, and head would all come together and there would be a real person where there had once been a function or a functionary, a part person, a bit player in other people's plays.

The final contradictions had to do with people.

In the political theory of the life I had led, the abilities of people to control their own lives were seen as sharply divided. On the one hand people were said to have enough sense to run their lives without the interference of a lot of government bureaucrats. But on the other hand they were not seen as able to govern their lives without a lot of corporate bosses. The privileges, prerogatives, and almost divine rights of corporate owners were seen as not only properly above the people generally for legal reasons but for moral reasons: the people could not work without being managed.

The people are said, at least in conservative political prose, to be fit to rule. But they are not fit to manage. Actually, as you face the contradiction posed here, it becomes clear that conservatism is just a version of modern liberalism in its attitude toward people generally. The liberals say that people generally cannot handle politics, and thus must be served and led by bureaucracies. The conservatives say they cannot handle production and thus must be managed.

In life, everyday life, neither is the case. People can and do manage themselves and can and do perform the actions which are needed for their own well-being, the stability of their neighborhoods, and the continuation of their culture. They do these things where it is necessary. They can and are talked out of doing them by those who reap a profit—in politics or money—from making them behave as though powerless and mindless.

At work daily, with other welders, mechanics, truck and heavy-equipment operators, carpenters, steel riggers, electricians, pipe fitters, and engineers, I discovered (imagine, discovering something like this in your forties!) that people have absolutely the capacity to manage themselves in the accomplishment of productive work, that they are not insular and competitive and selfish when dealing with concrete situations—but that they tend to take on those traits when dealing with abstractions.

Faced with a concrete situation, working people try to find an effective way to solve problems and advance the work. Far from being mean or competitive they enjoy, as I certainly enjoyed, any solution that appears to be better than the usual or familiar. A new way to accomplish something is a point of joy and pride for the entire working group, and not just for the author of the idea, if one person, or the skill group, if one of several groups is responsible.

Also, in the small talk of everyday work there is an intense interest in philosophically important rather than trivial matters. Honesty, courage, breadth of spirit, wisdom, prudence, love (that's right, truck drivers and welders know about love) are the subjects of everyday conversation. I have rarely seen it fail, for instance, that when the lusty talk of just plain sex is exhausted, there emerges a story or two of deep and abiding love and that people are affected by them, not titillated in the manner of the sophisticated to whom every warm, human relationship is reduced eventually to gossip.

Why then, some have asked me, don't these working people show delicate and sensitive discrimination in, for instance, their reading habits? Why do they read the *Reader's Digest* or go to Western movies instead of reading Pynchon and viewing Bergman? I am convinced that the reason is not lack of sensibility at all. It is lack of interest and the failure to share a vocabulary. That's the charitable reason. The less charitable is that most people have decided that the highbrow literature is just a cryptic and frivolous way of stating simple, common-sense truths which they know anyway. This is not to say that cryptic writing is not fun and frolicsome for people who live mainly in their vocabularies. It is to say that judging the sensibilities of others by that gauge alone is unsound.

The great problem is when working people—or any people —confuse the real world and the abstractions which are advanced to regulate it. The *Reader's Digest*, for instance, does contain much material, unambiguous material, about the real world—even the cute stuff about Jane's Kidney and Joe's Elbow—but it also contains material about that abstraction, Patriotism.

An important dividing line seems to be that common sense prevails in considering abstractions that pertain to the specific behavior or character of specific humans or discrete groups; on the other hand, sentiment and simple side-taking overwhelms common sense when considering abstractions that pertain to institutions such as nations, corporate bodies, teams, races. People-centered abstractions are usually measured against the actual actions of people, actual people in concrete situations. Common sense prevails. Institution-centered abstractions endow the institution with intrinsic value which is not necessarily judged by concrete action. By and large, people are judged for what they do. The prim talker is not immune from criticism as an active lecher. The mean talker is often excused because of kind acts. Institutions, however, are not judged so much as they are respected. It is not so much what they do as whether or not they do a lot of it. The Congress that passes a lot of legislation is a good one. The legislation is judged, if at all, as somehow separate. The military is probably the most respected American institution despite the scandals that annually are exposed in it, or debacles such as the Indo-Chinese war. It is respected as an institution, not judged for its actions. Also, the flag is respected. What it may stand for at any particular time is not considered. The nation takes on a life and an image separate from reality. It is the purest sort of ideal and abstraction.

On the job I discovered that the introduction of any such institution-centered abstraction into a conversation meant the immediate end of common sense and the beginning of sheer side-taking. But of course exactly the same thing is true in much intellectual work. While working as a welder I also attended many seminars at the Institute for Policy Studies where, on occasion, some Marxist-Leninist purist would demand an explanation of where someone stood in regard to this or that purely abstract line. (How the hell, in America, can you glibly say where you stand in regard to the *lumpenproletariat?*—The what? Or armed struggle?—What arms?) Most seminars, at such a point, break down into the historians arguing about who said what and when, the purists arguing about where you stand in history, and the majority of the other folks retreating into either stunned silence outraged wisecracking, or futile attempts to argue reason in the face of sentiment and allegiances.

So it is under a truck body or beside a bulldozer. Sensible

people in such situations often understand fully that, for instance, people can be self-managing, that party politics is self-serving and deceptive—and paid for by working people—and any number of other ordinary truths. There is even a widespread, and wearied, understanding that the rich benefit from wars fought by the working people. Yet every such consciousness can be and usually is destroyed by the sorts of things that could be called the abstract party lines of patriotism:

"Somebody has got to run things." (The President of the U.S. or of the company.)

"You can't fight city hall." (You're lucky to get the least of two evils.)

"It's your duty to your country." (How should I know whether the war is right or wrong?)

Working American men and women are often shafted by intellectuals for falling into these unexamined positions. But the intellectuals make the same headlong plunges themselves:

"Democratic centralism means that the best people will rule in the name of the people." (Who, us? Replace one ruling class with another? Obstructionist.)

"There are forces of history (or karma, or production, or economics, or gravity, or stellar juxtaposition, you name it) to which we can only respond." (We're the vanguard of history and it's either us, baby, or them.)

"You must serve the people." (Oh, you *are* the people! Well, you know what we mean.)

Lest anyone get the notion that using what could be called left-wing intellectual examples is meant to be an exclusionary exercise, let me restate those points from a right-wing view:

"If we don't have a Republic in which the best can rule, we will have a mob in which the worst will rule." (Who, us? A ruling class? Nonsense, we can't help it if we were born to better things.)

"Human nature being what it is. . . . " (Don't ask me

why, if human nature is basically evil, you get good people at the top, but that's the way it is.)

"All we want is an honest day's work for an honest day's wages." (The time-study people, the pension planners, the budget committee, and my brother's aunt, the majority stockholder, have just announced that, in order to keep the beer-sodden working folk out of the pool room, we have lengthened the working day to twenty-five hours, pending approval by our friends in Congress.)

On the whole, however, working people, practical people, are content to avoid abstractions and so, day after day, I grew more and more convinced that American party politics, treating people generally like retarded humans or flawed humans, was wrong, unhealthy, and unsuited to the human truth—which is the truth of the great potential of people for good works, creative work, loving care, and joyous cooperation.

And while learning that at work, I was learning at the Institute that there was a movement or at least some people, off to the side of politics, many of whom shared that same optimism. It was called the New Left.

Quickly, then, because I want to talk about the New Left in more detail elsewhere, let me sketch in the other practical and material manifestations of interior change.

Separation and then divorce was a major exterior change with profound interior meaning. It was not a separation from a person I did not like but a break with a way of life. Its deepest effect was to teach me that in marriage as in every other social relationship, domination and hierarchy not only dehumanize the subjected people but also corrupt the oppressor. Marriage had deprived my wife of a full life as an independent person. And the deprivation had fed my own vanity and selfishness.

In work there had been a similar situation; the past had been in a world of vanity and competition. The present was in a world of far different values. My work as a welder was enriched, for instance, by experience in a fully cooperative, voluntaristic and quite spontaneous community: a boat community, on the Anacostia River, in which about fifty people shared all the chores of community housekeeping (garbage, fuel deliveries, most food purchasing, and mutual care of the boats which were our homes). Also, the community shared work projects, ranging from boat repairs to light metal construction to dock construction. It was all unstructured, leaderless, and a complete and constant joy. Leaderless, of course, did not mean without any regard for skill. As the best welder, I could be said to lead, when welding was needed. There was a magnificent cabinet maker there and he led, you could say, when small wood joints were the problem. Same with a competent electrician, and so forth.

But skill at one thing was never confused with or accepted as the same as right to command in regard to some other thing.

While it lasted, I say without reservation, it was the most satisfactory of ways to live and to work. It ceased to exist not because of internal weakness, incidentally, but because of the external pressure of the state itself. For reasons which were never explained beyond saying, "It's regulations," the government agency in charge of the Washington waterfront area, the Park Service, ruled that no one could live aboard a boat, at least at our boatyard. The residents of actual yachts, not far away, were never disturbed, nor was the permanent crew aboard the Presidential yacht, docked less than a mile away, in the same river. We fought the action as hard as we could but, in the end, after several years aboard the boats and working in the most pleasant surroundings and most satisfying way, the boat community was shattered and scattered. Its dream, however, surely persists for everyone who lived and worked there.

During the same period I began a small act of resistance

which has had large repercussions in ways I could not imagine when the resistance began. I decided to stop paying taxes.

It was not for an heroic theoretical reason or for any other reason which, in the long run, could be called effective or well thought out.

While working as a welder, I was called in by the Internal Revenue Service to be audited for returns filed while working in politics. The auditing of the losers in a political campaign has by now become simple routine for the victors.

On point after point, it seemed to me, the adding machine person doing the auditing would almost angrily reject any discussion of whether or not a particular decision was just or fair. Instead, the phrase "it's the rule" was a constant rejoinder. Now I am sure that there are people who get themselves so heavily involved in a job that they cannot, in fact, ever act counter to the rules of their superiors. But even in such cases, at least at an industrial level, you find people who will bitch mightily and discuss lengthily the morality or sense of a rule, even if and as they obey it and force it on others. Not so with the little, pinched people of the Internal Revenue Service. In the course of a long audit of many years of returns, I met many of these people. Not one of them seemed to have retained a shred of human decency in the way they worked. They were totally subservient to the corporate demands of their agency, extensions of corporate machine planning, and absolutely nothing else. The easy, sophisticated habit of castigating soldiers for being robots has never really been justified, to my mind. Throughout the Indo-Chinese war there were resistances by soldiers. Every war is full of stories in which ordinary decency breaks through the most incredibly barbarous situations to turn soldiers into human beings, if only for an instant.

But never has it come to my attention or been part of my experience that a revenue agent, a tax collector, has put humanity above regulation. They are, again in my own experience, the most abjectly humorless, dehumanized, order-taking, weak-charactered, easily vicious, almost casually amoral people I have met. If you want to look for a fascist constituency in America, I would suggest that you turn away from ordinary working people, from the small towns, from the neighborhood bullies even, and focus with prudential fear on the hollow men and women who are the cold cogs of federal bureaucracies such as the Internal Revenue Service.

At any rate, to deal with them is to loathe them. And it was while dealing with them, and loathing them, that the most stubborn part of my conservative background hammered its way to the surface. After years of writing against the creeping, creepy power of the federal bureaucracy, after years of theory about the nature of bureaucrats and the dynamics of bureaucratic organization, I suddenly found myself (1) in a face-to-face, significant confrontation with actual, not theoretical, bureaucrats and (2) at a point where I could actually take an action in relation to the bureaucrats rather than just strike a rhetorical pose in regard to them.

Several things about such a moment. It comes, like anger, quickly and without much warning. It usually reflects your general disposition and not any particularly exact need of that disposition. It is not, in short, a utilitarian anger, it is simply an anger.

And so, without urging that it is something everybody should do (though I wish they would) and certainly without claiming that it's the best action a person can take (it actually causes the rebel more trouble, I suppose, than it causes the bureaucrats, since they use the rebellions to justify expanding their own power), without making any extravagant claims for the practice, I can only say that I chose, face-to-face with these prime agents of the state, to tell them "No." I became a tax resister, not simply because of war, not simply because of corruption, not simply because of wanting to emulate the tax-free status of so many big corporations, and certainly not because of a precise political position. I became a tax resister, at that particular moment, because I got mad and because somewhere in everybody's life there probably is a line in the real world which you will not or cannot cross and which, often with the sort of sudden anger I felt, you balk at, stand on, and fight on. In a world of power and command and regimentation and regulation these lines appear with greater frequency. The rate at which they offend people is the rate of movement toward revolutionary change, I suppose.

Although aware that the decision to stop paying taxes grew out of general anger, I did think that there were particular and publicly responsible reasons for doing it. The Declaration of Independence spells out some of those reasons. I referred to it in the first of my letters to the IRS, refusing to pay taxes assessed in the past or demanded in the future.

The Declaration is really so clear. Perhaps that's why the Constitution is taught diligently in school while the Declaration, which is our most fundamental political statement, is treated casually. The Constitution tells us, in effect, why we cannot or should not act in our own self-interest—we must depend on duly-appointed others to do it for us. The Declaration tells us that there comes a time when we must stop taking orders and start taking our lives back into our own hands.

The Declaration points out that the only reason to institute a government is to advance the well-being of the people who get together to do it. Should there come a time when the government ceases to advance the general welfare but, instead, usurps the power of the people, reduces them to wards of power, and serves special interests, then the Declaration says that the people should overthrow that power and replace it with something more practical.

In terms of the federal government, I and many other conservatives had for years been writing that it already had reached a point of absolute usurpation of power. But still the conservatives spoke of the Constitution, not the Declaration. And there was another great contradiction: they spoke of using the Constitution to diminish the power of people who have gained that power precisely through the Constitutional process.

On the left, also, federal power had been attacked for years as having supported armed intervention around the world, as well as at home, in suppressing popular organizations.

We all talk about it. But here, as I said, was a time of being face-to-face with it. And so the Declaration did seem appropriate. I sent a copy of it to the IRS and pointed out that I had concluded, in all conscience, that the tax money was used for a warfare system that killed to preserve the power of the privileged few and a welfare system that regimented the poor for the same purpose, all within a federal system that had absolutely taken over and overpowered every right of individual or community-based freedom that had been envisioned in the settlement of the country.

I have done that now for seven years. The results have been predictable in one way, astonishing in another.

The predictable is that the IRS would not be interested in a declaration of conscience. (Interesting contrast: people who, for reasons of conscience, will not kill are exempted from *military* service. But no one is exempted, through taxes, from general service to the very state that orders the killing in the first place! The state, it seems, takes money more seriously than life.)

Over the years, in pursuit of its many pounds of flesh, the IRS has systematically slapped a 100 percent lien on every piece of my life they could locate. First came bank accounts. They got very little because I have very little. Then came salaries. For a time I was making a salary as a Visiting Fellow at the Institute for Policy Studies. The IRS confiscated it all. So I quit, preferring to remain close to the Institute as a friend rather than as a full-time worker for the government. Once, when I asked the IRS how I might handle a situation in which they took 100 percent of everything I earned while the corner grocer still demanded a smidgen for rutabagas, the IRS robot facing me at the moment replied, with simple clarity: "That's not our problem."

It quickly became apparent that the only way to survive at all is to work in ways by which labor can be swapped directly for sustenance. I have done that ever since, even while dutifully filing with the IRS an annual statement refusing to pay taxes.

The unexpected results of all this have to do with financial convenience and with property.

Not having a checking account, for instance, is an inconvenience. It also is an education and the basis for, I believe, alternative ways of handling money altogether.

A bank account emphasizes money as part of a bookkeeping system rather than a work system. It keeps one more part of your life compartmentalized. The bank account takes on a life of its own. Work has a life of *its* own. So has family. So has passion. So has play. And so forth. Bank accounts also reinforce the sense of unlimited credit, of eternal debt, on which much of our commerce coasts and crashes. The checks float in some limbo of accounts, people learn to manipulate the timing of deposits and spending, overspending is a bookkeeping and not a moral exercise, and vast coupon books of debt slips are repaid with other vast coupon books filled with personal checks stoked by other paper from other corporations, and so forth.

Not having a bank account suggests among other things that cash is better. The direct connection between work, money tokens derived from it or, just as good, barter items, is a reminder that there is such a thing as a real economy, well beyond the bookkeeping of the banks. And even the storage of cash can be handled cooperatively, with a single safe place being shared.

But can you trust anyone but an institution with your money? The answer is that there are many people you can trust with your money if you are living with people whose standards and morality are based upon human interaction rather than on corporate regulations. If a supposed friend betrays a trust, the friendship is lost, and I will now affirm very eagerly that strong friendships and loving relationships are far more useful and precious than money anyway and that there are substantial numbers of people who agree to the extent that they never would betray the one for the other. So, yes, you can trust people if you are living in the same culture and if that culture bases its ethics on how people behave with one another and not on how they behave in relation to abstract rules.

Property is another thing. I now understand that, because of my tax resistance, I can never legally own a single piece of property beyond the simplest personal items. If I did, the IRS, with its insistence that 100 percent of everything I might own or ever earn is rightfully theirs, would confiscate it. So, no property.

At first this seemed to me to be depressing. Again, because of my conservative background I felt that property was truly important and that, as a matter of fact, there were even philosophical reasons to treasure it: ownership assures freedom, and all that; property is the reward for work, and so forth. Even on the left there are strong interests in property. One whole sector of the left, for instance, is based upon the expropriation of property from present holders in order to confer it on new holders. Liberals, of course, combine the worst qualities of all sides and come up with such incredible positions as that of the Kennedy Administration's version of public welfare in which, as one spokesman put it, the government (tax money) would take the risks of scientific research in order that private industry (the people, so far as liberals are concerned) could reap the benefits. Liberals, of course, also explain that they will tax the private industry—sometimes even as much as they tax the poor—in order to pay for welfare programs to feed the impoverished.

What would it mean, then, not to own any property? Unless you feel that your property, and not you, should do work, then owning or not owning property is virtually meaningless, it seems to me. It is not the ownership of property that is important for day-to-day work and life. It is the use of property. Property viewed as an end in itself also becomes a master in itself, looming over the owner and taking on an importance to which the owner's own life becomes devoted and, as a consequence, secondary.

Yet there is an obvious reason for property taking over so many lives. There is a feeling, among many, that only what they own can be counted on as a base for security. What they *do* is usually under someone else's control. The idea of a tiny piece of real estate and an annuity makes a lot of sense when the goal of so many people is to quit work, which they merely tolerate, and to live apart from the life that occupies their most productive years. First of all, of course, this shows the deep estrangement of people from work with which they can or would wish to identify and from which they could derive great inner satisfaction. Among other things, a person would never want to quit work that is satisfying.

Being denied property and being denied also the possibility of even having property as a base for security sends you in search of other values and bases.

First, it puts you in closer touch than ever with the most basic "property" of all—your own life, the one thing which, for sure and certain, you can be said to own; the one thing, for sure, which you had better own, lest it become the property of the state, the corporation, or the party.

When you are thrown into yourself and away from property relationships, new notions of self can emerge. One is that property is properly a tool of your life, rather than your life being a tool of property.

The tool concept of property implies also a skill sense of creativity—that the way you use property will be a consequence of the way you use your life and develop the skills of that life. Skill, whether of the more rarefied variety such as abstract mathematics or the earthier type such as welding or medicine, can be seen in a purely utilitarian and instrumental sense: Will the skill enable me to play a leading role in corporate or state life? Or it can be seen in a social sense: Will the skill make possible a community in which I can live with others? There is sometimes a romantically envisioned third choice: Will the skill enable me to be totally independent? The answer, of course, is, "only if you care to be a hermit." Any and all situations other than being a hermit mean there is no possibility of total independence and every reason for some interrelationship. Anyone who thinks, for instance, that Beethoven or Einstein, because of unique genius, also were uniquely independent forgets the courts of Europe whose orchestras performed the maestro's work, or Princeton University. The brooding loner, separated from everyone by genius, is a romantic figment in literature, never existing in life.

In life, the interconnections are everywhere. For some they are chains. For others they can be the healthy veins of a healthy community, in which healthy and self-reliant but not self-enfolded and separated people live, love, and learn.

Being without property makes it much easier to think of yourself and your skills as more important than any other property. I am sure that I could not, for instance, ever seriously

again entertain an argument about human rights versus property rights. If there is a society in which there is even the
possibility of such an argument, it is one that I would carefully
avoid and which, I would bet, is doomed to simple dysfunc-
tional extinction in the long run. The fact seems to be that
people everywhere are becoming very conscious of being people
and of wanting not to be in bondage to abstractions and to
rules. Property, as it is treated in a commercial society or in
a state socialist society, is not one side of an argument—human
rights versus property rights—it is the negation of even a
difference. In commercial systems it is said that property rights
are human rights and that the ownership of a share of General
Motors stock is as sacred as the ownership of your life. In fact,
given the choice between the laws that support the stock and
the necessity that might bring workers, for instance, into col-
lision with that ownership in order to save their lives by demanding certain costly safety precautions, the commercial
system invariably replies that property rights (which they
again insist are the rights of owning humans) must come first
because only in that priority can the system itself be maintained.
State socialists, who treat state property as sacred, and will kill
people for "misusing" it, also feel that the principle of property
ownership is superior to the claims of ordinary human life.

Both the commercial system and the state system, therefore,
it seems to me, are obsolescent. Human relationships will replace them—and for quite practical reasons, which are discussed elsewhere.

In sum, in regard to the property question, the deprivation
of property has led me to the most meaningful sense of my
own life and skill and my own relationships with other people
as being superior to my old concerns for property simply as
property.

There was a time when house, car, and bank account seemed
the absolute measure of security and success. Each of those,

however, was for me and is also for millions a measure just as surely of the most abject dependency. The house involves an abject relationship to the mortgaging bank. The car has a similar relationship to the bad craftsmanship of the corporations on the one hand and the pharoah-like roadbuilding of the state on the other hand. The average auto owner, it has been estimated, must work about 1,000 hours a year to buy, maintain, and pay for the roads of this agency of freedom. How free is that?

The point is not to demean people who truly value their houses or their cars or any material signs of success. The point is to question closely the prices paid and the roles played. In particular it is to put possessions into perspective. If a person is identified by possessions, then the person and the possessions would seem to be mere objects, the person no more vital than the inanimate possessions. That is too high a price and too dehumanized a role.

The human use of possessions should not obscure the human character. The possessions should be merely adornments of that character and tools of its purposes; purposes which, to avoid demeaning the possessor at all, should be consonant with all of those attributes which, throughout known history, most people in most places have openly described as virtues: kindness, cooperativeness, creativity, the capacity to love and be loved, honesty, friendliness. It should avoid those attributes which, also throughout our known history, people have identified as vile: greed, violence, dishonesty, arrogance, and parasitism.

Finally, property should assume creation and work as well as use. Something that you did not create or did not work for, and do not use, certainly should not be called your property. By this test, most working Americans come out pretty well. The very rich, particularly the inheritor rich, certainly do not.

The price that people pay for the commercial system on

which they see their lives depending may be the forfeiture of actual values which they themselves see as making life worthwhile. The forfeiture may be seen as some sort of social given, an unbreakable rule. Many are questioning that rule today. More may tomorrow. And it is out of that exact questioning that great changes certainly may come. It was out of such questioning that the changes came for me.

From work came the questions about the hierarchical and top-down organization of work and society. I had already questioned it in regard to society and politics. That's why I had become a Republican. Working as a welder made me start questioning it in the world of work. That's why I stopped being a Republican.

From associations at the Institute for Policy Studies, I began questioning my past fears of what I had known as the "left," discovering that its traditions and even some current tendencies were in fact the heartbeat of a decentralized, free society, of the historic attack against power itself. And that's why I identified with and worked with the movement known as the New Left.

From Richard Barnet's fine book, *Intervention and Revolution,* I drew and faced the most difficult political questions of all, difficult because of the years of emotional concrete hardened around them: the questions of unthinking patriotism and the attitude of "my country right or wrong." Barnet's book, which should be a required test of the conviction of any reflexively patriotic person, simply and without polemic rancor or recourse to anything but what could be called historical journalism, sees the course of American foreign policy without its stars-and-stripes clothes on, so to speak. It is a look at the Empire without clothes, the naked power-wielding, gunboating, market-shielding, expansionist empire of big money, big politics, and big plans paid for in the blood of plain people. Oddly or even ironically enough it was people called conservatives who made some of the earliest, harshest analyses of that empire posing as a protector of freedom. Barnet's book, bringing up to date with the most scrupulous scholarship the fullest outline of the imperial nature of American foreign policy was, thus, a voice from the so-called New Left which echoed some conservative good sense which, in that unqualified zeal called anticommunism, at least this conservative had altogether overlooked.

Reviewing Barnet's book for the *Washington Post* newspaper, I commented along those lines and thus, quite publicly, announced that I was forsaking the last bastion of my old conservatism: unqualified patriotism and the notion that every action of the government, if committed beyond the three-mile limit, was good and noble.

Raskin remarked, after that review, that I had frankly blown my cover. Until then it was certainly possible to argue that I was siding with the New Left because I shared with them a revulsion against state power and, specifically, federal power. But that could have been limited to domestic policy where, in fact, the New Left criticism of past liberal policies was much sharper than any conservative criticism. By siding also with the New Left criticism of the state for its foreign policy, and describing that policy as old-fashioned empire building, there really was no reason left to think of myself as a conservative in any important sense. The ideas that best suited my entire disposition against concentrated power were now ideas, foreign and domestic, which were basic on the New Left, and mere shadows on the conservative side.

Nevertheless, when Barry Goldwater ran for the Senate in 1968, and despite the fact that I was then a member of the Students for a Democratic Society, he asked that I come to Arizona and write some speeches for him and I was glad to do it—with what, in relation to any other politician I can imagine, must have seemed a remarkable proviso: that I would not write anything about the so-called law and order issue or the Indo-Chinese war. As I frankly discussed with the Senator, I was certainly opposed to American policy in the war, and could not separate the law and order issue from the, to me, unwholesome growth of sheer state power that was being justified in the name of law and order.

What I could write about with unchanged zeal would be opposition to state power in the mode of the "old Goldwater." The Senator was pleased. His campaign manager, Dean Burch, seemed pleased also and, in long and serious conversations, used to appear very interested in my new views, particularly on law and order. Burch, as an attorney, had recently defended a number of cases in which the arrests of young people with marijuana could be seen as clear cases of entrapment, in which government informers had sold the dope so that other government agents could make the arrest. Burch, a decent and thoughtful man throughout all the years I had known him, took very seriously the need to think well beyond party slogans in considering such matters. He was also interested in, if skeptical of, the experiences I was having in SDS and, although pleased with the decentralist nature of so much of SDS theorizing, was still offended by the easy recourse to heckling and even a low level of violence on so many campuses. Later, as a very special assistant and chief defender of the beleaguered President Nixon, he displayed no such sensitivity, at least publicly, for the political violence of the Nixon Administration. But then conservatives generally have a hard time understanding that to silence people by the intimidations of vast government power, even if more august, is morally trashy, whereas the catcalls of students or their sitting down in a dean's office are more in the nature of petty larcenies on the political scale— the difference between a Mafia caper and a kid shoplifting.

During the Senator's campaign there was one most wondrous incident. We spoke of SDS and of the New Left and he too was pleased with much of the decentralist and anti-authoritarian motion in the movement. In recognition of this he even said, in a speech at the University of Arizona, that he had "much in common with the anarchist wing of SDS." And, indeed, he did, at least so far as his opposition to federal power went. Unfortunately it didn't go all the way. Along with his election, of course, there was the election of Richard M. Nixon to the Presidency. Senator Goldwater had been grateful to Nixon ever since the 1964 campaign when Nixon had refused to join the anti-Goldwater Republican pack led by Nelson Rockefeller and his staff (probably including that Rockefeller stalwart, Henry Kissinger). Senator Goldwater does not take gratitude lightly. So, when Nixon was elected, Senator Goldwater was all in his corner and stayed there far past what some might have considered the bitter end.

Shortly after the election I asked the Senator if he did not think that it would be appropriate for his first legislative proposal to be an end to the draft. (I personally favored, by then, a Constitutional amendment to make it forever impossible to force Americans unwillingly to serve the federal government, but a simple end of the draft would be a good start.) Senator Goldwater's reply was the *only* one he could have made that would have convinced me that our time together was over. I'm sure I could have stuck through any other answer, to try and continue our dialogue about right and left. But what he said was, simply, "Well, let's wait and see what Dick Nixon wants to do about it." Loyalty, of course. But so misplaced, even then. Richard Nixon was not and never has been ankle high to Senator Goldwater in moral stature, openheartedness, breadth of spirit or intelligence beyond the measure of sheer animal cunning, a measure in which Senator Goldwater is gloriously deficient.

We did not speak again until several years later when we met while I was being arrested at the U.S. Senate during a protest against the clearly illegal nature of the Indo-Chinese war. Senator Goldwater talked with the protesters, the only Senator to do so in friendly interest if not agreement, and asked if I was somewhere in the bunch. Locating me, he came over to chat —two old friends who simply hadn't seen each other for a long time. I was both touched by that simple gesture of friendship and saddened by this fresh reminder that Barry Goldwater had twice lost the chance uniquely to influence American political life—once in his failed campaign for Congressional government in 1964 and once for the possibility of making an essential American opening to the left which, I honestly feel, he was capable of making in 1968 but which his election and his service to the unworthy Richard Nixon wiped out.

By an opening to the left, I mean that Barry Goldwater, and perhaps only Barry Goldwater, could have gone to the millions of so-called conservatives who supported him and said, in effect:

> We can no longer blind ourselves to the fact that concentrated economic power has become as reckless and ruthless and coercive as concentrated political power.
>
> We can no longer attack subsidies for the poor while supporting even greater subsidies for the rich.
>
> We can no longer speak of protecting freedom in the world by turning the world into protective hamlets. We can no longer oppose tyranny by emulating it.
>
> We cannot speak of individual freedom and free communities, self-reliance and self-responsibility, while honoring the assembly line, promoting urban demolition, and making a fetish of commodities. We cannot speak of honest work while honest working people are alienated from that work and treated as mere extensions of their machines.
>
> We cannot attack the abuses of arrogant and bureaucratic labor leaders without attacking the abuses of arrogant and bureaucratic industrial and business leaders.
>
> We cannot speak of a land of liberty and a national-

security state in the same breath—we must defend freedom at home if we are ever to have freedom in the world.

We cannot speak of a sweet land of liberty when the very land is soured by the greed of those who turn the landscape into real estate, who turn the rivers into open sewers, who see in every living thing nothing but a dollar in process.

Goldwater, I honestly believe, has thought about those things and in his heart knows that, historically, he is not right. He is a man, deep down, of at least a leaning toward the humanist left. And he is the one man who could have turned a discussion of a new direction in American politics into one which could have included and respectfully considered the grave concerns of the conservatives *and* the surging vision of the left, could have united the discussion in a final and conclusive abandonment of the failed programs of liberalism and, so importantly, even begun the dismantling of the American Empire in favor of a free America.

But he did not. No one did or has. And so the debate goes on where it does little good and the problems go on where their discussion makes little difference.

One reason for the failure of politicians generally to be able to make the breakthroughs in discussion which times sometimes demand is probably their inability to break the bonds of their own most close culture, their life-style.

There probably came a moment in Senator Goldwater's own consideration of his old friend Karl Hess when those bonds must have closed in like soft cords to strangle the possibility of serious change.

It is fine to speak, as he did to his eternal credit, frankly and openly about touchy matters such as civil rights (which he said would never be gained by blacks as a gift from white liberal legislation but rather through actual black political power) or social security (as when he told the elderly that the federal government was treating their funds recklessly). Yet those still are the speeches of a politician talking down to people, speeches that still are comfortably couched in familiar and reformist terms such as "get out the black vote" and "turn social security into a true insurance system."

To speak about the nature of actual power in America, about the return of power to people where they live and how they live, about the reordering of actual priorities, about restating the social contract so to speak, you cannot in any way talk down to people—you have to talk with them and be with them. The turn to such a position cannot be made without a turn in your life as well. Senator Goldwater has, probably, the internal self-assurance and stamina to do it but he also has old habits and long-accustomed and comfortable ways of life. I did too. And I did not abandon them out of some act of superior will or conscience. I was squeezed out and away, slowly, sometimes painfully.

I have never been able to blame or be angry at those who are still where I was. I can only be doubly thankful that I am not there with them.

And the reasons are not just those described so far. There are these very personal reasons, mentioned here simply because I find them so much more important than I ever did in the past and because it is the melting together of politics and living, of words and way, that I find, finally, to be the most satisfying aspect of life on the left.

Life on the right was competitive in the very worst sense. People jealously protected position and privilege. Secrecy and self-serving pretenses were simply the way people related. The ideologues with the sweatiest brow and the most fevered speech, the crusaders for the light, were all of them as brownnosing and self-seeking as any junior corporate executive when it came to jobs, incomes, rising up the ladder of success and maintaining their own prideful positions. It is, I am sure, one reason that the right will never successfully develop a way of talking to and with people about earthy matters. Its own ideologues are not with the people generally, they are simply job holders looking for bigger houses, better cars, and a secure retirement. If there are exceptions that I overlook, I apologize. I simply can't think of any. In my memory, it is all an endless repetition of the quintessential moment when, during cocktails at Bill Buckley's home one evening, an ardent anticommunist on his payroll looked intently at Buckley and, when the attention of the others in the room was drawn to his staring, said in awed tones, "Bill, you have the profile of a young Caesar." How many million young vice-presidents have said something embarrassingly similar to how many bosses? Well, let me testify that I did it and so did everyone I knew on the right; fawning on the rich who supported our writing and our speaking and our crusades, bending to their whims and prejudices, ascribing to them wisdoms and wonders. Paid mouths. Paid heads. The new centurions of the oldest profession.

There are, of course, prima donnas on the left and, from time to time, there emerge the entertainers of the left who rise up as great monsters threatening the peace of the countryside and giving the audience luscious thrills and chills, or scrawling political obscenities on the walls like wild kids trying to shock the old folks. They come and they go, and everyone knows who they are and what they are.

But the left persists. With people who have worked all their lives for union democracy and will never stop. With people who have worked all their lives against war and will never stop. With people who have worked all their lives to bring the poor from the impoverishing programs of the welfarists into the world of real self-reliance and who will never stop. With people who have fought entrenched privilege all their lives and will never stop.

And to this I will swear: I do not personally know an active, persistent person on the left who is in for the money, the glory, or the personal power. On the right I knew scarcely anyone who was not.

I think of another sort of incident that is typical of the difference. When groups on the right such as Young Americans for Freedom decide to take an action, they beat the billionaire bushes for heavy money, insisting on a proper office, a staff of secretaries, expense accounts, and ample salaries before their crusade takes flight. They are careerists, simply and only. When young people on the left, typically, decide to take an action they simply take it—because they believe in it, with what they have on hand and with no thought of anything beyond the work at hand. And, incidentally, very many of the young people I have known on the left got there, as I did, from the Goldwater campaign of 1964. Where else could they go?

My point is not that everyone on the left is good and kind and pure of heart. It is that I have found many who are just that. On the right, I didn't. Nor, come to think of it, did I deserve to.

There is even a contrast in personal conduct which is striking to me because it is such a sharp contrast. On the right there is an almost universal saturation with booze and promiscuity. Not everyone, of course. But it is a heavy part of the atmosphere. Presidential campaigns, in particular, are as notable for their shifting bed partners as for their shifting promises.

People on the left are hardly prudes but, and again I swear this to be impressively true, I have never heard women discussed as sexual trade goods. On the right it was commonplace. Alcoholism simply isn't a problem either, although there was a time when drugs might have seemed to be a substitute. Today, except for casual marijuana use, I have a strong impression that drugs of all sorts are far more a general middle-class preoccupation than a practice of the political left. Right political ideologues are job holders or seekers. Left political ideologues are social changers, already having changed their lives, seeking to change the conditions that bind others. There is simply less difference between the way people talk and the way they live, full time, on the left.

On the right, for example, the sharing of a political way of life by a man and woman living together is not only not necessary, it is downright uncommon. The women attend to their things, the men to theirs. And they often live together in gin-soaked oblivion to what those things really are. Who cares? It's a job.

I do not know many men and women living together on the left who do not share their entire lives. The casualties between men and women on the left are for reasons quite different than on the right. The men and women on the left who separate do it because they cannot share some point or preoccupation. On the right, where life may be lived one way during office hours, another at the club, another whoring around, another at the bar, and a tiny other at home, the sharing of anything between men and women is of little consequence and certainly of little discussion.

On the left, with its constant insistence on narrowing the gap between politics and life-style, between being and doing, there is either sharing or there is separation. And that seems to me importantly honest and decent. And that, in turn, seems to me the essence of the left-right difference at the personal level. The way people live is important to the left. The way people "behave" is important on the right.

That leaves, in rounding out the personal, before turning to the more general, just one profoundly important matter: the life I live with the woman who is my closest friend and dearest comrade, Therese Machotka. I knew her when I was a thorough conservative and she used to infuriate me then with common-sense questions about why I supported war while talking about freedom and creativity. I used to tell her that I was privy to state secrets, that women couldn't understand, and all of the other profound arguments which are familiar in regular American politics.

Later, after I had lived a year or so on a boat, had survived the dope craze of the sixties, and had become thoroughly situated on the left, we met again, and this time without any of my old pomp and pride. I found, and she found, that where there are no cultural constraints to subordinate women—as surely there are on the right—and where there is an absolute commitment to openness—no poses, no role playing—there is a rich opportunity for a man and woman to live together in a creative and supportive way, without exploitation and without domination. And that's the way it is.

The nature of the social change that it seems to me is best imaginable by turning to the left is simply the sort of change that makes life whole again, the way it is for me, for so many of my friends, and for Therese.

5

THE "RED" YEARS

If we could look at our politics over the past twenty years without labels and without being satisfied with standard explanations, we might all be (1) better off, (2) surprised at who the real heroes, villains, and victims were, and (3) amazed at some of the folks we might find at our sides in making the kind of future we want. We might be amazed, saddened, but certainly wiser to discover where we fitted into it all, who benefited most when we thought we did, who suffered most when we thought someone else did, and always, who actually paid the bills, skimmed off the gravy, and died for it all.

My own political career—and until now it has been a career, separate from the regular, decent demands of citizenship in which every one of us should participate fully—my own political career carried me from young socialist to professional Republican, to full-time right-winger, also professionally, to the right-wing populism of Senator Barry Goldwater, to disillusion, to unattached rebellion, to militant left-wing advocacy, to slow recognition of my own real place in the world and the sort of world of communities in which it seems most people, and certainly the sort of people I know and live with, would live best. Finally, now, it seems to me that it has all come together in a coalition of interest and perception that combines the best of the American revolutionary tradition with the indispensable good sense of socialist economic analysis and

the equally indispensable good sense of libertarian and cooperative social practice which also has roots deep in the American
experience. And through it all there is laced the very good old
right-wing distaste for bureaucracy which, at its best, is a sure
key to liberty but which, unfortunately, often is simply a cover
for an agenda of special privilege for groups which, though
not called bureaucratic, have much in common with bureaucracies.

The view from the far right of the Roosevelt years was
one of unrelieved disaster. Quite accurately, that view included
the social fascism of those years—with the government's bureaucracy becoming the focus and factory of the social goals and
practices of the people. The term fascist seems appropriate
because it is the important base-point of fascism that the state
is, indeed, the people rather than the other way around. Fascism,
either of Hitler's or of Roosevelt's sort, actually begins with the
absolute nationalization of the people, the absolute placing of
the people at the disposal of the state. Also, in both cases, the
programs began as social welfare programs. Hitler promised
to subdue social unrest by instituting social security programs,
pensions, welfare. So did Roosevelt. Hitler did it, as Bismarck
had advised earlier, to build a powerfully supportive base for
a powerful military force. Roosevelt did it for obviously more
benign and less bellicose reasons—to subdue social unrest by
the same programs but without, at first, the major goal of
military strength.

There is nothing in this to even suggest that the regimes of
Roosevelt and Hitler were altogether the same. Far from it.
Hitler's was mad and murderous. Roosevelt's was not cruel,
certainly wasn't crazy, certainly was kind and helpful for many,
and certainly was to serve a purpose which could be called
peaceful if compared to Hitler. Roosevelt sought the perpetuation of American power and privilege pretty much as it
stood. Hitler sought new power and a new order.

But most Americans know about the differences in such regimes. The trick is to see the points of similarity because, in the long run, they are what you have to contend with. And the most important point of all is to see that whenever we talk about regimes or rule, or administrations or reigns or what have you, we are talking in one way about the same thing, no matter how good or how bad the performances involved. We are talking about the separation of power and people into two distinct groups, the group that gives the orders and the group that takes the orders, about them and about us.

In the time of the New Deal, the "Them" and the "Us" became more separated than ever—but within an overall performance that left a lot of "Us" very confused about it all.

Some of us (me, for example) made the mistake of thinking that the Roosevelt years were radical, actually radical; that they were transferring power from the industrious and working people of the nation (in which category I hastily and mistakenly also lumped all managers and owners) and giving it to the shiftless and the undesirable.

In particular we made a mistake about the role of the intellectuals in the Roosevelt years. Because there were many professorial advisors to that President, and to all subsequent ones, the impression could be gained that the intellectuals were making the policies and actually steering the course that the state would take.

It now appears, and it has been my own experience in government, that the intellectuals merely add the details, provide the rhetoric, and in general dress up the plans of the politicians and the bankers and their friends—and then take the lead in peddling those plans to the people.

There is also a handy process of self-deception involved which helps. Probably most of the intellectuals involved in the New Deal and in subsequent Administrations have had some sort of inner, glowing desire to help what they consider to be the poor, benighted ordinary people of the land and to represent those people against what they consider to be the reactionary parts of the system. My notion that there is self-deception involved in this is based upon a rather solid feeling, unshattered by any experience in politics, that these same intellectuals are actually most concerned with the power of their own personalities and, more generally, with the power of their own "sort." They have, it has been my experience, a firm conviction that only they, because of their superior education and refined sensibilities, can "lead" the ordinary people to glory. And, in this, it is not only assumed that someone who likes Beethoven and Bach better than Bluegrass *is* a better person, but it also is assumed, quite incorrectly, that anyone who does like Bluegrass is incapable of liking Beethoven and Bach. The snooty point of it all is that to most of the intellectuals who have entered politics, Americans are a rather dumb lot who, without the help of the elite, would squander their resources, wreck their families, litter the streets, be impolite to their neighbors, lynch everybody in sight, burn the books, break the violins, sack the museums, spit on the pavement, smell, eat garlic, drink beer, belch in public, be unkind to dogs, use abstract paintings as designs for the kitchen linoleum, watch baseball, go to movies with happy endings, scratch themselves, dress unstylishly, and otherwise be hopeless clods.

I have found little difference in this attitude between intellectuals who call themselves conservative and those who call themselves liberal. On the other hand, it is not true that all intellectuals feel this way. On the contrary, the people who have most effectively criticized such intellectuals are, not surprisingly, other intellectuals who, although they work with their heads instead of their hands, understand that they *are* working, that they have a lot in common with, and are not superior to or separate from, people who do other kinds of work. A physicist or a historian is, of course, more likely to be a better physicist or historian than a welder but that may be precisely where the "better" argument starts and should stop— not forgetting that the welder may be a better welder and that, very probably, they'll all be quite equal in virtually every other skill of living, honesty, decency, regard for others, and so forth. Also, they may be either male or female, white or black, Caucasian or Asian, short or tall, quiet or noisy, sensuous or shy.

For the intellectuals of the Roosevelt years, however, the main point must have been to save the great industrial, banking, and owning system that was threatened by the rising discontent of people generally and by, particularly, the very good chance that working people would organize to demand control of industry and not merely better wages.

The radicals of the left were the most noisy. But they could be dealt with either by outright suppression, by some suppression and some compromise, or by a lot of compromise and, mainly, co-optation—the process of taking over their promises in order to retain the power to make the performance of those promises serve, not the left, but the establishment powers themselves.

There was a concern on the right as well—the rigid right, the unbending right, particularly among the old fortunes and the old and cautious banks. Such people had great power, were peers in the actual control of the nation, and did not want the government to take any new power over anything or anyone except the unruly working people. The right always has argued against government controls on the one hand while arguing for government *power* on the other, so long as that power is funneled into the police function of keeping the population generally in line.

The decision, with the election of Roosevelt, swung toward co-optation. It meant reform rather than radical change or absolute preservation of the status quo. The left was called criminal with liberals taking over the "acceptable" parts of the left program. And, handily, in the process there was every excuse to present a bold front against the unyielding right. To satisfy important parts of the population, as a matter of fact, the rigid right had to be bent or broken and it was. The attack against this particular part of the ruling establishment was widely misinterpreted, even by some theoreticians *on* the right, as being an attack against the system itself. Far from it. It saved the system.

But look at the array of impressions that could be had, just for the wishful thinking:

Liberals (in the sense of those who, like the nice ladies and proper gents of the reform movements in the big cities, wanted to do good for the common folk without letting the common folk do good for themselves) loved the idea of a government that would poke a few rich snoots and let a lot of sociologists and college professors assume titles of governmental grandeur —and spend the poor folks' money for the poor folks' own good.

A lot of working people, who had not thought about their situation long enough or hard enough to see anything basically wrong with the ownership and acquisition system but only thought it needed better rules, welcomed the Administration that promised those rules.

Other working people, perhaps tired of fighting over basic issues, and even though they suspected or recognized basic flaws in the system, may have felt that, what the heck, Roosevelt was better than anything else, one step forward was better than two steps back, so hurrah.

Many poor and, particularly, unemployed people, of whom there were plenty, welcomed the rhetoric. Relief programs were started all over the place, food was distributed, jobs were created, even if only sweeping streets or chopping trees in remote government camps. But, at least, someone seemed to care.

Blacks, especially, seemed to have heard the trumpets of salvation in the noise of the Roosevelt years. And, in fact, part of that noise was passing strange—it included respectful mention of black people as though they *were* people and it even included enough actual attention to the black nation within the nation to make Roosevelt appear to be the devil incarnate to white supremacists. (The confusing truth of the matter was that black Americans were, at that time, being turned into what they would remain for many years, a special constituency of the Democratic Party, a party which also would be based upon solid white supremacist political bossism in the south, thus giving one of history's better examples of just how shallow principle is in the stream of American politics, the most pragmatic and power-centered of any in the world.

From the other side of the street the view was as wonderfully varied.

Die-hard conservative and rich people were convinced that Roosevelt was a communist or, worse, in league with the devil to miscegenate and level the country. All they could see were changes which, indeed, worked hardships on many medium-sized fortunes, on some genteel but relatively shabby inheritances, but which also brought to Washington pushy sorts of people who did not belong to the best clubs, did not have particularly neat pedigrees, and who trailed behind them, like an evil vapor, suggestions and hints of licentious behavior, racy reading, and disrespect for country-squire manners and mentalities.

Practically anyone disposed to dislike concentrated power would also abhor the new rulers, for they were, indeed, hell-bent on grabbing power, and no doubt about that, and despite the good motives for which they claimed to be doing it.

In those years, I am convinced, because of this wide range of possible views, and because of the seeming impossibility of discussing anything *across* the gaps of those perceptions, there developed the fundamental confusion with which our politics has been plagued ever since: the fundamental confusion between a radical but American analysis and a liberal/conservative holding tactic.

In the process, also, there has developed what seemed to me in my own experience to be the main language problem in American politics: the identification that many Americans automatically make between radical, liberal and collectivist on the one hand and individualistic, conservative, and noncoercive on the other.

The fact of the matter, apparent just from looking at the times in which we live, is that the Roosevelt years, supposed to be radical, liberal, and collectivist, did nothing to basically change the system of power and privilege in this country. Those years modified the system, made it more palatable, to be sure, and most importantly took off the rough edges at a time when those edges might have torn apart the fabric of public obedience.

In an important sense, what the Roosevelt years did was to provide machinery through which government could mediate the potentially dangerous competition between industrialists and financiers which many saw as a cause, for instance, of the Great Depression. Rather than competition among the *very* rich, cooperation could be achieved, through various government agencies which could regulate production, oversee pricing policies, prevent unduly harsh raids of one business against another, even prevent titanic battles to form new monopolies (which might threaten the old ones!). Also, the New Deal went along with the trade union movement, but in such a way as to encourage the least dangerous part of it—the part concerned solely with wages and contracts—and discourage the most dangerous part—the part concerned with decisions, ownership, work conditions, nature of products, and the whole idea of working for wages rather than, for instance, sharing in the entire enterprise. The left!

At the end of it all—and the proof of such pudding *is* in the eating—American corporations emerged as the most powerful on earth, despite a long war or, some would say, because of it; and the government bureaucracy, more powerful than ever also, was still obviously subservient to the interests of the rich.

What happened in the war (the Roosevelt or Second World War as distinguished from the Truman wars in Greece and Korea, the Eisenhower Cold War of nerves, the Kennedy war in Indochina, the Johnson war in Indochina or the Nixon war in Indochina) was that millions of individual Americans were asked to sacrifice quite a bit, many their lives. The unions were pressed, finally, into the first surrender of what is now their habitual surrender of the right to strike, working people were told over and over that their "greed" should not interfere with national purposes, and voting people were told that they really should trust their leaders and that not to trust them would aid the enemy. And most Americans were hit with the first series of tax jolts in what would be, from then on, a never-ending assault on their productive lives.

But the corporations fared differently. Government contracts and tax-built facilities poured billions of new public capital into privately-owned business. And the always hazy line between economic and political power began to grow more fuzzy and even disappear. (Today, for instance, huge aerospace companies are said to be national necessities when they are in trouble, and thus get public money, but become strictly private a little later when the profits are divvied up, thus shifting back and forth very conveniently between the world of politics and the world of private finance.)

Human beings are often drafted in this country. Individual houses are often confiscated either for nonpayment of taxes or to make way for a road or even a shopping center. Industry is never drafted. Banks are never confiscated to make way for a cooperative savings plan. Factories are not confiscated to make way for a village industry. And the rich are never subjected to the tax confiscations of the poor.

What changes, then, is not the basic structure of power. What changes are just the exterior trims and the locks on the doors.

In all the years of wild talk about radicals and liberals, conservatives and reactionaries in or out of power in Washington, nothing really has changed way down in the command centers of power and privilege.

At the most visible level, for instance, the distribution of income in the country has remained almost absolutely stable since the end of the Second World War. According to Census Bureau figures, the poorest fifth of the people received 5 percent of the money income in 1947 and 5.5 percent in 1970. In 1947 the richest fifth received 43 percent of all money income; in 1970 they received 41.6 percent.

In between, the second fifth received 11.8 percent in 1947, 12 percent in 1970; the middle fifth got 17 percent back then, 17.4 percent more recently; the fourth fifth got 23.1 percent in 1947 and 23.5 percent in 1970.

Rather than being the shifting, seething land of change that some Chamber of Commerce types try to sell, the economics of America, liberal or conservative politicians notwithstanding, is virtually a standstill economy in terms of sharing. Some call it stable. Some call it stuck. You can take your choice of names but not of facts. The economy does produce more and more —but at greater and greater costs to working people generally, who pay higher and higher taxes, who go deeper and deeper into debt, who suffer the accidents and tediums of increased production—but the economy does not *distribute* that productivity in ways that reflect anything but existing patterns of ownership. Genius is not the criterion. Industriousness is not the criterion. If they were, then couldn't we expect that the patterns of income would shift wildly, given the wild differences between what a first class inventor contributes to a productive process, or a first class machine operator, as compared to a person who contributes nothing but an inherited fortune with which that person had nothing creative to do in the first place?

Exactly where did liberalism stand in this equation of actual stability for the rich? It really did not challenge the very rich at all. Its programs have never been financed by the corporations and their taxes. Individual taxation has outpaced corporate taxes by two to one throughout the so-called liberal era. Working people have paid a far higher proportion of their incomes in taxes than have people who live off investments and other unearned income. The controls on which many of the plans have depended have actually affected working people far more than owning people who, among other things, always can buy the expertise to evade controls if they get too tight.

And, most importantly, the liberal plans have simply failed.

By making the poor dependents and wards of the various levels of government, from federal to state, being poor has become a profession as well as a field for professional employment. The poor have become a constituency for politicians and "clients" for bureaucratic social workers. The poor also have remained poor.

By applying at every accessible level of government the liberal idea of concentrated managerial power (the "good" people making decisions for the people generally), the cities have become collapsing and unmanageable jungles, neighborhoods have been abandoned and disbanded, locality has been blighted, localism has been scoffed into obsolescence—and the quality of life has become more trying and less satisfying for more and more people.

Also, by assuming that the defeat of socialism in the world

was the main task of foreign policy, the liberals have led us into war after war.

This is not to settle down for an attack on American liberalism. It stands discredited without any help. The point is raised because of that deadly confusion of liberalism with the left.

A further point is that, although thoroughly discredited, the main thrusts of liberalism, particularly the grand assumptions about centralized management decisions, continue to live a lusty life even though clothed in the business suits of the reigning politicians who call themselves conservatives.

All along, while the American liberal notion was becoming the main, and even sole, notion of American politics, at least of successful American politicians, the left was talking about something entirely different. For good reason, however, not very many people bothered to listen—the reason being that most Americans probably felt there was no need to listen to anyone else calling themselves leftists when the liberals were in power anyway.

The actual left message in America still reverberated from Eugene V. Debs, the American Socialists, and such voices as that of the most romantic and consistent of all left voices, the Wobblies, the Industrial Workers of the World.

That message went to the heart of the matter, to the roots, to radical change. In essence it attacked the almost accidental accumulations of power that left the means of production in America in the control of a relatively few immensely rich families. It attacked *capitalism,* not America, not Americans, not Americanism. It agreed with Marx that capitalism had been the historic force needed to smash that other system of accumulation, feudalism. It even agreed with Marx that capitalism had produced fantastic productive facilities in the great commercial nations. But it said that the need for that sort of accumulation had passed, that the time for cooperation rather than destructive competition had come and that if people were to reap the benefits of modern industry they would have to be real partners in it, not wage slaves of it. The IWW based much of its attack on the wage system specifically, pointing out that people who work for wages are endlessly at the mercy of people who own but do not necessarily work.

The economic attack made by the radicals was so emphatic that other parts of the attack seemed secondary. Yet, from the Debsian, IWW-style American left, the most typically *American* left, there was a steadfast attack against political concentrations of power also. In particular, the Stalinist bureaucracy in the Soviet Union was viewed by them as a betrayal of and not a fulfillment of socialism. There was, throughout the American left then, as well as today, a most pronounced bias against central authority and an enthusiasm for localism, for the rank and file against the union bureaucracy and the management, for the neighborhood against the politicians downtown, for the farmer versus the railroads and the banks, and so forth.

There was similar fervor on the part of the right, where right-wing individualists kept banging away against the growing liberal tendency toward concentrated political power. At the outset many of the people on the right attacked concentrations of power in the economic area as well.

The complication of the growing importance of Soviet Communism, Stalinism, intruded, however, to make impossible an alliance (which should have been natural) between the right-wing individualists and the American socialists. Just as liberalism became mistakenly equated with the left, so did anti-Stalinism become mistakenly attributed as an almost exclusive function of *pro*capitalists. To be against Stalin meant you were for capitalism.

The reasoning was convincing enough for political rhetoric, for a good deal of school teaching, plenty of broadcast propaganda, and sermons. It went like this: Stalinist communism seeks the destruction of freedom (and, since it had pretty much accomplished it in the Soviet Union itself, there wasn't much argument on that point). But, even though it is Stalinism that might be the visible enemy, it appears that *any* form of socialism is likely to lead to Stalinism (after all, the goals of the Russian Revolution were good but look what happened). If Stalinism is so bad, then what it is *against* must not only be good but must also be the first line of defense against it. And what were the Stalinists against? The same thing socialists were against: capitalism. Therefore, capitalism comes out good, and socialism (now, *any* kind of socialism) comes out bad.

For a lot of Americans, the inherently unpleasant behavior of liberals just added weight to this wonderful equation. Everything they did was described as some form of creeping socialism.

At any rate, a lot of people who might have and should have listened more closely to the socialist analysis of concentrated economic power, and its links with concentrated political power, preferred to face outward, toward Stalinism, to devote their major energies to fighting it and, if even just by default, to end up defending *everything that Stalinism was against, beginning with capitalism itself.*

To be an anticommunist, a pure and holy one, became a more specialized position every year. It meant less and less concern with anything in the world *except* communism. No defect of the noncapitalist world could be closely examined if it gave any credence whatsoever to any communist claim; no social change could be countenanced if it resembled in any way anything ever done behind the Iron Curtain.

There may be a myriad of very fancy explanations of this and, indeed, there is at least one shelf in every public library that has a half dozen or so volumes explaining American anticommunism in terms from the psychological to the theological.

I think there is a less gaudy factor. There certainly was in the anticommunist circles in which I traveled.

To be involved in anything as purely political as full-time anticommunism, a person must either be independently supported or make a living from the act of anticommunism itself. It is imaginable that a person could be a doctor or a waitress or a bricklayer all day and then do anticommunist crusading all night, and indeed, that happens. But for the most highly energized, the hustlers, the ideal is to be a political hero full-time and without mundane worries. After all, the person who is good enough to want to save the world shouldn't be bothered with details.

By far the easiest way to be a full-time political person, and specifically, to be a full-time anticommunist political person, is to find somebody with money who will support you. Who has that sort of money? Naturally, people who benefit from the status quo, who derive a surplus from the system as it stands.

When such people support an anticommunist effort there are always two factors involved, not just the single factor of anticommunism. They may hate communism in the abstract or for some entirely separate reasons, but they also must defend *capitalism* and, particularly, capitalism as it exists in the modern corporate sense, for it is from that source that they derive the surplus with which to finance their political causes.

And so, at the best-funded levels, anticommunism is not *just* anticommunism, it also is procapitalism. There is an important difference there, because it wipes out the possible alliance of those who opposed Stalinism because of its concentrated power —but also opposed capitalism for the same reasons—and those who *just* opposed Stalinism without thinking very deeply about any other power problems.

There is also a lesson in there for people who feel that individualism, that most treasured of American talking traits, can be maintained without any reference to the surrounding social system. Indeed, many who hated Stalinism or any other power monopoly, as they were drawn deeper and deeper into the procapitalist support of their cause, began to excuse and then applaud everything that was against Stalinism even though it might have about it important aspects of the very sort of centralized authority supposedly so repulsive.

Some of the most important anticommunists with whom I have been associated have been in the oil business, for instance. That industry feeds very distinctly upon the sort of centralized authority, power, and even politics that, you might think, would be the very things you would find most obnoxious about Stalinism. Special laws pertaining to mineral rights give special advantages to the prospector—and it has been many a romantic day since prospector meant the grizzled loner and his burro—the individual. Prospector now means corporation. It means big money and big power. Tax advantages abound for the oil folks. Special regulations are available to hold down production or to boost it, to keep out imports or to let them in—in short, to do everything needed to keep oil a fantastically profitable business. And, rather than the flowering of opportunity that would be the schoolbook American ideal, this industry exhibits a galloping corporate tendency toward fewer and fewer dominating giants.

Yet, beyond any question, men such as H. L. Hunt (for whom I worked briefly in Dallas designing a format for his *Facts Forum* magazine) are against the central authority of Stalinism. They find it evil beyond belief. But what sort of central authority do they find good? They find the central authority of the military most attractive, and support the expansion of the military budget particularly if it is spent toward the ultimate goal of destroying some socialist government or another somewhere. This business of destroying someone else's government, of course, is no exercise in libertarianism. It requires a goodly sort of garrison outlook instead. To defeat a garrison state, therefore, such anticommunists are more than willing to accept—a garrison state!

One reason that it is understandable for this contradiction to arise is that the rich are not the ones regimented in most garrison states. We can recall, for instance, that the greatly rich Krupp family of Germany owned a huge hunk of the country when Hitler came to power, operated much of the German industrial enterprise while he was in power, and turned out to still own much of it after Hitler was defeated.

Similarly, it must not be conceivable to a man like H. L. Hunt that he would be personally burdened or harassed in the sort of garrison state necessary to wage a protracted war against the Soviet Union in particular or socialism generally.

In brilliant point of fact, such a garrison state has been at least partially erected anyway and, also in point of fact, H. L. Hunt and his friends have been very little inconvenienced by it even while many other Americans have been.

Hunt also is a firm believer in another tenet of the very Stalinism that he otherwise abhors. He is a great believer in hierarchy, privilege, and authority. He has proposed, for instance, that Americans should be given numbers of votes commensurate with their money-worth. As one of the most wealthy single individuals in the world, this would give Mr. Hunt exactly the sort of special advantage that a commissar might enjoy in the Soviet Union. The difference, he might say, would be that he earned his special privilege, authority, and place atop most other people. I would say that the commissar earned his in much the same way—manipulating existing political arrangements to his own advantage, accumulating power even as the oilman accumulates money, and operating in the purely speculative world of political arrangement rather than being a direct producer, even as the oilman operates in the purely speculative world of leases, tax breaks, etc., while the drillers, geologists, and truck drivers do the *work* of turning that speculation into productive activity while rarely getting a decent share of what is produced, much less a share equal to their contribution

Hunt himself often is held up as example and proof of the

wonders of the American economic system. I must admit I viewed him that way myself in the very impressionable days when I worked with him.

Americans who have managed to get over a reverence for royalty still may not have got over a reverence for money, I find, and being in the presence of a man whose weekly income is one million dollars has a bad effect on your critical faculties. Instead of wondering what the heck he could do that is *worth* a million dollars a week, the impressionable person, and I was certainly one, is just awed into silence by the thought of the money itself, those heaped up, glittering piles of loot that represent the worth and wealth of literally millions of working Americans.

But, one might say, if H. L. Hunt, himself once a working man, a plantation manager, a wildcatter, if he can become so rich then so can anyone. What a grand system. The flaw is rather like the flaw in the argument that anyone can become President. H. L. Hunt's wealth is based upon control of vast areas of land and the minerals under them. No matter how you slice it, there just isn't enough of that land to go around in any way that could make a reality out of the statement that if he could do it so could anyone. When a person like H. L. Hunt *does* do it, the actual fact is that the chance for anyone else doing it is vastly reduced. Opportunity is not made, it is closed.

But, even if that is an unfortunate statistical truth, what about the lesson in principle—that anyone can get ahead by hard work and perseverence? Well, any example in the oil industry, or any of the mineral industries as a matter of fact, suggests quite the opposite. Stumbling across oil land, or winning some in a poker game, as H. L. Hunt is often quoted as saying he did, is more like winning a game of chance.

The difference between hard work, honest labor, brilliant creativity and sheer good fortune should be kept firmly in mind.

What most Americans want is a system that rewards the work. What most have is some slot in a system which, for most, is just a gamble.

A working American, to be sure, can save enough money to set up a small business. Fine. But what of the success of that business? It *can* depend just on hard work. But more likely it will depend on the toss of political dice, such as the location of a new road, the demolition of or the erection of housing—in short, upon social matters rather than individualistic matters.

There is a commonsense question about getting ahead that most Americans probably do ask themselves and even answer in one way or another. The question is whether anyone really expects that just anyone can get to be a Rockefeller or a Morgan or a Mellon or a DuPont by hard work. Well, the commonsense answer, of course, is that the only way to be one of those is to be born one or marry one. So, most Americans might then say they would settle for just being an ordinary millionaire. Admittedly, that is a field with some openings. A few Americans every year nose into that class, at least technically. Stories in our newspapers day after day tell us that the fact of the matter is that such fortunes are often fortunes of debt and wild speculation, not hard work at all. (The only millionaire working person I can recall having made it recently, as a matter of fact, is the ingenious inventor of the Polaroid camera. The inventor of the basic xerography process on which the multibillion-dollar copying business is based didn't make it; corporations which exploited the patent did. And so it goes.) The final comfort, however, is that thousands of Americans, it is true, can make it past poverty every year, and even into some semblance of security. But even there the gambler's system is like a ghost over all of us—click, the dice go this way and illness wipes it all out; click, the dice go that way and a tax increase wipes it out; click, and the neighborhood and the house are demolished by a new high rise; click, and a freeway does the job; click, click, click. It is rather more like living on a roulette wheel than living in that world of golden work-hard opportunity that the books told us about as children.

There was a time in Mr. Hunt's own political development when he must have been concerned far more with what could be seen as truly liberty-seeking activity. I was told, while working there, that he had once thought of using his vast landholdings, acquired incidental to his oil leasing, to establish small farming communities where young people could go to learn practical farming. His vision was of more and more Americans learning to become self-sufficient as farmers. In that, this veritable symbol of hidebound reaction was actually a premature hippy, preaching the virtues of a return to nature just like the long-haired youngsters he must so despise because of their disrespect for authority. At any rate, it was not to be. Someone else, using the reasoning that it wouldn't do any good for people to learn how to be free so long as communism existed as the ultimate threat to freedom, convinced him to save the world from the Reds instead.

Going along on such a trip is very tempting. For one thing, it takes care of the bills. It also means that many of the very annoying contradictions that arise can be sent scuttling without any hard thinking, the sort of hard thinking that might even threaten your life-style.

And anticommunism becomes your business. And the business of anticommunism also becomes the business of defending business itself.

The pattern became bitingly clear even toward the end of the Roosevelt years, and the end of the Second World War.

With the purpose of the New Deal brilliantly achieved, and with American corporations not only back on their feet but standing on top of the entire world, the role of government changed from one of mediating disputes between discontented people and the economically powerful, to one of opening new frontiers for the powerful.

The excuse of a war was no longer an ever-present reason for subordinating the actions of individual Americans to the actions of the government. Working people could not be pushed back for that handy reason alone. The new reason was anti-communism. First of all, of course, it was perfectly reasonable insofar as it meant recognizing that the Soviet Union was in the grip of police state tyranny. It also was reasonable insofar as it meant recognizing that there were agents of that police state actively at work in America. There is a long step, however, between those very specific concerns and the all-encompassing, broad range of concerns that came to be lumped together under the anticommunist fervor. My own experience in the fervor came from working with several major contributors to that fervor. (I was for a time an editor and writer for the "standard" anticommunist newsletter, *Counterattack*—a publication widely used in business and industry as the basis for attacks against "left wingers," particularly in trade unions and in social welfare movements—and the author of numerous anticommunist "exposé" articles for national publications.)

At one point, particularly, I recall working for a Chicago "management consulting" firm that assisted employers in either breaking or rebuffing union organization in their plants. Of particular concern to the project I was hired for was the United Auto Workers. The project itself was designed to provide information that would smear the UAW's leadership as procommunist and therefore beyond the pale.

Consider then the sort of formula this type of thinking establishes. First there is the obvious fact of the Soviet police state, a fact most notably confirmed, finally, by the anti-Stalinist leaders in the Soviet Union itself. Then there is the fact that many people in America who were interested in social change in their own country also had had an interest in or were knowledgeable about Russia or Russians. This should not have seemed strange. After all, the Russian Revolution did exist, it was one of the epochal events of our time, it did involve social change, it proceeded from socialist theory, and it also proceeded from some of the theory of the American Revolution. Of course it touched everyone, somewhere.

With the recognition of the Stalinist perversion of that Revolution, however, the very name communism became a dirty one. Thus, also, the name of anyone who ever had anything to do with it became dirty. And then, for the final and most confusing touch, the word itself became applicable to anyone or to anything that was not foursquare pro-American. But what kind of pro-American. The answer, I found, was the kind of pro-American defined by those with the money to pay for it; the pro-Americanism of the corporations, the banks, and the political establishment.

So, as in the case of Walter Reuther and the United Auto Workers, it was only necessary to show some connection with the Soviet, first of all. That was easy with Reuther, who had worked for a time in a factory there as part of his own youthful questing for the meaning of social change. Add to that the fact that Reuther and his union kept pecking away at actual *social* issues rather than simply at wages and hours. Result: He became an enemy of the system and a Red, all in one fell swoop. A fairly substantial business developed just writing scare stories about Reuther as a Red of some sort or another. Add to Reuther everyone pushing against the status quo and the thing becomes not only a good business but a growth industry.

And, let me repeat and emphasize, it was a business at least based on solid concern. Stalinism was a grave peril—but more so to the Russian people than to the Americans!

But anticommunism went quickly beyond that and became an

expanding shield for all existing power arrangements in America. Some other examples come to mind.

Rather than having to answer socialist and other criticisms factually, business and political leaders could and did simply attack all forms of criticism from such quarters as being "pink," being covert communism, being designed to weaken the fabric of the nation at a time when the nation stood imperiled by the great red menace, and so forth.

Of crucial importance was the matter of militancy in the trade unions, militancy far more meaningful than Walter Reuther's rather tame, even conservative concerns about welfare programs and so forth. Some unions persistently attacked the heart of the new American direction and policy. They saw the Cold War as, most importantly, a cover for the suppression of individual American needs and for the glorification of political and corporate needs. They would not accept the idea that the Soviet was about to pour its armies over the borders of America and they certainly wouldn't accept that as a good reason for foregoing their own demands or for preaching the growth of trade unionism beyond wage demands into a social movement with demands about working conditions, ownership, sharing, and so forth.

The expansion of American corporations into new world markets, the dominant fact of corporate growth during the Cold War, could not tolerate activities at home which might be supportive of native, national and socialist movements in the new market areas. Although the corporations had no objection to national regimes that practiced socialism under a central dictatorship, such as a military junta, they would be seriously imperiled by nationalist movements that involved a distribution of ownership and power back down the line, toward the people generally. From such movements come demands for the expulsion of foreign exploiters of raw materials and for the development of local needs ahead of the development of outside corporate needs.

The militant American unions all had in common some degree of support for such national movements, as well as support for the same sorts of priorities in this country. They spoke of the needs of working Americans *ahead* of the needs of the Cold War and the goals of the corporate and political leaders.

They had to go.

Since all unions were vulnerable to political charges of pro-communism—since everyone who challenged *any* capitalist proposition was, ipso facto, a communist in the eyes of many powerful Americans—many of the unions themselves recognized a need to put on a bold, red-white-and-blue front. One way was to single out the most militant, the most vulnerable unions and expel them as a grand gesture of anticommunism. Eleven were so expelled from the CIO and the possibility of the trade union movement becoming a serious brake against corporate interests in the Cold War ended. In fact, from that point on, most American trade unions fell all over themselves in cooperating with the government, with the CIA, even with management groups in attacking trade unions anywhere on earth if those unions were basically critical of capitalist action and not just content to negotiate for their piece of the action.

Just to make sure that the unions stayed honest on that score, it remained a profitable and popular part of anticommunist theorizing and writing to knock any union member who got so far out of line as to be basically critical of the system.

For anyone who might recall that expulsion of the CIO unions with some sort of anticommunist pleasure, it should be instructive to point out that all of those unions continued to represent American workers, that American workers continued to join those unions, that some of them continued to raise essentially radical questions, and some still do, and that so far as even a detailed dissection of our society can reveal we have not been harmed by them. Most are now considered quite respectable. Were they ever actually perils to us? They certainly were annoying to certain politicians and to certain corporations.

I recall in the same light the many attacks against Pete Seeger, the folk singer. He was harassed over the years for procommunist activities. What were they? Opposing war, advocating the sorts of social change in which people could successfully take back power from both the corporations and the politicians, opposing racial restrictions. Much of his advocacy was done in association with people known to be communists or at rallies involving the support of communists. How, you can ask in retrospect and regret, could it have been otherwise? Embarrassingly enough, it does seem that wherever there was an action, particularly in the fifties and sixties, against injustice, for peace, against the excesses of the powerful, there *were* communists involved. The terrible question for so many of us today must be, "And where were we?"

At any rate, Pete Seeger remains the same man today but, as sanity has replaced the craziness of the indiscriminate anticommunist crusade, he is widely respected as a convincing advocate of clean-water projects, an interest he shares with a number of upper-class trout fishermen.

What has changed is not so much Seeger as public good sense on the subject.

Another still startling example, for me, of the confused nature of anticommunism during its heyday is the matter of the Council on Foreign Relations, a very high-class group of businessmen and academics whose regular pronouncements on American foreign policy carry tremendous weight and quite often form the policy itself.

During the fifties, when the anticommunist crusade was at its craziest pitch, some of us in the anticommunist business, and notably Dan Smoot, an ex-FBI agent turned Red-ripping journalist under the wing of H. L. Hunt, latched onto the CFR as a most sinister example of communist infiltration of the highest reaches of government.

The reasoning, roughly, was that the CFR advocated, roughly, coming to terms with the greatest communist power, the Soviet, so as to proceed most smoothly with developing *American* power this side of the Soviet Empire.

Compromise with communism? It was enough to set off every alarm in the anticommunist firehouse. And it did. Who were these sinister folk? Well, they turned out to be such worthies as John J. McCloy who once had *negotiated* with the communists as an official of the occupation in Germany. Ahah, Germany. Wasn't Germany even now divided, half occupied by the terrible Red? Of course. And wasn't any such triumph of Red expansionism to be explained by hanky-panky since communism has no force or merit of its own? Of course. So, ahah, McCloy, the infamous official of the German situation which resulted in a red split of the country, is involved with the CFR. Therefore—obvious, eh?—the CFR must be guilty of red perfidy.

Now the thing the CFR is, was, and perhaps always will be guilty of is having an undue influence on U.S. foreign policy but with no equivalent responsibility. It never stands for election, or even questioning. It rides, undeterred, on the rails of its rich and powerful membership.

But the anticommunists attacked it only for being somehow communist for wanting, in effect, to divide the world along existing East-West lines, grabbing everything left over, particularly in the underdeveloped areas, for "our" side, and making a nice bundle along the way. It was a mistaken perception if ever there was one.

What the anticommunists should have attacked, if they were real friends of human liberty, for instance, was the commercial aspects of the CFR. Later, the New Left, represented by such publications as *Ramparts* magazine, did effectively analyze the commercial aspects of CFR and convincingly displayed its main role as *being* procapitalist, far from being procommunist. To be sure, the CFR has always tilted toward the Big Communists rather than the little communists, but hardly from some socialist viewpoint—rather only from a hard-nosed capitalist viewpoint. The Big Communists make deals. They even deal, when necessary, just like Big Business. The little communists, the national liberation movements and socialists such as those in much of the not-yet-industrialized world, are not only harder to deal with but also often have a direct bearing on American corporate investments such as in mines, plantations, and plants in areas only recently held as wholly-controllable colonies.

American foreign policy, as most bloodily obvious in Indochina, always has been to be tough in those areas and conciliatory in the areas of the Big Communists, such as the Soviet.

The most useful perspective for Americans who are always being asked to be anticommunist is simply to ask "why?" Is it sensible, for instance, to accept a garrison state here in order to fight one there? Is it sensible to see government policy aimed at virtually the destruction of small-time socialist or communist regimes while making the most extraordinary overtures to major communist powers? If the big ones are to be friends, why are the little ones so deadly? Who benefits from such a business? Might it *be* business and might it not be significant that the places where we are asked to be most anticommunist are places where there is a maximum threat to some specific corporate interest rather than to Americans in general?

Another useful example comes to mind, just along those lines. One of the most active and durable anticommunist groups is the American Security Council. Again, even if one accepts the notion that all of their anticommunist activities might be desirable, it should be fair to ask if that activity also covers another agenda of interest, such as corporate profit. In the case of the American Security Council the answer seems obvious. It is backed, primarily, by large corporate donations. Just as with every significant anticommunist group I can think of, the center of support comes from corporate money, not from widespread individual support. Its anticommunism is not mere opposition, it has a very positive side, the side of maintaining the largest possible defense budget. And, most significantly, it is the size of the budget far more than the nature of the budget that preoccupies them. People who fight against waste in the budget are not heroes to the Security Council. People who fight against failed weapons systems are not, either. What the Council advocates is money, money, and more money in the defense budget as a principal way to fight communism.

The ironic result is that the American Security Council actually is the main rooting section for the most, not the least, Stalinist sector of the national economy. The Pentagon is, of course, a state socialist organization. It is a socialized function, under the absolute control of state bureaucrats, and totally devoted to state purposes. Its supreme boss is not the people generally, but the single person of the President, the Commander in Chief.

Those who serve the military serve under conditions of total control, rather like those we think common in communist nations. They have little freedom of speech or action. They operate inside an Iron Curtain of secrecy. To criticize their leaders is to risk the charge of treason.

The anticommunism of the American Security Council does far more to support that totalitarian system, it seems to me, than it does in actual fact to oppose totalitarianism elsewhere. And how, in fairness, could it be otherwise? The problem of dismantling tyranny in any nation abroad is—unless we are endlessly prepared to launch war after war after war—essentially a problem of the people involved. Our main struggle against totalitarianism, our *practical* struggle against it must be right here, at home. In that struggle, the loudest anticommunists remain squarely on the side of the most rigidly regimented side of the society, the military and the Presidential bureaucracy, the defense corporations. They loudly oppose central authority in the Soviet Union. They loudly support it and help build it here.

A good American question might simply be to ask whether devotion to freedom should be measured so much by the bluster of global anticommunism as by the performance of politicians and corporations right here at home.

And the most general American question of all would be to compare what you have had to give up, in the name of anti-communism, with what you have gained. For most of us the answer is a special kind of red ink. Our freedoms at home have become subject to more and more political control. Huge corporations and politics have come to dominate everything—because only big this and big that can combat big communism, the argument goes. The cities decay. The farms molder as agribusiness takes over, reaping plastic foods for us. The schools, which devoted so much time to molding proper citizens, turned out to have spent very little time in teaching skills—or decent regard for one another. The hot competitiveness that marked the Cold War has become the ceaseless standard of conduct for all. Distrust of one another has become commonplace. There are Reds everywhere, remember! And the defense contractors have grown rich while the politicians of both America and the Soviet now face, in growing friendship, dissent from their own ruled populations.

For the sake of this argument, however, suppose that every ounce of energy ever devoted by anyone to being anticommunist was well spent. Even in that situation, I cannot see that there would be equal justification for that energy being used to *defend* everything that communism was against—but that was exactly what happened.

6

YEARS OF ANOTHER COLOR

After years of fighting the left, moving *to* the left might seem a shocking experience, a great political trauma full of wails and anguish, soul searching, garment rending, lonely vigils, fasts, and almost mystical revelations. People who have moved in the other direction, from the left to the right, often describe their experiences in such epic terms. Many see their experience in exactly religious terms, worshiping some left ideology blindly and zealously at one point, perhaps even committing crimes on its behalf, then repenting those crimes but merely shifting the blind devotion to a new religious zeal—Christianity, maybe, or capitalism seen as divinely inspired, or American nationalism seen as divinely ordained.

It is, all of it, against the American grain, that hard old grain of common sense that winks knowingly when a repentant sinner sings the hymns a bit too loud, or when the meanest person in town makes a special display of Sunday piety.

Moving left, for me, was at every step a matter of ordinary and not extraordinary human experience. Certainly it was not a mystical experience. A lot of my "beliefs" on the right had, to be sure, become pretty much matters of faith, of following leaders, of accepting conventional wisdom, of just going along and, above all, of applying the most high-sounding philosophical wrappings to the most self-serving, practical and partisan matters. And it is surely true that there is similar blind faith and obedience on the left—plenty of it—but it has been my very good fortune, so far as I can see, to avoid most of that. The way to avoid it, right or left, is to be healthily skeptical. Not cynical, denying everything, knowing nothing. Just skeptical. Always ready to question, not to carp, really to question, and to be prepared to move, change, or stay where you are depending on what you learn.

For faith, through most of my life, I have always wanted to substitute knowledge. Knowledge, to me, is a usable array of thoughts which are observably consistent with the real material world. Faith can deal in absolutes. Knowledge cannot. Knowledge is what you can observe, or what has been observed, about either the behavior of people, dandelions, or subatomic displays of energy. If any of the material conditions change, then so might the knowledge. The dandelion withers when plucked and so the knowledge that dandelions grow is now enlarged by the knowledge that they also do *not* grow under certain changed conditions. The ancient concept that all material things possessed the distinct characteristics of fire, earth, air, or water gave way to the picking and probing that observed that all those things, instead, possessed more important things in common—such as detectable electrical properties.

Faith deals in matters beyond observation and thus beyond change and even beyond human grasp. Humans do not have to understand matters of faith. They merely have to subscribe to them. Faith might be said to be an opinion about the nature of reality (including the opinion that there is no reality) while knowledge might be said to involve only a process of observing things, then making statements about them (to share knowledge with others), then testing those statements regularly in light of other observations and, finally, being prepared to make new statements where common sense indicates.

Such points may seem a far cry from looking at the purely down-to-earth reasons for a shift in political outlook, but bear with them for a moment because in order to *be* down-to-earth it is very important to know what kind of earth, what kind of ground, the speaker is standing on in the first place.

If, indeed, political positions and nationality and even class position are felt to be matters of faith, explained by forces and ordinations beyond the understanding and even the capacity of human beings, matters of pure belief, matters of absolute right and absolute wrong, then the appropriate action is merely to take a side, or to know that you are on one side or the other. Matters of such faith are fit for conflict rather than argument. They are, literally, life or death matters. Above all, such positions do not require explanations. They require only declarations. In such positions you are identified by what you say you believe in rather than by what you do.

A small but striking example might be in the matter of displaying the names and photographs of great leaders in public places.

In virtually every public office in America there will be a photograph of the current most powerful leader (president, governor, mayor) with a direct impact on that office. The accomplishments of every federal agency are announced in the name of the President, just as the work of most state agencies is publicized in the name of the governor (as in the literally hundreds of thousands of road construction signs all bearing the name of a governor, as though the governor might have been hard at work with a pick and shovel, or at least paper and pencil, on a road which, in fact, the governor might not even know exists). When the leaders change, the photographs change, almost instantly, and by the hundreds of thousands.

This we accept as part of a free society.

In the Soviet Union, however, when we observe precisely the same sort of goings on (Stalin's picture is everywhere one day, nowhere the next) we recoil in horror and say that the public display of the pictures of a leader is worship of Big Brother.

Faith tells us that it is okay when we do it, bad when they do it. Knowledge might ask us why, might sort through the differences. (Our leaders are elevated by the selection of two parties, theirs by the selection of one; our parties have separate organizations but often very similar factions within those organizations, while their party has an unvarying overall organization but tough factionalism within it; and so forth.) Then knowledge, skeptical of the judgment of faith, would wonder if the public display of the leader's face everywhere might not lead to the sort of Big Brother idolatry that we ascribe to "them." At very least, common sense should tell us that there is nothing especially sacred about the face of a leader, that the display of the photographs should be carefully weighed against cost and against the possibility of idolatry, and so forth. Through such an approach you might gain knowledge not only of what happens when you display such pictures but of why such displays are called for in the first place. And, finally, you would reject the explanation of faith that says it is good when we do it, bad when they do it. Exactly the same sort of process might save us in such other examples as applauding when George Corlie Wallace says he wants a policeman on every corner and booing when we discover that in some other country they damn near *do* have one on every corner.

It was this kind of thinking and not some sudden lightning bolt of revelation that moved me from right to left. It was not, in short, a conversion. It was simply a movement.

And the most crucial point of that movement cannot, to my mind, be restated too often. It had to do with how correct the right was in regard to its knowledge of political power and how actually thoughtless it was in regard to economic power, not even seeking knowledge of such power but rather accepting the desirability of its concentration as a matter of faith.

But errors of this sort are reflections of something far deeper than what we see on the surface: politics, economics, partisanship, nationalism. They are reflections of an attitude which subordinates humans to hierarchy, which places institutions above people, which seeks order through rules rather than through civility, which substitutes state power for social agreements, which asks not what a person is or does, but asks instead just what a person *has* (money, power, titles, status).

On the right I had always had some sort of idea, more vague as time went on, that I was fighting that sort of subordination of person to pomp and privilege. As I met people on the left, they pointed to the many contradictions with which I had been content to live and was content to ignore as I made my living doing it! And always, that nagging contradiction between our right wing attacks on political power and our supine attitude before equally awesome economic, corporate power was the one I could not answer, could not wriggle out of, could not explain or rationalize to myself or—and this is where it becomes publicly noticeable—to anyone else.

And, believe me, it was all very confusing.

There were, for instance, the Students for a Democratic Society. They had been organizing while I was working with Senator Goldwater. At first they seemed just another Communist front, and, of course, with our early information coming mainly from friends in the FBI—agents whose special job it is to keep legislators up to date on the latest FBI version of current events—there was never any reason to think otherwise.

Yet the clues and the contradictions were there. If only people on the right had been able to see them more clearly! If only some of the old wisdom of the right had been added to the sharp, incisive, new statements of the New Left! If, if, if, if, if, if.

There was the old right, preaching mightily about the encroachment of the federal establishment into every area of local life. And there was SDS, in its very earliest organizing projects, working for, of all things, *neighborhood* self-reliance and independence. There were, along the way, some perceptive SDS theorists, such as Carl Oglesby (later to become a warm and admired friend) writing that there is a "moral confluence" between the old right and the new left.

And there were the Panthers.

The Black Panther Party for Self Defense, as it was in its beginning days in Oakland, was a nightmare to the right wing. The famed picture of armed black men standing proudly/arrogantly (take your choice according to bias) in the California State House sent shivers down our spines. But they were such wrong shivers. They were shivers of fear. They should have been shivers of pride and admiration. What right winger worthy of his extremist position and his place on the liberal blacklist had not dreamed at one time or another of that final, can't-stand-it-any-longer day when aroused Americans, like their revolutionary forefathers, would take up their muskets again and say NO to the bureaucrats?

The liberals, in every way possible, had always characterized the right as a bunch of trigger-happy, armed primitives ready to defend their positions recklessly and even violently. Actually, I have met very few right wingers in my entire life who would have the actual fortitude to defend their positions with anything more substantial than a small contribution of money —but the image of being throwbacks to the days of the Revolution certainly was prevalent and most right wingers at least relished it.

And, so, here were black men acting out the fantasy, actually telling a gang of bureaucrats that they would not be disarmed (a constant right-wing pride), that they would not be shoved around by the police (the right wing, of course, would never say police, because of shallow analysis, but would, instead, say politicians or bureaucrats, forgetting who backs up the politicians and the bureaucrats). In short, here were black men saying, in actual fact, that they did not consider extremism in the defense of their freedom to be a vice or moderation in the pursuit of justice to be a virtue.

Even more, the Black Panthers were neighborhood-oriented! They did not even at the outset preach a doctrine of global communism or world government or even set as a goal the assumption of national power. They wanted, instead, freedom where they lived, freedom to have communities rather than colonies.

The right should have cheered. Instead, it called the cops.

And, just as I listened to the FBI and detested the SDS, I didn't listen at all to what the Panthers were saying—and detested them.

But, more and more now, I was attending seminars at the Institute for Policy Studies and coming closer and closer to the most trying of times: the time of meeting in person people I had previously hated in theory. I am sure there are hides thick enough, prejudices deep enough, to withstand such experiences. I possessed neither.

When I started visiting the Institute I had what I regard as the most commonplace prejudice in American politics: the notion that liberals represent a position on the left, that liberals are even procommunist, that liberals are left wingers, and that all left wingers are alike.

The Institute, specifically because it was filled with people of the left who were anything but all alike, offered a wonderfully instructive transition. First of all, it did not face me with a sudden reversal of everything I had believed. Far from it. There were liberals there quick to fume about my role in resisting grand federal bureaucratic plans. There were state-socialist leftists too, quick and long to argue the virtues of central planning and state power and loudly to condemn as anarchism or—horrors—individualism any notion of liberty. There were professional blacks, always eager to dump loads of guilt on any available white head and, although they clearly preferred liberals as a dumping ground (they writhe so well), they obviously didn't mind having a right winger on hand so that the liberals could gasp aloud at the spectacle of a white who did not feel guilty.

But there were so many others. Black men and women who had survived the actual terror of community organizing under the guns of political bosses and their hired thugs in certain Southern sheriffs' offices, and who persisted in working for black independence and self-reliance rather than welfare dependency, who worked still in Mississippi towns, in basement schools in urban ghettos, wherever and however their neighbors were working for freedom and not just for crumbs from white liberal tables of power. There were men and women who had moved from liberalism, and even from positions of power in liberal politics, to the left of real alternatives and actual opposition to liberal programs. Men and women who spoke, curiously, it seemed to me, of so many of the things we on the right had spoken of—but with more understanding, more study, and far more consistency in terms of human social organization as a whole and not just a series of partisanly-fragmented parts.

This New Left that I met there was deeply compelling and deeply moving.

From people like Michael Maccoby there came long, serious discussions of the place of individuals in society, a place that begins with secure and healthy understanding that we are each of us individual people with individual personalities and minds but that we are individuals within and not outside of a society of many other individuals, that we have an absolutely individual interior life and identity which can enable us to be cooperative rather than competitive with others, that it is from this interior sense that we derive our most basic human orientation, either moving toward and loving life and living or retreating into the deathlike orientation in which all are viewed as enemies, in which material possessions become, like a tomb, the measure of our worth and ambitions, and in which crushing power over others is the goal of action, lest they (the lurking, feared "they") do us in first.

From others whom I have already mentioned—Raskin, Barnet, Kotler—and then Hannah Arendt, Martha and Mike Tabor, Paul Goodman, Arthur Waskow, Sam Rosencrantz, Rob Burlage, and so many others, the clearest attribute of the New Left emerged for me: a growing body of thoughtful, principled, and then active opposition to the very notion of hierarchy, the very notion of people giving up power to institutions rather than retaining that power in the fullest and most participatory forms of citizenship. Even those who most earnestly sought to retain the forms of existing institutions, in order to make the most pacific and orderly transitions to enlarged freedom, spoke of "reforms" which were radically decentralizing in nature. To Raskin, for instance, a national tax structure could even be retained in a free society—but every citizen would have to be accorded the right to designate areas in which the citizen's money could or could not be spent and in what proportions. To Kotler, national enterprises could be preserved but could be made fit for free citizens by basing political power in the neighborhoods, and in government by town meetings, by assemblies of the entire people, with regional and national actions stemming from federated activities of the politically independent but socially interdependent neighborhoods.

And there were people in transition, even as I was. Gar Alperovitz, whom I had first known as virtually a technocrat of the liberal establishment, moved away from great central planning toward a notion of what he called regional socialism, in which people in naturally defined areas, with naturally congruent problems and interests, could socially own critical facilities while still retaining a government close enough to everyone to include everyone. And Dick Barnet moved from an incisive, I think definitive, critique of the cold-war bureaucracy toward an equally incisive and probably even more important analysis of the role played by giant, multinational corporations in shaping decisions which become public policy and assume the rhetoric of national-security necessity. Ralph Stavins, a fairly hard-line advocate of central planning power when I arrived at the Institute, moved toward a detailed analysis of the state of almost martial law which the federal bureaucracy can and does impose under the guise of national security and thence to a series of scholarly probes of the possibilities of participatory democracy, local political sovereignty, and small or human-scale social organization. Also, very memorably, he led a seminar once on gun controls which left liberals howling in horror and some right wingers whirling in confusion because here, from an avowed man of the left, there emerged the most reasonable defense of a citizenry armed not against vague prowlers and foreign invaders, but against the steadily encroaching power of the police and the state itself.

Just as crucial for me, however, were, finally, meeting with the dreaded SDS and the fearful Panthers. I don't suppose I will ever recover from them. So far I have had no reason to even want to.

The first SDS meeting I ever attended was notable for two discussions. One was in regard to the fact that someone had just heard a speech by George Wallace and was amazed to hear him say many of the things SDS had been saying. He had, reportedly, attacked the big banks and big government—both major targets of SDS. The difference between George Wallace's attack, however, and SDS's is simply that SDS people had studied what they were saying, could put their attacks in an overall and consistent political context, and could relate it all to a social goal and to human terms. Wallace spoke as a partisan, attacking the overwhelming power of "their" government while earnestly trying to build the power of his; attacking the giant corporations which did not support him while earnestly envisioning a system in which others would support him. In short, SDS was attacking power and privilege itself. Wallace was attacking to *gain* power and privilege.

This is not to say there were not factions in SDS that shared precisely the Wallaceite notion of grabbing rather than diminishing power. The bitter infighting that eventually destroyed the organization was fought largely along just those lines, between people who, in the founding spirit of the group, wanted to attack power itself and to build a society of participatory rather than representative democracy (town meetings, for instance, versus city halls) and those who wanted to seize power and exercise it and who wanted to do it precisely as Wallace and other politicians always want to do it—in the name of "the people." But when I first attended SDS meetings, becoming a member, the impulse toward liberty and against central authority was clear and strong.

That very impulse, as a matter of fact, was the basis of the second of the discussions that so impressed me at my first meeting. The discussion was whether to cooperate with the Communist Party! Here was a group which, from official FBI statements (the sort on which most right-wing and probably even liberal politicians depend) was seen as a virtual communist front, but a group which was deeply divided over the question, in effect, of whether even to be caught talking to the Communist Party. That too was a debate that never died within SDS.

State communists were considered by most SDS members I knew to be actually reactionary, to have renounced the fervor of true reform and revolution in favor of the deadening partisanship of supporting the Soviet Union. Many members of SDS considered themselves to be communists. To them, the official Communist Party was not much more communist than any other establishment party. If they favored a form of communism other than the sort of native version they wanted (a decentralized, locally based ownership-in-common of the means of production), it was Chinese communism, with its persistent emphasis on village organization and even village autonomy or, at least, near-autonomy.

Actually, just about every SDS meeting I attended contained some sort of sharp criticism of both the factions which, earlier, and like so many Americans, I had assumed to *be* the left: Democratic Party liberalism and official Communism. The criticism was far more penetrating than any I had heard on the right. There was no misguided belief that American liberals were trying to turn the country over to working people. There was, instead, a clear understanding that liberalism in America was helping regiment working people into bureaucratic trade unions whose policies were in absolute long-range accord with management (preservation of the existing ownership and control system). There was a clear understanding that liberal welfare programs simply organized the unemployed into a welfare clientele where they would present no restless challenge to the system. There was a clear understanding that it was supposedly liberal politicians like John Kennedy who had most advanced the cold war and even turned it into hot war on occasion.

And there was no misguided belief that the Communist Party was the patent medicine for what ails us in America.

There was, instead, an intense, somehow wholly American, belief in the ability of people generally to make their own history, control their own lives, set and reach their own goals, and work cooperatively and peacefully—although, to be sure, there was from the outset a growing feeling, among many of the very young members in particular, that in the final analysis nothing *could* be accomplished peacefully and that only violence and confrontation would start the process of change.

It is still difficult to assess what impact these young people had. Their violence on campus obviously turned many Americans, and particularly working-class Americans, against what they perceived to be "the left." On the other hand, the black violence in Watts, Detroit, and Washington turned the country in ways still difficult to assess but nevertheless impossible to assign zero impact. The violence of SDS, which welled up after —significantly *after*—it had vested substantial energy in the most constructive neighborhood organizing projects, must have had some long-range effect also. Although it might not exactly counterbalance the alienation of the working people, the SDS impact must be weighed in the entire process by which Americans of every walk of life began to prepare themselves for what may be seen today as an epic disillusionment with the representative political process and, in the face of incredible inflation plus incredible profits, a disillusionment also with corporate capitalism.

My personal assessment is that if SDS had been able to withstand the many official assaults against its neighborhood projects, and had established a solid base in first a few and then many ordinary neighborhoods rather than retreating so completely to the easy haven of the campus, its impact would have been even greater. But no matter, it left America not only scarred but changed, even if just a bit.

Today I know of students who have moved back into neighborhood projects, even while continuing in school. They can and do offer to local groups the special skills of research and presentation which come easily for college people. Actually those skills are quickly grasped by working people generally. But the young students often help break the ice. College students never really had a prayer of leading working people. Why should they? Working people are generally far wiser. Students may have more access to information. Together they may make good neighbors, good co-workers in various causes. The establishment which seemed virtually hysterical at the work of SDS actually has far more to worry about today with all the old arrogance gone, with quiet determination setting in, with cooperation and not competition between factory and campus at least a possibility.

One example which is very close to my heart and mind concerns an undergraduate in a midwestern university. Hearing that some nearby farmers were threatened with eviction from their land because of a government project, he simply went out into the community, told them he could do legal research, could help with publicity, and just generally lend a hand because he believed in their fight to save their land. He was accepted. Many of the farmers, as he quickly discovered, were extremely right-wing in their politics generally—but in the concrete case of the threat to their land they were as against the "law and order" that was about to evict them as any flaming radicals you could imagine.

The farmers and the student had been working together for months when I last saw the young man. They had taught him not to be so quick and harsh in judging middle-class Americans or in assuming that their political attitudes were incapable of change. He had taught them, by hard work and patient research, that the so-called free enterprise system which they so blindly supported was, in fact, now a corporate system in which the interests of the big rich and the big politicians invariably conspired to destroy the people in the middle—the honest, hardworking Americans.

Multiplied again and again, such alliances between idealistic and radical young people and threatened, disillusioned, hardpressed older working people, on farms, in factories, even in small, besieged businesses, are far more of a threat to the reign of the corporations and the established politicians than most street demonstrations. Yet who is to say absolutely that the dedication of young people to change today would be as patient and as serious as I am convinced it is, without the shouting, the fighting, the turmoil of the recent past? It was as though we had to get a fever out of our system, a fever brought on so much by the enormity of the Indo-Chinese war, in order to recover not the status quo but a new level of determination.

The Black Panthers have followed a similar course.

When I first met members of the Black Panther Party there was an air of incredible romanticism and heroism about them and everything they did. From the unbelievable armed saunter through the California State House, through the streetcorner confrontations of Huey Newton, to the black leather "uniforms," to the states of siege raised by various local police departments around Panther headquarters, these people seemed so much bigger than life that, like them or hate them, it was hard to see their true dimension.

I worked as closely as I could with them, mostly in Washington, raising money, speaking at public meetings on their behalf, helping with pamphlets and speeches. I recognize it simply as what it is, a personal testimony, but I will say this: I have never worked with or known a finer or more conscientious group of people in any political work that I have done. I know that there were scoundrels in the Party. I didn't happen to work with any of them. I know that there were purely violent people in the Party and I didn't happen to work with them either—and quite a few turned out to be police provocateurs anyway.

As a white man, I was impressed very much by the fact that the Panthers with whom I worked were not racists, did not hate white people, clearly saw that class and not race was crucial to the long-term developments of change in this country, and were rooted to the idea that change must be based in the places where people live and work and not high up in the sky of political moralizing, abstraction, and theory. Just as in SDS, as a matter of fact, a major struggle within the Party was with those who felt otherwise, who wanted a more stern Marxist-Leninist politics and discipline, and whose eyes were focused on the faraway horizons of history and destiny and not on the mean streets of home.

Unlike SDS, the Panthers have survived this struggle and, today, moving in the regular politics of Oakland, and with the Panthers being firm and quick in their denunciation of such possibly police-provoked adventurism as that of the Symbionese Liberation Army, it seems to me that there is an enduring role for them to play in the development of a new political sovereignty and a new participatory democracy in America.

I recall standing in front of a church in Washington and hearing a Panther speak of why he did not want the Panthers to be involved in an "international movement." International, he said, meant something between nations. He was not interested in nations, he said. He wanted a world where relations were between communities. Intercommunalism was the phrase he used.

It was a haunting echo. Gandhi had spoken of a world of villages, relating one to another without the artificial restrictions of political systems and borders. Goldwater, even though an ardent nationalist, had made speech after speech suggesting the dream of people living in communities of self-reliance and self-responsibility. The antifederalists of the American Revolution, preferring the Articles of Confederation to the nation-binding Constitution, also had obviously dreamed of a land which might never be a great and powerful *nation* but which could be a sweet and free *country* of towns and villages and farms.

The Panther who spoke so clearly of genuine freedom that night was the same Panther who just a while earlier, I had to remind myself, I had seen as a communist villain, a black menace—because I had been carefully taught and told to see him that way.

How I wish, constantly, that more and more of my old right-wing friends could stop listening to what the professional anti-leftists have to say about such people. How I wish they could meet and talk directly with such people. They would, I sincerely believe, find friends, not enemies. And America would find a growing and spreading alliance, cutting across imagined class lines, across racial lines, across old partisan lines—the sort of alliance that would start us all working and organizing on our own behalf and not lining up as docile sheep to be fleeced by the corporations and the politicians operating and well organized in their own self interest.

There could be equally fruitful, and surprising, meetings between many Americans and something else they probably have come to fear and hate without ever seeing it close up: Marxism. As an "ism," it is as distasteful to me as to others. There is no reason for it or for any philosophical work to be an "ism." "Isms" are the monkey wrenches in the gears of history, diverting people from making their own history and tempting them to accept someone else's, second hand.

History, I believe, should be made from the social action of people serving their own perceived needs rather than from following the blueprints of remote authority, whether that authority is as remote as heaven or as immediate as a bureaucratic office, or as handy as the codifications of a book.

The historical analyses of others, the philosophical speculation of others, are and should be tools used to help living people forge their own structures of life and living. They should help with the building but not substitute for the thoughtful decisions of the people who, because they must occupy the space in history themselves, must take the responsibility for its proximate contours.

So, as a guide to the future, I would absolutely reject Marxism. As a tool to grasp the dimensions of the past and some of the *possibilities* of the future, I would no more reject the work of Karl Marx than I would that of Aristotle, Tom Paine, John Dewey, Peter Kropotkin, or anyone else who has thought long and hard on the condition of being human. Or the Bible, with its many extraordinarily commonsensical perceptions. One need not be a Marxist to appreciate Marx or a Christian to appreciate the Bible. I would not follow either. Nor would I ignore either.

In a book that I wrote just after the 1964 Goldwater campaign, I stated rather strongly my perception of what Marx had been talking about. It is an embarrassing reminder, today, that I wrote it on the basis of what FBI briefings told me Marx had said and not on the basis of my own knowledge and reading. At any rate, my notion then was that Marx had laid out the proposition that humans were like animals in general, mostly creatures of sheer appetite. It was my impression that Marx had established the notion of the human as an economic unit, to be manipulated like the cog in a machine, for purely economic reasons and for economic reasons, additionally, which would be established by a state bureaucracy.

No matter the use Marx has been put to by regimes which rule by police power and which treat people as mere cogs in the state machine, what Marx himself wrote about is strikingly different from what most Americans seem to think he wrote about.

At a time when many historians were persisting in seeing the human story as just a chronicle of kings and queens, Marx dug deep enough to find the people generally and to see their role in history as shaped in the long run not so much by the capers of the kings as by the relationship of people generally to productive life, to ways of working (from gatherers and hunters to farmers to feudal peasants to factory workers). He saw, also, that the great sickness of society was the increasing separation, alienation, of people from their work; separation in fact, by more and more people doing smaller and smaller and usually inexplicable parts of a process, becoming mere extensions of machines, and separation economically by working in a system in which the full value of their labor could never be realized by workers themselves due to the demands of owners to skim so much off the top.

Above all, he saw that human beings were vitally and essentially social in nature, deeply desirous of living in communities, with other people, and capable of open cooperation among themselves if not alienated from their human roles by intervening institutions such as capitalism or the state which, in Marx's eyes, was the executive committee of the economic ruling elite.

Now, in the most familiar American terms the essence of the writings of Karl Marx deals with the people as special creatures, uniquely human, and not as mere cogs in either a clockwork universe or a divine plan. Perhaps the insistence that humans are part of a history which they themselves make, and not part of a divine plan, would be offensive to devout Christian believers and they could debate that exact point. But that is not what most devout Christians do debate about Marx. They debate, instead, the false notion that Marx wrote about people as being "mere" animals. Far from it. Marx exalted people *as human beings* and as very, very special creatures indeed. Also, devout capitalists cry out that Marx writes about turning "their property" over to the mob. Far from it again. Marx wrote about the historical process in which property and wealth created by the labor of many is steadily expropriated by the few in collusion with the politicians. He wrote of the little mob of capitalists, as a matter of fact, systematically stealing from the labors of the many. How many commonsense Americans, seeing small businesses falling steadily by the wayside, watching mergers on top of mergers, watching profits endlessly rising, watching the rich grow richer and the poor grow poorer, how many Americans really disagree in their own experience and in their own statements with what Marx actually wrote about? Most who abhor even the mention of the name actually abhor not what the name really covers but what they have been told it covers.

This is a defense of the value of what Marx did write and not at all a defense of Marxism. Marxism has come to denote, for me, a mind-set in which reality must be hammered into the shape demanded by this or that official version of Marxist literature, a mind-set in which a correct line is far more important than correct, or decent, actions. It has become cant and cabala, political theology. It has become, more than that, distinctly anti-Marxist, in the sense that Marx wrote so often of seeing the world fresh and fully and without the distortions of past orthodoxy. For the writings of Marx, which raged against the hold that official histories had fastened on people, to now *become* an official and orthodox history and analysis is supremely ironic.

Nor should a discussion of Marx be continued too long for fear that, as with the raging Marxist, it will appear that nothing else in human thought is consequential. The point is just this: Distortions of Marx, both by the right and by the left, have been used for terribly bad purposes—to justify police repressions on both sides of the fence, for instance. To avoid falling prey to such distortions it would be wise to read Marx's writing for yourself or, if you prefer not to, not to let what others say about it become a determining factor in your actions.

There is, finally, what was, when I was on the right, the dread phrase which could be hauled up from its dark forbidding place to frighten the daylights out of anyone, to end any argument, to silence any question, to unify any ranks, to cause any doubters to straighten up and start chanting that craziest of slogans, "Better dead than Red."

The dread phrase is "dialectical materialism." Like some nutty Vincent Price horror-movie device, dialectical materialism seems to have some sort of paralyzingly different but terrible meaning for each person who recoils from it.

Yet, I will bet you, if you ask the next person who bandies it about just what it means, you will get either an answer you do not understand, because the person doesn't understand it, or you will get some weird and special misstatement.

On the right, I have heard the term tossed around so constantly over the years that it has lost any real meaning. It just means something bad and it means it in whatever context you happen to be talking. If you listen to your loudest anticommunist neighbor, somewhere along the line you will probably get belted with it. It is the sort of phrase that is like a password, denoting membership in some inner circle of deep understanding of the evils of all things leftist. You hear things like:

"Look here. It goes deeper than just political differences. After all, the Reds are DIALECTICAL MATERIALISTS. God knows we can't compromise with that."

"Sure, they may be talking out of a different side of their mouths now, but that's just DIALECTICAL MATERIALISM. You'll see. They never change."

"I don't care what they say, it's the way they think that's evil. They're DIALECTICAL MATERIALISTS."

"They are against everything we stand for. They are DIALECTICAL MATERIALISTS."

"Why am I against them, no matter what they do? I'll tell you why. I don't want my kinds to grow up under DIALECTICAL MATERIALISM."

When pressed for explanations, most of the people who rant and rave about dialectical materialism do it on the basis of definitions such as:

"Dialectical means that it's okay to lie; that it's okay to twist any meaning to whatever you want it to be. Materialism means that all you care about is material possessions and running things. So dialectical materialism means it's okay to do anything in order to get power and turn everybody else into slaves."

Funny thing about that sort of definition. I have heard renowned defenders of corporate capitalism say that the only responsibility of a company is to make a profit. That its only function is material, its only goal the accumulation of material wealth. Then I have heard highly placed people in government say that it is all right to lie in the name of the government. And I have heard virtually every politician in the land admit that when all is said and done the only function of a political party in America is to gain power. Winning, they say, is the name of the game. And *only* winning.

And, finally, I have heard more and more Americans taking more and more seriously the common phrase that "all we are in the system is a bunch of wage slaves." Or slaves to machines.

Perhaps it is inevitable that what we hate most is more easily seen and criticized in distant places and in distant, abstract language—so that many Americans accurately describe their own growing pain but then transfer it to a condition which they say exists somewhere else and for some fancy reason such as dialectical materialism.

The best way to expose, for the foolishness that it is, the mystical right-wing fear of dialectical materialism is simply to state what dialectical materialism is. Like so much that so many of us have come to fear unreasonably, its fearsome face doesn't look nearly so bad in the light of some knowledge.

The notion of dialectical reasoning (it just means argument or discourse) goes back to Aristotle and beyond. To Aristotle it meant the kind of thinking that would take some accepted notion and then critically examine it, holding it up to the real world to see if it fitted facts that could be observed rather than just opinions which could be stated but never tested. He was an especial foe of what he saw as the opposite of dialectical thinking, in which a person would make some statement arbitrarily for some self-serving reason and then force everyone to argue on the basis of it.

If the phrase "Better dead than Red" is used as an example,

the dialectical approach would be wholly critical, looking as closely at what it means to be dead, as Red, wondering if being dead might not, come to think of it, preclude any chance of ever being un-Red, and fully defining the conditions of being Red so that an apt evaluation could be made of the entire equation. The approach that Aristotle so abhorred, the *non-*dialectical approach, would be to state "Better dead than Red" as some absolute, unexamined, virtually religiously revealed truth and then make all subsequent arguments on the basis of fully accepting it (without ever dialectically, or critically, examining it).

In the American tradition there is no more absolutely dialectical summation than the good old Missouri slogan, "Show me." Yankee skepticism, one of our folk heritages, may be seen as a dialectical approach.

With the work of Marx and Engels and Hegel, the idea of dialectics assumed a special meaning to social change. It became the name for the idea that, after critical examination of historical evidence, every part of existence is a process in which conflicting, or contradictory, forces surge against one another, finally merging or penetrating one another to produce a new situation which, although it has brand-new qualities, is nevertheless a melding of the old qualities, a synthesis. But inherent in the new quality, this position states, are new contradictions and conflicting forces which surge, join, change, to keep the process going through infinite changes and versions.

An example might be seen in the growth of machine technology. At first, people and their machines got along well, with cottage industries springing up to loom wool and cotton, for instance. Then the conflicts and contradictions emerged between machines that could serve cottagers but also could be exploited by large landowners with, say, large holdings of cotton grown by colonial slaves. The interests of the people generally would pull one way, the interests of the aristocracy would pull another. Finally they begin to join in a new con-struction: the machines become dominated by the rich and the powerful but the former cottage industry people are not totally destroyed, they are simply assimilated into a new system in which instead of being independent they become employees of a company. They don't get anywhere near all the wealth they produce—but they get some. The company doesn't get all it wants, but then it doesn't have to fight constant uprisings either, it just jiggers or "reforms" the shares of the wealth which the workers produce. The state, meantime, goes through a similar dialectical change, surging through the conflicts be-tween absolute monarchies and the rising power of new mer-chant princes, to name just one. From the contradicting forces emerges a new sort of state, no longer absolute, but still power-ful enough to preserve itself against most forces and creating with the merchant princes a new sort of power in which, to cite a famous American slogan, "business is the business" of the state.

And even now, this dialectical view would have it, the grow-ing contradictions among interests in society, between working people, for instance, and the owners of people and property, are coming together, struggling and churning, and will soon produce new structures altogether unlike the old but containing elements of it and also containing new contradictions which will be worked out in further push and shove.

Whether you agree or disagree with the proposition, it scarcely seems that this dialectical statement is so different from many ordinary, everyday conceptions as to require Americans to fall in a faint whenever they hear the word. Instead, they ought critically to examine it. Dialectically, you might say. Also, dialectically, it strikes me as most American to understand that there *are* contradictions between what is supposed to be the way of life here and what it actually is.

The definition of materialism in all this is no more terrifying.

It is not, emphatically *not*, the definition of materialism which we very commonly and very wisely apply to our corporate system, the definition in which the almighty dollar reigns supreme and in which profit is the be-all and end-all of corporate life, assuming an importance which we all either secretly or outspokenly know to be greater than the importance attached to such human values as peace of mind, creative freedom, love, friendship, trust and tolerance and even delight in differences.

Materialism, as a philosophical position, is altogether different. Its "material" refers not to creature comforts and money but specifically to the "real world," the world of matter and energy, the material world. Its fundamental proposition is that the real world exists independent of any supernatural or mystical origin or reason, that it should be accepted "without reservation" and that, furthermore, it exists independent of the mind of man, that it is not, as some philosophers claim, just a result of human perception. Materialism is the root notion of much of what we generally accept in science today—without shuddering; such ideas as that of evolution, in which matter is believed to have existed prior to the human mind. Now, materialists might say, humans are simply that form of material life which is conscious of itself, studies itself and all other forms of existence, matter, and energy.

Materialism is simply a way of thinking about the world which is directly different from, say, mysticism and supernaturalism. To that extent, of course, it is a denial of the supernatural *basis* of religion. But it is not, emphatically *not*, a denial of the religion. In a materialist view, religion would be seen as a cultural reality. Some materialists would rail against it. Others would not. The important point would be the denial of the supernatural nature of religious truth, not a denial of the cultural power of religious statement.

Taken together, then, dialectical materialism sees the real world as matter and energy with (as the ecological view has lately made popular) everything dynamically interconnected, and with opposing factors and forces constantly forcing changes.

Everyday life easily accepts dialectical materialism. The worker understands that even if he or she dropped dead tomorrow the world would go on and that even if we all dropped dead, the world would still spin around a sun which, in turn, would move in its galactic place in a broader universe which is subjected to endless speculation and not just shrugged off as unknowable. Yet, the worker also understands that his or her death would cause changes, that lives are interconnected even as environmental systems are interconnected and even as certain electrical characteristics interconnect matter. Too, the worker understands that no matter how intense a person's loyalty to a boss or a company, there are times when contradictions and conflicts arise and that, just as surely as there have always been changes in the past, there will be changes in the future.

Now it is true that from the notion of materialism you can derive things which may appall and frighten you. Its denial of the supernatural is, admittedly, a withdrawal of divine authority for *any* religious statement. The deeply religious might well resent it for that, and understandably. They might also fear what it could lead to, as in the official discouragement of, although not abolition of, religion in certain countries. But the intellectual conflict between the real and the supernatural world has been going on for millennia, and not just since such names as materialism and the dialectic were applied to phases of it.

On the other hand, the materialist position and the dialectical method of probing conventional wisdom could as easily encompass religious tolerance, and even demand it in the name of *cultural* reality.

A deeply religious farmer, for instance, might hold an unshakeable religious faith as an inner conviction and yet be an absolute materialist, and even dialectical, in insisting on testing various techniques, in not trusting to luck in planting, in trying to pin down every real possibility of botanical and biological knowledge as applicable to the farm.

Many scientists, thorough materialists in the laboratory, nevertheless profess profound religious beliefs although they are not known simply to pray for experimental results. For those results they endlessly argue, test, compare, analyze. The religious scientists are, in fact, embodiments of the very sorts of contradictions which dialectical materialism, as applied to historical change, would accept and even predict, adding that sooner or later the abiding contradictions between the supernatural and the materially scientific will bring forth new concepts, formed out of but possibly not at all like the strongest parts of the old positions. The entirely new position, however, will also contain entirely new contradictions.

Again, Americans—whose heritage literally includes the best that the old world could offer, a land which is itself a dialectical result, you might say, of synthesizing old contradictions and producing new ones—have little to fear from such notions as dialectical materialism or the analysis of Marx. Rather, Americans can learn, discard the useless, confront the contradictory, struggle for the new, and make their own history—to precisely the extent that they will engage themselves in the project.

Fear, in a largely literate and still amazingly self-reliant and responsible group of people such as the Americans, is just a nightmare that is not worthy of us. I think that America not only could but should absorb, not recklessly reject, Marx, the anarchists, dialectical materialism, and all the other so-called leftist "isms" from which we recoil without reflection.

It was the American Declaration of Independence, we should not forget, which far ahead of Marx and Engel's *Communist Manifesto* rejected any notion of divine sanction for rulers, which assigned to the state the purely functional role of serving the people, which set the people themselves absolutely above all institutions, even urging them to replace the government itself if it ever got too big for them to control. And if there ever was a proper materialist in the philosophical sense it was none other than our own (not *their*) Tom Paine.

In many ways, the pragmatic, skeptical, down-to-earth approach of many people in this country has been more Marxist than the actions of many foreign Marxists, with their harsh denials of creativity and their insistence on state power as superior to immediate human needs and desires.

Marx himself, on the other hand, flatly said that so long as the state exists there is no liberty, and when there is liberty there will be no need for a state. The fact that more and more Americans, weary to death of the exercise of state power over their lives, weary to death of pompous promises and failed programs, are beginning to share this notion doesn't mean we are or should be Marxists. Rather, it seems to me, our role in the surge of conflicting forces is to be the people who finally take the great step or leap forward to new freedoms, without overwhelming institutional power, without hierarchical organization, but with work in which we fully participate and from which we are in no way alienated, with communities in which we also fully participate without lazy delegations of our citizenship, with a new and bursting respect for and joy in the infinitely creative nature of the human mind and in the as yet barely-touched horizons of self-respecting and responsible societies of mutual aid and myriad diversity.

If there is a place for this step to be taken first, it seems to me it is very close to home—not in so-called mass parties or national organizations, but in the neighborhoods where, no matter how far we may roam, we actually live much of our lives and where the people with whom we live must necessarily be seen as living human beings and not political abstractions or cogs in a machine.

Revolutionary social change, like charity, begins at home.

7

THE LONELY RUNNERS

Perhaps, like a sinner converted, I will seem to make too much of this next point, to deal with it too harshly, too sweepingly, to generalize about it, to fume and to fuss. True. But I am convinced that it is the point on which the entire direction of social change in this country will turn. If, in the matter of work, most Americans can be convinced that their best interests lie with those of the present owners of industry, then all possible social change will be along liberal lines at best and some sort of fascist line at worst. Change will be simply to consolidate the status quo, tranquilizing people with welfare programs on the one hand or putting them into line with national security programs on the other.

If, however, the vast majority of Americans whose lives depend most directly on work rather than ownership take a different tack, then so will the country.

In essence, I think, the struggle will be over whether to continue to separate or to bring together the political and economic parts of our lives. The political part of our lives already has one well-defined theme: that political democracy is desirable. Realized or not, the ideal of political democracy is the central public theme of our politics. We have retained active examples of the most radical forms of political democracy, the town meetings. And, even though the town meeting, or participatory democracy, has been beaten back in most places by representative democracy (the democracy of legislatures rather than of assemblies), it is true, nevertheless, that all arguments for political democracy, even the radical ones, are both acceptable and familiar. The militia is not called out to encircle people meeting to debate the formation of a town meeting.

The militia has often been called out, however, to encircle and even attack people who have met to discuss another form of democracy: industrial democracy.

There is no wider discrepancy in American life than between the familiar and accepted rhetoric of political democracy and the rejection as overly radical of the ideas of industrial democracy. Yet, I have come to feel, there can be no *actual* democracy of any sort so long as the work people do and the lives people lead are separated by law and custom into airtight compartments.

Industrial democracy simply says that people who work should participate in the decisions of work just as they should participate in the decisions of community. It says that *doing* work entitles a person to this participation, just as *being* in a community entitles a person to participation there.

Industrial democracy faces a barrier that political democracy does not. It faces an unbroken history of opposition at every level, rhetorical and actual, by major cultural influences: media, schools, government, advertising, and all other organs of commercial influence. The crux of that opposition has been to blur the lines of self-interest in the country.

The rich and the powerful always have been well organized in America. They know, obviously, the effectiveness of getting together in their own self-interest. They know how lost they would be if, instead, each of them stood alone, wary of the other, so frightened of their own shadows that they couldn't see the shadows of real threats lengthening all around them. The rich and the powerful do fight among themselves, of course. One way they do it is to become either Democrat or Republican and thus contend for control of the political machinery which they depend upon to serve their economic machinery. One group may prefer to do it the Democratic way, through make-work projects, professionalization of welfare, war, and high taxes for the middle and lower classes but with at least the rhetoric of high taxes for the upper class. Or they may choose the Republican way, with high profits, turning welfare operations over to private companies, relatively high taxes for the middle and lower classes and, lately, war.

The major difference between the two parties that I have been able to observe during and after a quarter century of rather devoted service to partisan politics—always as a professional Republican propagandist—is that the Democrats tend to bend toward the special needs of the more modern ownership groups, at least in the north, while responding to political clans in the south. The Republicans, on the other hand, seem to bend more toward the older, usually land-based fortunes and the old mercantile fortunes. Each has the highest regard for the bankers in general, with one group of bankers (the more cautious) coming to the fore during Republican regimes and the flashier (international, expansionist) during Democrat regimes.

In actual operating terms there really isn't much difference at all. Corporate profits, no matter who is in power politically, continue to rise to record levels.

Each industry produces a well-financed trade organization which operates in much the way a union does, providing a mechanism for the concerted action of owners and managers in the same way that a union provides for the concerted action of working people.

Prestigious groups such as the Council on Foreign Relations give the bankers and the major corporations an organized way to press for the foreign policies most favorable to their international expansion—an expansion which is now the major growth area of American industry as more and more of its efforts and cash go sailing across the ocean to pastures far greener than the hardscrabble remains of the saturated American market. Such domestic groups as the Council on Economic Development and the various groups officially organized to advise the President on business matters, and the Chamber of Commerce, of course, bring the rich and powerful together in ways to push the best and hardest for favorable tax, regulatory and other internal policies, and bigger and better subsidies and government loans to business and industry. The American Banking Association, the trade union of those hardworking folks with all the problems of what to do with all *your* money, is as effective in getting raises for bankers as is the UAW in getting raises for auto workers—except that the bankers don't have to split the take quite so many ways. (There are only 13,000 banks in the whole country and, although they employ a million people, it seems fairly safe to say that the big beneficiaries in the banking profession are a smaller number, as a glance at the staff of any bank, with the panelled back room of the president and the perched stools of the tellers, will tell you. On the other hand the UAW has a membership of 1,500,000 who must divide up raises fairly equally, excepting only some far out-of-balance salaries for the union officials themselves.)

At no time has there been a discernible outcry from the great corporate owners of America against the principle of organization. Far from it. They have run that principle as far into the ground as they can, beginning with the early monopolies and extending right up to the most modern conglomerate; beginning with the first primitive lobbying group right up to the most sophisticated modern educational campaigns to defend high profits on television.

Yet, let anyone *else* organize and the screams may be heard from here to there. That is particularly and crucially true of people who work. When they organize they are said to be disrupting the classless society, betraying the American Dream, and wallowing in divisive selfishness.

I can remember having written and said all of those things while a propagandist for corporate interests and for the Republican Party. One glowing image that I conjured up in a speech for an industrialist was that of a mighty ocean liner—America. The bridge of the mighty ship, I wrote, could be compared to modern, forward-looking American management and the system of ownership under which that management serves, the good old free enterprise system. The engine room of the mighty ship could be compared to American working people. Now, I continued, there were sinister forces loose in the land who wanted to sink the bridge of the ship, who wanted to take away the power and the privileges of the people on the bridge. Then, in a triumphant phrase which gained considerable currency in other industrial speeches, I wrote that YOU CANNOT SINK THE BRIDGE WITHOUT SINKING THE ENGINE ROOM AS WELL!

The incredible thing is that just such slick phrases actually do have an impact. The system of ownership which actually depends upon the agreement and the hard work of everyone in the engine room is twisted around so that it appears, instead, that everyone in the engine room is dependent on the people on the bridge.

Actually, the question that normally hardheaded and commonsensical Americans should keep asking is who built the ship in the first place. It was not the people on the bridge, much less the people in the panelled offices. It was shipbuilders.

But divide and conquer continues to be the main approach insofar as the owners and the people who work are concerned or, rather, unite at the top, divide at the bottom, and conquer everywhere.

People who own the business and industry of America, as

already pointed out, do organize regularly. They understand that despite many differences they may have—even such differences as being Democrat or Republican, or being in aerospace or in highways (two heavily- and directly-subsidized industries)—they have interests more fundamental. They're rich and they own. Most people are far from being rich and own nothing, in the sense of productive facilities.

Only about 10 percent of all Americans, for instance, own even so much as a share of stock in American industry. But 1.6 percent of the adult population owns 82 percent of all stock, and thus actually owns American business and industry.

In a very real sense, that tiny 1 percent of the population faces the other 99 percent across a barrier of very real self-interest. That tiny 1 percent has been accumulating more as the years go on, not less. The key to that accumulation is assuring that the people who make up the other 99 percent are sharply restricted in what power and privilege they accumulate. Of course, there is always room and energy enough, it is said, to increase the total amount of the take, so that all have more. But there isn't enough to share it around so that the size of the shares themselves level out. At least it is true that the people in the tiny 1 percent who own it all effectively, and own more incessantly, have never lost control over the affairs of the nation to the extent that the shares *have* changed.

Whatever you choose to call that—class interest, caste, group solidarity, organized greed, or whatever—it is a fact beyond theory and beyond special labels. It is the system of accumulation which we all are called upon to serve and increase.

And so the formula is evolved that says that any organization to perpetuate the system of accumulation is good, any organization to upset it is bad. Since we know that the rich and the powerful get the most out of this, it should be fair to ask what the rest of the people get. It is the job of the propagandist for this system to come up with overwhelming answers.

The first answer, of course, is right in front of your nose.

Americans have more material possessions than any other people on earth. It can be argued that they must work more skillfully and more productively than any other people to get them, and that the things are not exactly gifts from a grateful system. But the fact remains—we have a lot of things. There is a growing doubt about how much good or pleasure or, contrariwise, actual harm we may be deriving from those things—but the things are there and it doesn't take a genius or a poet to convince most Americans that they are better off than anybody else. Various spokesmen for industry and politics, including some I've written speeches for, do try to rise to almost poetic heights, however, with such eloquent imagery as that the poorest American has things at his disposal, such as the automobile and the television, which not even the richest king of old could command—a magnificent flight into anachronism, like saying everyone alive today is smarter than Sir Isaac Newton because they can go to a book and look up the laws of motion which he had to invent, plus a few he couldn't even have imagined. And there also is the great comparative statement about the poorest person in America being downright middle class when compared to the starving untouchables of India or the dying children of Biafra. The use of the starving Chinese as the invariable example in this little game has been abandoned totally since it was discovered, to the West's chagrin, that no one is starving in China any more—and that, even more shockingly, people in China can leave their doors unlocked without fear of being robbed. Of such disturbing facts are entire new views of the world formed.

It is easy, therefore, to defend the system of accumulation and ownership, the entire commercial system, on the basis of its output of material goods. Karl Marx had good reason to point to that output as epochal even in his time. And Soviet propaganda, to this day, urges Communists to overtake America in terms of purely commercial production.

Looking closely, however, it occurs to me that what is being defended is not just the material output or any system that guarantees it. What is defended, way down deep in all of the propaganda, is the *privilege* of those who own, the *right* to own more and more while doing less and less—the right, in short, to retain an economic aristocracy which is every bit as worthless and parasitic as any aristocracy of antiquity. It is an aristocracy which, at best, might excuse itself, as did the old ones, by the "virtue" of supporting charities which would not be needed were it not for the aristocrats. Or they are defended as patrons of culture. But, were it not for the aristocrats, art could flourish throughout the countryside rather than just in the salons of the cities.

A commonsense test of this claim is to listen to any speech by any bosses, managerial or political, on the subject of the great system that produces all of our material well-being. Does that speech explain how the system did it? Does it explain even how it works? Or does it just leap from the fact of the productivity to a generalized justification of everything associated with it?

Most such speeches, and I guess I have written a thousand of them, say such things as only the risk-taking initiative of the rich provides jobs and industrial increase.

Now, to begin with, there is little alternative for the rich. They must invest in order to increase their holdings. Otherwise, just living off their capital, they or their children might someday spend themselves into having to go to work.

But even so, the speeches press ahead, if there was no system of reward for the rich to invest, they would not invest and everything would come to a halt. Why?

Suppose every rich person in the country clamped shut every fat purse in the country. Suppose they just said, well, we're shutting up business and all you poor people can go whistle. It is a nightmare on the order of that often used to scare working people out of organizing unions, for instance. It is a familiar device, politically, for explaining why politicians simply cannot put too tight clamps on the rich—this fear of the rich getting mad and shutting off the money.

First of all, the rich depend on money to avoid having to be like the rest of us. This means that they must have us around to do the things they don't want to do and don't know how to do, like building things. If they just shut down all their factories, one effect, obviously, would be that there wouldn't be anyone building the things that *they* want. But, you might say, they could always buy those things from other working people in other lands. That's true. As a matter of fact there is a tendency of the rich to do just that, anyway.

So, isn't the argument convincing? Wouldn't we all just starve to death if the rich closed the factories because they were unhappy about not making enough profits because, for instance, of some darnfool union agitators?

I cannot imagine the folks in a commonsense neighborhood starving to death just because some rich owner said that he was closing the factory, fencing off the farmland, and closing the valves on the waterworks. The folks in such a neighborhood, I am pretty sure, would say, sorry, but we are going to have to plant some crops, build some plows, and open the tap because that is what life is about. It is not just about owning and accumulating. Life is for living, not for legal theories. And the rights of ownership, stemming as they do from human action, surely can't be said to be superior to human action or human life.

What *does* create things, wealth, worthwhile life, and so forth? Is it the bank accounts of the rich and their willingness to spend? If so, how did the country develop? The pioneers risked something other than money. The inventors contributed something other than money. Work and creativity is what built the country—not money. Money, as a matter of fact, was a rather late system, at least on a national basis, with the national currency, replacing local and even private currency, not being official until well into the development of the nation.

Money is a way of keeping track of things. It is not in itself a productive force. It is a tool more like a bookkeeping ledger than like an axe or a milling machine, or a computer.

Work and creativity, then, seem to be the things that actually build and those are attributes not of the reigning rich at all but of the population generally, of the working people rather than the owning people. You know this. Your senses tell you this, and yet propagandists for the rich can come along, as I did and others still do, and tell you time after time that without the rich you would starve, that without the rich the factories would close, that without the rich the farms would wither, that without the rich we would all be forced back to a primitive and animal existence.

Is it possible, on the contrary, to imagine America, with its incredibly skilled working people, its array of machines which they designed and built and operate, with its sturdy history of independence, is it possible, to imagine this land going *backwards* because the Rockefellers, the DuPonts, the Morgans, and the Mellons were dispossessed of their great wealth?

If, as a matter of fact, the rich are so incredibly much better than the rest of us, what difference would it make? If they are so smart they don't *need* all that money. They would show us all up anyway and be rich again almost overnight no matter what. As much as I hate to admit it, in retrospect, I have even used that incredible argument in defending the status quo of the people of status. How wasteful, such a speech goes, to dismantle the great economic aristocracy because it is an aristocracy of genuine merit. The smartest people are the richest people. The smartest people always will be rich, and so let's just leave things the way they are.

How this argument can be made with a straight face is a

tribute to the hypnotic effect of working for the wealthy and to the rather subordinate position that your own common sense comes to occupy when it begins to jostle your bank account.

The propagandists for the rich who make such arguments have before them all of the evidence of their own senses to tell them the truth about the situation. If rich people are so gifted, energetic, and creative then why do they not display those gifts in great personal achievement? Why do they even need two-bit intellectuals and hired guns to defend them? Why are not the great defenses of the system of accumulation written by the great accumulators? Why do they not design the machines that make their factories hum? Why are so few hard at work on the factory floor, in the laboratory, or even in the office?

Sometimes the denial of the evidence of our senses when it comes to the rich is because of the few people who are both rich and all of those other things. Several things must be said about such people, at least all of them that come to mind in my case. First, they are not among the truly great owners, nor are they or their heirs ever likely to be. They will be among the barons and the earls but not the crown princes. Or so it has been thus far in our history. Another thing is that the very ingenuity that led them to their fortunes, the very creativity, often is the same sort of itching, really irrespressible energy that often makes them become involved in schemes which most subvert, rather than support, the system of accumulation. Sometimes they are called ungrateful for doing this. I think that the truth is that truly creative people (and such a person as the fine mathematician, Max Palevsky, of computer and Xerox fame comes to mind) find the elder-family, idle-rich accumulation system actually repulsive. They enjoy working and creating. For such people the rewards have always been secondary to the work and they do not quail or flinch before the prospect of doing it all over again, or always being judged on their own personal accomplishments rather than on the size of their bank accounts. These extraordinary people, it is true, would be extraordinary under and in any system. But—and it seems to me this is a crucial "but"—there is ample evidence from talking with and working with many of them, that the rewards were not the prime incentive for their energy nor would they be the main reasons for their continuing to invent, create, probe, and produce. They enjoy what they do. They are craftsmen and it is only in this particular system, and because of it, that they so easily become confused with the idle and unproductive rich. They exist everywhere in the world, under every system and, to be sure, it is their work that often shines forth. Yet, more than the idle rich, surely, they understand fully that even the most outstanding talent shines on stages built by many other and varied talents. Also, it seems to me, such craftspeople are far, far more numerous than mere statistics would indicate. Each year, for instance, companies like DuPont are granted hundreds of significant patents on creatively brilliant things developed by such talented craftspeople—whose talent is totally absorbed into the corporate image, leaving us too little view of the individual reality.

But of what weight are the accomplishments of the people who really work, even if they pile up a few millions in the process, when it comes to the weight of those who merely manipulate and accumulate money? Ounces compared to pounds! It always does some good, for instance, to recall that (according to the most recent figures I have seen) the thirteen thousand U.S. banks control $607 BILLION of institutional investment, to recall that there are one thousand two hundred members of the DuPont family who together control such items as General Motors, to recall that the Rockefellers are said to sit on top of $15 BILLION, to recall that one Rockefeller alone (David) is boss of a bank (Chase Manhattan) which has assets of $24 BILLION, to recall that the forty-nine top banks hold potentially controlling hunks (at least 5 percent) of one or more classes of stock in five thousand, two hundred and seventy companies, and so forth.

That is meant to be and hopefully will be a sobering reminder that in all of these discussions rich (and idle rich—people who earn their income from simply having title to property) refers not to those superenergetic types who sometimes flash into the headlines or who actually invent things, but to a relatively small, long-powerful group of people who own most of this country and, consequently, own much of your life.

All of this is meant to keep whittling away at your identification with such people. They are not by the wildest stretch of the imagination like you, and you are not by the wildest stretch of the imagination going to be like them.

Yet, as I have been saying, paid propagandists keep building the impression that the fate of us all is linked inextricably to the fate of those few.

Communism, for instance, is the enemy, and efforts to expose it as such are widely supported exactly so long as the positions of the rich are challenged by some communist action or another, as with the expropriation of properties in various countries or as—most particularly—communist action for more militancy in American trade unions. But that opposition to communism, we can observe, comes suddenly to an end as soon as communist *markets* are opened. Much the same is true of the opposition to trade unions. The most deadly opposition to trade unions did not end in any way involving communism. It ended when the unions themselves stopped hitting at basic issues and contented themselves almost solely with wages and hours. The opposition flares up whenever and wherever unions go beyond that. The continuing attacks against trade unions are based largely upon opposition to interference with "management prerogatives" and that may freely be translated as the prerogatives of existing property relationships.

The continuing propaganda, then, is the propaganda that

tries to teach working Americans that they have nothing in common with one another but, instead, have a common interest with the owners; that they can best get ahead by competing with their neighbors and cooperating with their bosses.

Always, behind the pious political pronouncements, the appeal to material well-being, the American daydream of "owning a piece of the rock," there is that message: struggle to be better than your neighbor, get ahead, get away, get up—but cooperate with, agree with, bow to your boss. Your neighbor, this propaganda subtly suggests, is your enemy. Your boss is your way to salvation. Or, in a variant form, the only way for you to solve your problems is alone. Do not organize. Work hard, but alone. Do it yourself, the argument suggests, and it touches upon deep and real echoes of sturdy American independence and pride. But it doesn't mean quite the same. It just means isolation. It just means attaching yourself to the interests of the very rich rather than staying rooted to the interests of that very place where your own interests are best served in the long run, in your community, in the community of your own friends and working associates.

Ironically, this means that while hired propagandists write glowing speeches about standing on your own two feet—rather than joining a union, for instance—the company management making the statement is huddling *together* to fight you, is getting fat off special tax breaks and the general advantages of corporate law, is grabbing at every government plum in sight, and acting, in concert with other corporations, to protect their interests as a *group*.

This is a crucial point. Working people are urged to protect their interests as individuals, to feel somehow lower-class if they organize. Corporations are organized at the outset. They always treat unorganized people not as individuals of great worth but as individuals who may conveniently and consistently be ignored—as nothings.

The sense of guilt and shame that is fostered in connection with working people getting together—as the rich always have got together—and particularly with being conscious of being a working person rather than an owning person, has even become a sort of status symbol. For instance, there are otherwise perfectly sensible people who prefer to work in lower-paid but not unionized jobs because of what they fear (and I have had many people tell me this) as being the lower-class stigma of belonging to a union. They want *out* of the working class, they say. And one way to do it, they think, even if it means being a flunky for some manager, is to get away from those jobs even susceptible to union activity.

One of the most dependable allies that owners have always had in their efforts to keep employees fully subservient is this kind of snob appeal. Technicians, at least in the past, have been particularly easy to sell on this line. In the writing that I have done against union organizing, the technicians are so easily handled that they are rarely worth more than a few paragraphs. You just kiss them off with such wisdom as "professionally trained people must be true, first of all, to their great professional responsibilities and training. They are not mere ditch-diggers in our society, concerned with grubbing dollars out of the dirt. They are the torchbearers of knowledge and the future and must remain above the petty squabbling of labor."

It says very little for the good sense of technicians that many, perhaps most of them, have bought such nonsense at one time or another. It says nothing nice about intellectuals that any of them can concoct such nonsense. Today, however, the foolishness continues. Many professional associations continue to insist that their members remain isolated from the real world and from real self-interest and become instead just dependable, silent servants of whatever demands the owners and rulers put upon their professional services.

The deepest tragedy of this ongoing con game is not that

it prevents people from organizing in their own interest. The deep and intensely psychological damage is that it prevents people from thinking about themselves as having a common humanity with other people, of *being* working people and, above all, of being always the subjects of their own lives, the centers of their own history, rather than objects to be manipulated by others and in the interests of others.

All of us face this assault against our good common sense. The farmer sees the factory worker, organized into a trade union, as putting pressures on the economy that threaten farm incomes. Yet the same farmer feels that to organize with other farmers would mean getting into the sort of big-city life-style that the farmer abhors. The farmer may feel that to be a farmer is to be truly independent and that to organize would betray that independence.

If it were true that the farmer is fully independent, or that any of us are really independent of other people, then organizing together for anything *would* be foolish. Such autonomy and independence should not be disturbed. Nor should it be considered as real if, in fact, it is illusory.

And it is illusory. The farmer, unless subsistence alone is the function of the farming, is a person who does a certain kind of work in a certain kind of social setting, in a certain community. The farmer is part of and not isolated from that community.

What the farmer is isolated from is not the world of the factory worker but of the factory *owner*. The factory worker and the farmer, if they could talk, would probably find themselves talking as humans with greatly mutual interests, feelings, and problems. But the factory owner would be more likely to regard the farmer as a quaint bumpkin, a potential handyman or anything except a person just like the owner and the owner's friends.

In the many corporate and Republican speeches that I wrote, this appeal to the sturdy yeomanship of the farmer always was

considered dependable. Even when talking about farm subsidies, the sensitivities of people who were supposed to be
revered for being so isolated from the everyday strife of life
were respected by saying that since the government had got the
farmer into such a mess that subsidies were needed, it was up
to the government to get the farmers out. Republicans are
always quick to think of splendid rationalizations for the welfare programs directed to their friends, even while otherwise
making quite a fuss about welfare programs directed toward
anyone else. Democrats do the same thing when they scream for
aid to the poor, attack the rich, and then proceed to enact
programs that pour millions into industrial coffers and pennies
into the pockets of the poor, not bothering to point out that
the way they help the very poor is by overtaxing the nearly
poor.

Similar appeals were considered dependable when directed
anywhere in the middle class. Union members always were
attacked as a selfish minority in a great nation of selfless people
who did not need to pay any dues to get ahead and stay ahead
in the race of life.

The effort is always to make the union appear useless and
the members little better than worthless. Part of this effort is
enhanced by the origins of the unions among people who
worked with their hands as well as their heads. In turn, the
notion that people who do manual labor do not have to use their
heads is fostered eagerly by the propagandists of the owners
and managers. Nothing could be further from the truth. If one
does not use the head while working with the hand, the hand
will be chopped off or worn off. And anyone who believes that
a worker using a hydraulic press is somehow doing something
dumber than a clerk filing things under A to Z is just not
thinking clearly either.

Union members, then, are portrayed in the skillful speeches

of the hired hands of the managers as not only greedy but also unworthy.

The tempting allure of this sort of appeal is status. People who can be convinced by an advertising agency that they are somehow better people for owning an Oldsmobile rather than a Chevrolet, can also be convinced by corporate and political writers that they are somehow superior if they do not belong to a union but "make it on their own." Oh, what wonder there is in that phrase! Visions of the pioneers flash before the eyes, the indomitable figure in front of his indomitable rose-covered log cabin, with his indomitable rose-covered Cadillac in the indomitable garage. It is a veritable full-color vision of delight.

The truth, of course, if people so easily misled ever took the time and thought to examine the verbiage being served them, is that they never do solve their own problems sturdily on their own anyway. They are the servants of the mighty and they are never able to forget it, except in the dreams of being better than the poor slobs on the factory floor. They may have some illusion that they are being paid what they are worth, whereas the evil union member is being paid what he can extort from the long-suffering managers, but the truth is that they are being paid exactly what some personnel hotshots figure they can get away with, and they are treated as just the same sorts of cogs as the union people except that, from time to time, some management people must chuckle about how dumb they are to put up with it all.

Further strengthening the myth these days is the regular repetition of the "fact" that America is now a solidly middle-class, white-collar nation and that the blue-collar worker is a dying species. It is simply not true. Most Americans continue to do work that is basically manual. The white-collar figures that the corporations and the politicians use simply lie by excluding from the blue-collar category such working people as postal employees, stock clerks, other people who do manual work in retailing, and a host of others.

But even so, what is so intrinsically good about being a white-collar worker? What it usually means is being even more slavishly under someone's thumb than even the janitor in a factory. The janitor, at least, gets to shuck all the woes of the job, the jibes of the foreman, the snobbishness of the manager, and so forth, when the working day is done. The so-called white-collar workers must worry all night long about whether the boss smiled or frowned. They must be concerned about whether their hair is nice, their suits and dresses clean enough, their tones of voice properly oily, even whether the conduct of family members is likely to satisfy the manager. These white-collar workers, supposedly riding high on middle-class advantages and privileges, instead are being ridden to a frazzle, in most cases, by the twenty-four-hour-a-day demands and tensions of jobs which, in a not unfamiliar final irony, may not even pay better than a blue-collar job.

Again, however, such propositions as "it's better to be a white-collar worker" are not propositions that just grow like lilies of the field, wildly and whimsically. Far from it. They grow under the careful nourishment of people who have something to gain from having other people believe such a thing.

Anything that drives a wedge between working people and makes some of those working people more loyal, rather than less loyal, to the entire system of top-down, largely hereditary and aristocratic ownership and control is encouraged by the owners and by the hired hands who write and speak for them.

The wedge between white and blue collars is a way to make sure that those collars continue to be yokes to the system, no matter what color.

There are some people, of course, who don't care what color the collar may be. They are sent into fits of rage whenever the term "worker" is used to describe anyone.

"Who do they think they are?" "What do they want?" "What did they ever do?" Workers are said to be lazy, stupid, venal, greedy, uninspired, requiring harsh discipline and, above all, needing "to be kept in their place."

It is a particular fancy of the antiworker cult that workers never produce anything or, to be more precise, that they never "create" even if they do produce.

Thus, the typical answer to the question of who created the modern steel industry is Andrew Carnegie. Henry Bessemer, whose invention enabled the first effective steel production, is relegated to some sort of limbo. But, the antiworker faction may chorus, Bessemer merely invented the technology, it took Carnegie to invent the industry. That is rather like saying that Carnegie's organizational ideas—his emulation of state power in cornering a market by manipulation rather than by production—could have produced an industry *without* the technology.

There are important sides to this speculation. On the one side there is the manager. On the other side there is the worker. Carnegie was a manager. Bessemer was a worker, an inventor. The combination of their efforts produced a certain sort of industrial organization. The Bessemer converter produced steel. The steel can be made under many sorts of organization. But no organization could make steel with an organization chart alone!

The difference is crucial, I think. It seems to me that the great gulf in the world today, the gulf through which pour most of those things we regard as problems, and across which face the most significant of opposing views, is the gulf that separates workers from consumers, producers from users, managers from makers, performers from audience, doers from onlookers. I consider myself a worker now. When in politics, I was more of a manager, a stage manager, perhaps, but a manager rather than a creator, providing a service upon remote demand and specification rather than building something on the basis of my own and my neighbors' interests. Now, as a welder, and as a writer acting on behalf of my own and my neighbors' interests, rather than on behalf of any institutional grand view, I feel that my interests are more similar to, rather than different from, the interests of most who actually work in this world.

But, another argument goes, you are *not* just a worker. You are more like a "professional" person. This is said to put a person in the company of doctors, physicists, engineers, etc. Such people *can* provide their own leadership, but craft and manual workers can't, according to the familiar argument.

I have found that to be a wrong view, also. In working as a welder, more than eight years now, I have found that *without exception,* manual and craft workers are capable of and actually do exercise a high degree of creative self-management whenever forced to or whenever they have space to.

Craft and manual workers, in my experience, share many of the attitudes and capabilities of scientists, engineers, and poets. Their skills differ sharply but the *mode* of their work is similar. It involves problem solving (as distinctly opposed to what, in management, usually is credit taking and status improvement) for immediate and practical reasons. It involves a measure of cooperation (as opposed, again, to management competition which, it seems to me, often is merely competition for status rather than competition for actual excellence of performance and production). It also involves a tendency to be creative rather than doing things "by the book."

On the other hand, purely managerial types, with whom I also have had substantial experience, tend to deal with phantoms of reality rather than reality itself. Many, for instance, take a mystic view of time spent at work, asserting that long hours are the same as productive hours. They are rather like certain priests in that sense, equating prayer time with time actually being decent toward real people in the real world.

Managers often gauge their success simply by how they please their bosses just as the priests say they can gauge their effectiveness by how they please their theology rather than how they actually behave in the everyday world.

Rather than becoming agitated when a person is described as a worker, then, it might be useful to ponder what it is *not* to be a worker. To not work. To be a nonworker.

It is very deep in the American grain to respect work. People who will not work (as sharply different from people who cannot work) are not admired. But slowly, the good common sense of that good American perception has come to focus on the shiftless who are poor. The shiftless who are rich, thanks to years of glamorizing, in media owned by the very same rich people, have come to occupy a special place as virtual American heroes and heroines. The travels and revels of the immensely rich are fed to the people through the media as a form of public spectacle, as a sort of aspirin to make people forget the problems of their own lives by living vicariously the fantasy life of the rich. There is no more miserable product we have received from the very rich than the spectacle of their ostentatiously wasteful and pampered lives being held forth in invidious advertising and four-color puffery as the summit of civilization and the epitome of the American Dream.

In his 1964 speech accepting the Republican nomination for the Presidency, Barry Goldwater spoke of a day when the young people in America would once again admire scientists, artists, engineers, and teachers rather than the slick and the sly and the glamorous. He should have gone further. He should have spoken of admiring all workers, not just a few of them. And he should have singled out for more scorn than he did the people of fashion and fortune.

The old populists did it in many of their political statements, attacking at one and the same time the two great categories of shiftless people in the country: bums and millionaires.

The message has never been more appropriate. There are people who work and work hard in this country. They create its wealth. They build. They invent. They are workers.

The most sure gauge of the possibilities of social change in this country is the extent to which workers of all sorts, as opposed to owners of the major sort, begin to act as though they understand where they stand; that the miner coughing out his lungs working for the mine owner has more in common with the scientist slowly blowing out his brains for the chemical tycoon than either has in common with the owners themselves. So long as the owners can convince them otherwise, as they surely have for so long, then the coal miner and the scientist will both work as they are told—and the owners will laugh all the way to their banks. They will continue so long as workers can be deluded into thinking of themselves as sharing all the interests of property just because they own some stock, an extra house, an insurance policy—so long as a little ownership can buy up workers themselves as defenders of the great owners of vast property.

Tragically, there is one group of Americans who are caught in a particularly cruel part of this confusion between who is and who is not a worker. They are the older people, workers retired on social security or hard-earned pensions. When Barry Goldwater warned, as more and more responsible people, right and left, are now doing, that social security as presently constituted is in precarious financial shape, older people reacted as though he was against the idea of security itself. They acted like people who might object to a fire inspector because he warned that the attic was junky and might catch on fire, feeling that what was being attacked was the attic itself and not just the hazard in it.

It is the same with the reaction of many older people against anything called leftist. They hear, it seems, only the ominous edges of the political discussions. The left is against capitalism, against the very system out of which, currently, retirement pensions are being paid. The quick assumption then seems to be that the left is against the security of the elderly.

The same reaction obviously spills over into other places. The hardworking home owner, perhaps fresh from a tough day in a factory, may hear a leftist orator of the more shrill variety attacking private property. What is the factory worker to think? What he hears is an attack on his own home, his own hard work as concretized in savings or something else. He doesn't hear an attack on the property that is really crucial, the property of the idle rich, the great owners, the super-capitalists.

Thus the left itself to a sad degree continues the false divisions among Americans which the capitalists themselves have spent so much to foster.

In a commonsense sort of world, it seems to me, a person would have to view the world from the center of that person's own consciousness. Your eyes do not look out from some abstract place, they look out from the very concrete place called your brain, the place where all of the information gathered by your senses is stored, sorted, made the basis for some sort of action or reflection. This place, this brain of yours, is obviously a most personal possession. It does not and cannot exist anywhere but inside your own head. It not only is *yours*, it might even be said to be *you*. It is the activity of that most splendid organ that permits forming the thought that there even is a you.

From that point of view, from the point of view of "you" looking out through your senses to the world generally, you are unique, single, alone, individual, self-contained. But only from that point of view. The absolutely private self is the absolutely interior self, the inside. If it never came in contact with anything else, it could remain that way.

Instead, however, in the fullness and variety of real life, that private and interior self comes in contact with many things and, most importantly, with many other "selfs," each looking out from some other interior, each sensing you the way you sense them.

From the time any human being becomes aware of any other human being, individualism gives way to—what else can we call it?—social life, to acting in a world that cannot be shaped exclusively by what goes on inside your head but also must be—no matter what—shaped by the relationships of one person to another person, people to people, finally community to community.

The individual remains, of course. It is still from the individual that even the concept of the social life must proceed—but even if an individual chooses to deny the social life, that life persists, independent of individual will, dependent solely upon the existence of people aware of themselves and living in some sort of closeness.

Only by becoming a true hermit can an individual separate from social life and retreat into purely individualistic life.

People, as individuals, may disappear from view in various social theories, but they never disappear in social practice. They persist. They have names, or at least identities. They have passions, quirks, size, shape, hands and heads. They can be attached to the punched cards of a time clock or the identity cards of a police state, or the chains of a slave system. But they remain in reality. And even the most exalted leader, ruling from some distant mountain or palace, must sometimes know late in the night that the faceless mass actually has many faces. Such faces, I hope, always haunt great leaders and particularly those whose most inhumane acts are excused because "society" demanded it. Here the circle comes full turn, for leaders too are people, they are pressed by the real world around them but, like all people, they respond to that pressure as individuals. Leaders often loom as larger than the times around them, and the people generally seem so small as to be mere ants, not worthy of even a mention on the page of history. But they are all, actually, just *part* of those times. All have roles in it. The people submitting to the leader make the leader possible just as surely as the will of the leader makes that possible. The myths and legends handed on from the past, the customs, and, so importantly, the ownership of things all press against all people, helping to shape the way they act but never getting around the fact that, finally, it is the action of people that makes history and not the other way around. The people must accept the divinity of the king or the king will not rule. The people must surrender their power to become powerless, for what ruler actually possesses the strength, unaided by such a surrender, to render people powerless one by one? Revolutionary times seem simply those times when people who had previously been convinced that they were less than human in the ability to act, disagree and begin to act, as human beings capable of making their own history rather than having it handed to them—on a silver platter *or* at the end of a whip.

Corporate capitalism, however, maintains a doctrine that individuals are almost totally separated from one another, must act only in terms of individual self-interest, and actually achieve solely on the basis of individual effort. In the view of that doctrine there is no *social* life at all, simply economic life, in which each person is part of an impersonal ledger book, ticked off in terms of individual monetary worth.

American liberalism, while supporting the economic theories of the corporate capitalists and the corporate life-style in particular, adds not a social dimension but a political one to the economics of pure capitalism. The political dimension holds that, although the capitalist may be the sort best qualified for the grubby business of making steel and money, highly trained professionals in other fields are best qualified to establish the norms of what society should be and how people should behave in it. The liberal, therefore, admits a social life for people but does not permit the people to define it. Only the trained professionals can do that. From this emerges a crazy-quilt version of the individual and society. Some people, the liberals, are viewed as worthy individuals, fully capable of living a social life. Most other people, the clients, the masses, the voters, or what have you, are viewed as incapable of living such a social life and thus are not truly individuals at all, but lumps and clots of humanity requiring molding by the skillful hands of liberals.

Collectivists, in the sense, say, of the ruling bureaucrats of the Soviet Union, twist the view all the way in the opposite direction. Society becomes a real thing, but devoid of people. It is something that exists, apparently, all by itself. Society demands this. Society demands that. The person must do this for society, or that. The person and society somehow become separated and instead of society simply being the way in which individual people do live together, a structure which they build, society becomes a master, living in a bureaucratic temple somewhere and speaking to the lowly people through the mouths of leaders.

If, on the other hand, under the commercial definition of individualism, it is true that everyone gets exactly what he deserves out of the supposedly free enterprise system, then it follows as the day does the night that a rich man is more worthy than a poor man. Unless you choose to examine closely the process by which the one gets rich and the other remains poor, or is born poor, then the easiest thing to do is just accept the external evidence. And, particularly if you are raised in fairly close proximity to being poor, or are poor, then there is a purely aesthetic reaction that tells you rich is better. If rich is better, and if, indeed, the system is fair, then rich must be better because it deserves to be.

Also, there is external evidence everywhere that people, individual people, by individual effort, can better themselves.

The evidence is altogether external and quite superficial. It always treats, as I did for years, the efforts of any one individual as somehow strangely detached from the efforts of all others— as though, to repeat, there is no social life at all, but only individual life, rather than a social life lived by individuals.

Suppose, for instance, that a hardworking family saves and saves until it has enough money to buy a small store in a quiet neighborhood. For a time, the external evidence of their success through hard work is probably quite accurate. They did work hard. The store they bought is one which they operate by themselves. They don't gouge the customers. They provide a convenience and a real service. It is a small part of the American Dream and, it seems to me, a very decent one. But it is small, homey, comfortable and very local. Suppose, now, that this decent part of the Dream suddenly expands into the full-color, wide-screen Big Dream, the Jackpot, the Big Casino, the Daily Double. Is it still the same? The external evidence may say yes but perhaps this sort of thing actually is involved:

The neighborhood around the store includes a few lots owned by, say, a powerful political figure downtown, or by a big corporation or bank, that may have acquired the property in default of a loan, a default made necessary by some general economic dislocation. Other and varied, or *social,* factors begin to become apparent in this story of individual enterprise.

The lots now become the focus of a well-financed apartment project, made desirable, perhaps, by the need of the company to diversify or the need of the bank to get a new source of interest going—again, factors of a more general and social nature, involving the actions of many individuals, actions taken for varied reasons and scarcely seeming even to be related.

With the apartment project making a profound change in the neighborhood, the little store also changes, not because of the individual wills of the individuals running it, or because of their individual hard work, but because of this mounting set of social changes going on independent of the individuals in the store. They react to those changes but do not cause them. Their work is not part of those changes.

The store expands, takes on a deluxe rather than homey look, attracts a swanker clientele, begins to borrow money to modernize, becomes a familiar and good borrower at the bank, numbers "the right people" among its customers, has a friend here, a word of good advice there, and so on. Soon, the promoters of the apartment house in that neighborhood build another one elsewhere. There is no store near it. What is more natural, now, than to turn to the existing store and urge it to open a branch near the new apartment. Perhaps the apartment folks and the store folks even become partners. They are still not working harder. It is not their work, as a matter of fact, that is crucial anywhere along the line now—it is the work of thousands of people, the hard work, actual work, of the people who will pay rent in the apartment and buy in the store, the work of the architect, the work of the building crews, and so forth and so on.

But now the little store is a small chain. Then a big chain. First local, then national. Hard work? By whom? It is a complicated picture actually. To a propagandist for a cause, however, it can be made very simple.

It can be extolled as nothing less than an example of how hard work brought fortune to a humble family. The ingredients that are presented by the propagandist are undeniable. The family *was* humble. It *is* rich. They did operate the store all by themselves. They still own it, and so forth.

Such heartwarming stories have been successful in diverting us from examining any other part of the picture.

The other parts are conveniently shaded from view. The banks, for instance, never seem to enter into any of the cozy stories of individual enterprise. As I noted earlier, America's banking system, a politically designed and distributed system of plums and goodies, today controls $607 BILLION of institutional investment in the U.S. economy. That's a sum four times greater than the next largest institutional investment factor, the insurance companies, with $162 BILLION in investments.

Now somewhere along the line, I suppose, it would be possible to say that every bank and every insurance company began with a hardworking individual—but the line would have to go back very far indeed. Most of us know, or at least sense, that things like banks and insurance companies are rather the result of knowing the right politicians, having the right friends, and so forth. They are not the sorts of institutions which you and your neighbors put together. Unfortunately. If they were, they might be pleasantly different as, presumably, they were when insurance was a result of mutual aid group work.

At any rate, in the glowing examples of individual enterprise, the role of banks is usually obscured and for perfectly good reason. The bank weighs many more factors than just the weight of your perspiration when you apply for a loan such as the one wanted to modernize the little grocery store. Does the bank have some other, richer client that would be inconvenienced by the store? Does it have a client that might want to buy the location itself? If so, the loan is not likely to be a high-priority item and chances are that the little grocery store is going to have some strange troubles staying afloat in the days ahead. At any rate, some padded person in a padded chair, somewhere in the bank, obviously has a big say in how our little story of supposedly individual enterprise is going to turn out. The looming presence of that person is the first big contradiction of the idea that individual initiative is what is involved in American success.

But look beyond the banks. What of the other corporate entities involved in what are supposed to be stories of individual enterprise in a land of free private enterprise?

The little store and the apartment house both had to satisfy a political process that includes licensing and zoning as a widespread practice. As community after community has discovered, these processes may be widely advertised as existing to protect communities but they exist actually to change communities, even demolish them as the economic pressures of external forces, such as major corporations, dictate or as the political fortunes of a particular party or person dictate. In changing a community, of course, the wishes of the people in the community are widely ignored on the basis of another value which says something very strange indeed about the concept of individual freedom in this supposedly so-individualistic land. The value raised when a community is attacked is simply the value of our old friend "society." Society is said to demand that "progress" be made, for instance, over the dead body of some insignificant community. And a community of what? A community, alas, of individual human beings. And here is another case where we are asked to, and often do, forget that individuals are involved. Progress is said to be involved, not people. Were progress defined in exact terms, it would have to be in terms of the particular people advantaged—at which point we probably would get right back to our other old friends, the bankers, the corporate owners, the politicians.

But all around the neighborhood where the supposedly individualistic little store is about to launch itself on the path to "success," and self-made success at that, the idealized stories will tell us—all around it there are still other social forces. A highway either does or does not go through nearby. A school either is or is not convenient. Churches, too. Other stores. Certain sorts of places where certain sorts of people are employed, to give the neighborhood its economic base in the first place, and its character. Or the smoke from a factory blows across the neighborhood. It becomes drab, unpleasant. The smoke blows elsewhere. The lawns sparkle, the houses shine.

There is virtually no end to the social factors which intervene in what may seem an individual effort.

Yet the schoolbooks continue to teach that the only real differences among human situations are differences of hard work. Anybody can be President. Anybody can be a multimillionaire. There is therefore a secret guilt about not being great, or rich. The fault, we are carefully taught, lies within us. If we really got out there and rattled our bones, we could make it. After all, some have. Honest working people, thus, are led to look at the high-flying sports of the business world and say such things as, "I don't resent those guys. They worked for it. I could have all that too, but I just haven't got that kind of drive." What kind of drive? The hardworking people of the country, the scientists, the teachers, the steel-foundry workers, the farmers, the small business people, the truck drivers, the waiters and waitressses, the cab drivers, the laundry workers, the hospital workers, the artists, the carpenters, the pipe benders, the crane operators, the 'dozer operators—all of those people work very hard. They rouse themselves with aches and pains at the crack of dawn. They put up with miserable traffic getting to work. They put up with miserable managers, bureaucrats, and bosses, with rain, sleet, and hail, with uncertainty of income, with every conceivable rigor and pressure, and yet they keep coming back, honestly, decently, working hard day after day and year after year. How crazy to say they have no drive. How crazy to say they just don't work hard enough. And how crazy also for anyone not to recognize the fact of the matter which is—no matter the upward possibilities which do exist—that there always in this land are people who have it and get more while the great, great majority of people actually produce it all, put it all together, keep it all together, but still just feel lucky if they can keep their heads above water.

Let's admit that anyone *can* become President and thus join the ranks of those who do the ordering and escape completely the ranks of those who must take the orders. There are two hundred and twenty million men, women and children in this country. Of them, some seventy million adults or so are perfectly eligible to be President. How many can be? One, out of seventy or so million, and then only once every fourth year.

No matter the theoretical pleasure of thinking that you or your kin could be President, the reality is different. Only ten or so people in the lifetime of any one of us will be President, ten or so out of millions upon millions. It is a rare office.

The same can be said for any of the great offices that so sweepingly control our lives. They are occupied by few people. Those people, in association with the people whose ranks remain closed by virtue of birth—the great owners—run the country and, consequently, run you. They are a group apart. They constitute a group of people with little interest in the rest of the people except what they can get out of them—votes in the case of most of the politicians, work and endless debt and consuming in the case of the owners and bankers.

Great confusion results, it seems to me, from the fact that despite the separation of power from the people generally, there are illusions of power and realities of great comfort which sometimes obscure that separation, which make many people feel that, indeed, the American society is an altogether classless society, that everyone is just as good as everyone else, that everyone is equal before the law, that everyone has a voice which can be and must be heard, that everyone is master of his own fate.

At every level this is more illusion than reality.

You do not have any effective voice, for instance, in the major expenditure of your own money. Americans used to spend most of their income for housing. Now it is spent for taxes. Taxes at every level gobble up about a third of our income. Most Americans work well into April to pay taxes before, in gross terms, they earn a cent for themselves or those who depend upon them. The rich who pay only the taxes for which their highly paid lawyers find no loopholes are excepted, of course.

Have you voted for many taxes? Sometimes there is the opportunity to vote for a local tax. Fine. But not for national taxes. You vote for representatives who pledge to hold spending or even cut it. They rarely have. The federal budget does not shrink. It grows, feeding on itself. It is the creature not of the Congress, as a matter of fact, but of the President, that isolated man surrounded by flunkies, totally removed from the lives of Americans generally, usually preoccupied not with America at all but with Destiny, Greatness, and the World.

Also, the government long ago arranged it so that the real voice of the people absolutely could not be heard in matters of taxation. Most Americans now realize that if it were not for the withholding tax—in which taxes are taken in advance, before you ever get your hands on the cash—most now realize that if it were not for this systematic theft of paychecks, most Americans simply would not be able to pay their federal tax bill on tax day. It means that the load of taxation is so staggering and probably odious that Americans would not prepare for it the way they might for a debt they had willingly and enthusiastically assumed. The taxes would not get paid.

The clear implication is that the government itself feels that most Americans, given the freedom and the space to deny their money to the government, would fail to come up with the cash.

I have never talked to a politician or government official who did not agree absolutely that the only device that keeps the government afloat is the withholding tax. Without this systematic advance drain against the earnings of people generally, the government simply could not continue to operate at its present level—because *the people would not support it if given a choice.* And so you are denied a choice and a voice. It is possible to mutter. It is even possible to be represented in Congress by one of the half dozen or so men, out of seven hundred, who regularly speak for cutting back government spending. It is more likely that you will be represented by one of the great majority who talk frugality when votes are sought and who vote profligacy when favors are sought.

In the economic area the closed circle that rings most of America is more subtle but just as visible with a close look.

Every working person, it is true, can save enough, if desired, to go into business, to be independent. But look at your own hometown. How much independence, in fact, is left in its business? The chain markets steadily dominate the grocery scene. Even the small "convenience" stores, once the great citadel of the small merchant, now come packaged by a distant franchiser. The hamburger stand is another similar and notable example. Even the car wash is plugged into a distant corporation.

Gasoline stations, laundries, hardware stores, dairy operations, soft drinks—the list goes on and on. Independent business is dying in America. Big business soaks it up at every turn and off every platter.

So become a *big* businessman! There the illusion is as great as anywhere. The really big business people remain the great inheritors, the huge stockholding families. The managers, to be sure, have vast powers, but compared to the owners those powers are transitory. No *great* new fortunes emerge. Many small ones do, but always to rest under the castle shadows of the great ones. Great managers emerge as well. But is there a banker who worked his way up and who fulfilled the supposed American Dream, who could ever dream of being a David Rockefeller at Chase Manhattan? Or a Rothschild? Or a Lever?

J. Paul Getty, often called the richest man in the world, probably would still have to tug the forelock when standing in front of a Mellon, a Morgan, or a Rockefeller, men to whom mere vulgar richness is for servants. I recall the way Getty once referred to the president of one of his great oil companies, a man who must to the rest of us seem a figure of great awe and success. Getty said, "He's a messenger boy."

I recall the bitter awakening of a friend who at the time owned one of the largest individual agricultural operations in the land. After meeting with the officials of a great food processing company, he said, "They treated me the same way I treat my tenant farmers!" Good. Even though the gulf separating him from the farmers is great, it is not quite so great as the gulf that separates even the upper reaches of the *working* rich from the heights of the truly exalted and usually idle rich.

The most important reality for many Americans, however, is the reality that comfort can be achieved by hard work. Sometimes the comfort is even great enough to carry with it very real illusions of "belonging" to the upper reaches of society. Even if not that, the honest working person with a decent salary can think "I've got it made" with a car or two in the garage, a good vacation, toys aplenty for children and adults alike, everything from power lawnmowers to snowmobiles to electronic organs. Money in the bank. Paid-up insurance. Not too much left on the mortgage, perhaps just ten years' worth. In such circumstances it is quite unlikely that the person would think very seriously about changing the system. That's understandable. People who do want to change the system should know that—and not grudgingly, but understandingly.

Obviously, some new American language of unity and of purpose, centered on a commonsense American view of work and workers, needs to be spoken loudly and clearly. When it is, to be a worker will once again be as proud a claim as to be an American. And the separation between the lives of individuals and the social life will be healed.

8

PROGRESS AND PROCESS

Local freedom, freedom in and of neighborhoods, is a popular rhetoric of people who call themselves right-wingers. Democracy in the workplace is a popular rhetoric of people who call themselves left-wingers. Science, technology and progress are heavily emphasized in the rhetoric of the managers of capitalist enterprises. Science, technology, and progress are heavily emphasized in the rhetoric of socialists.

But many who call themselves rightists, leftists, capitalists, or socialists have profound difficulty in accepting the realities of any of those terms. I have observed this to be true in every facet of traditional politics which I have been able to view close up. There is emerging, however, a new alliance in political life which, absorbing much of the recent past, is moving in a new direction which clearly points to local freedom as a first principle, democracy in the workplace as a first result of that freedom, and the use of scientific method and technology as tools of the work. Finally, it is defining progress in terms of better, not more.

Briefly, the new alliance involves those factions of the New Left which always were and have remained steadfastly opposed to old left, central-planning dogmas; the people of the counter culture who either avoided altogether or survived and moved past the drug experience, incoherence, mysticism, group therapy as a way of life, and begging as an ethic; segments of the old right whose libertarian tendencies have broken them completely with Republicanism or with any dealing whatsoever with government authority; young factory workers who are forming rank-and-file caucuses in old-line unions not just to get more pay but to confront directly the entire condition that results from assembly lines—pollution, health problems, tedium and, finally, products which seem less and less sensible; independent craftsmen and very small businessmen, such as independent truckers, who live under a constant shadow of corporate domination; small farmers, living under the same shadow; some technical, scientific and health workers who produce "progress" but are seldom rewarded for it or, lately, even edified by it; and veterans of Vietnam who, in substantial numbers, feel angrily that they were had by the politicians.

People I know in all those sectors of American life have been able to accept, live with, and work with a politics of locality, an antihierarchical ethic, and a humanely-oriented technology.

In common, all such people share an enthusiasm for, of all things, work. New Left firebrands who once thought they could organize people just on the basis of a bullhorn and book-learned slogans have reemerged as artisans and craftspeople, doctors, lawyers, nurses, biologists, physicists, you name it—still working in local political settings but now more a part of the general working population, possessing new hard skills to go along with their rhetoric, and infinitely more respected as a result. Counter-culture survivors have undergone a similar growth. Food faddism, for some, has been modified into skillful farming. Hallucinations have dimmed and arts have grown. Crafts abound, and not just artsy-craftsy ones but earthier skills such as plumbing, carpentry and masonry. Graduates of the counter culture now operate thriving repair shops, garages, stores, and even community financial development funds, all sustained by the work of participants who enjoy full equality of voice and responsibility.

From those sectors particularly—the New Left and the counter culture—comes a broad agreement to abandon all old distinctions of sex, race, age, caste, and class. Hard work is admired but is not seen as a device to get ahead of other people. It is just a way to better fulfill the individual and to make the community a richer, better place.

Those attitudes probably will be longer coming to the other sectors of this broad alliance, which seems to be forming without formalization. At the moment, the attachment to hard work —but rejection of *drudgery*—is a beginning point for the alliance. Such people are fed up with slick political hypesters, with fat-cat corporation officials, with big bankers, wheelers and dealers, gangsters in custom-tailored armor. They all have in common a sense of themselves as people and a sense of the joyous possibilities of accomplishments which are self-fulfilling and not simply necessities. Also, with many of these people there is a stronger-than-ever sense of *place,* of living in a community.

The liberal disposition, with which many Americans still confuse the left, always was focused on administrative and manipulative skills and processes rather than on concrete work. Welfare programs, by liberals, always produced a better feeling for the bureaucrats than they produced sensible help for the poor. Also, the liberal disposition has always been cosmopolitan, not local, regarding life more as a series of jet stops than a progression of homes and towns and neighborhoods.

The impulses of the New Left and this broad alliance which I see flowing from it—or around it, if you will—are entirely away from that sort of administrative, cosmopolitan orientation. The poor (excepting the infirm, of course) are never considered helpless clients dependent upon bureaucratic benevolence. The notion of *all* the neighborhood organizing, with which I am currently familiar and which embodies alliances of New Left, counter culture, young workers, and independent producers, is that productive work in shared and cooperative settings is the answer to poverty just as it is a base for political and social freedom and innovation.

In sharp contrast to these emerging attitudes are the traditional attitudes of the left, right, capitalists and socialists toward work and its organization, and purpose, and the location of political power.

Conservatives, even while they have supported the most centralized economic, military and police power, have always been very wise in their spoken attacks against the federal government generally, central planning generally, and nonmilitary bureaucratic domination. They have at least given lip service to a warm regard for local control of this and that. The truth of the matter, however, as is now obvious, is that most people on the right never meant that *your* neighborhood should have freedom, just *theirs.* It is quite all right for Beverly Hills to have local autonomy, hardly all right for a "hippy neighborhood," or a black one or a Spanish-speaking one, or even a working-class one. Besides, the right has always hedged its every support of local freedom with overall support of every single police power that ever has been proposed—so long as that police power deals just with keeping working-class people and unions in line and does not extend to auditing the books of corporations.

Also, the right has always supported, more loyally than any other sector of the people, the most costly, most autocratic, and least controllable military establishment. Every single freedom that the right has tried to wrest from the federal government at one time or another, they have willingly, like grinning sheep, handed back if the demand for those freedoms were simply couched in terms of national security. The right, which speaks of personal freedom, has defended every increase in military power since the Second World War. (Prior to that time, interestingly, it was a right-wing characteristic to *oppose* military power or any other institutional demand that would cede more power to the federal establishment. The Cold War ended all that and dumped the right wing into the laps of the expanding federal establishment whether the right realized it or not. From my own experience, I can attest they did not realize it. They simply never have clearly seen support of U.S. foreign and military policy as support also of the broadest mandates for eventual and actual internal power.)

Today, in what will probably be its final ironic moments, the right—the Republican right—even supports the President in his every move, according him kingly status simply because he is felt to be on their side or, at least, not on "the other side." So discredited is the right by their own foolish and even cowardly retreats from principle that it would seem to me safe to say that they will never again play an important *moral* role in our life—except as they might still form the constituency for an actual military or paramilitary grab for raw power.

The right wing today seems to me to be characterized by smallness of spirit, vastness of fears and insecurities, and a total, final, and absolute abandonment of any old standards of self-reliance and self-respect in favor of a weak-kneed collapse into the arms of the national-security bureaucracy and every foreign adventure that they or their corporate friends can dream up. People of conscience on the right no longer have a home there. They must move. I would expect most of them to move into the new alliance of which I speak.

On the left there is a similar problem. Democracy has always been a left ideal, rhetorically. To the old left, however, from the major socialist to the communist parties, democracy was not a here-and-now thing but a somewhere-yonder thing. The working class might be the class to be served by social change, but it was not necessarily the class to control social change. Instead, the various vanguard parties arose as surrogates for the working class, as interim managers until, in that great by and by, the wicked had all been wiped out and the workers could be entrusted at last with their lives.

So long as the left was seen as a surrogate movement, speaking for the working class but not including it or actually trusting it, Americans could be excused a healthy dislike of it. The idea of swapping one set of rulers for another, no matter where you live, did not strike many Americans as a sensible deal—particularly when conditions generally were such that American workers didn't even think that control was worth talking about. Only wages seemed in contention.

But the main point is that just as the right is losing its vitality and appeal now because it obviously sold out cheap to a single politician who didn't even represent its positions, so has the left lost much of its vitality by talking to working people about freedom while practicing in its party structures and in its national bases the most harsh sorts of top-down authority.

Today, however, the left has an advantage that the right does not and cannot enjoy. It is showing signs of change, everywhere.

The left in the Scandinavian countries is moving further and further toward worker management of productive facilities and further and further away from old concepts of top-down authority and management. Participation has become a new way of life for many workers and a way of life which by all testimony has proved wonderfully rewarding. Even in Australia, which for years was the right wing's not-so-secret fantasy of Valhalla (some right-wingers actually emigrated there), one now sees workers in the openly left-political building trades insisting that they participate in the actual decisions of what will be built rather than just dickering for conditions after the fact. Their point is one that will be more and more heard here and probably everywhere—that the quality of life is important and cannot be taken for granted nor can it be prudently traded for sheer economic growth. The old left was never so particular. Its goal was power in the workplaces, not democracy in them. And the quality of life always was seen as secondary to the control of it for political advantage and purpose. Progress was defined sharply by the old left as increases of state power and not increases of people power.

Changes from that position are clear also in Yugoslavia where worker management, although flawed by the emergence of new managerial bureaucracies, has reached sufficient stature to oust that new class and even further to democratize the workplace. Whether it will or not is not absolutely crucial because the movement toward worker management is hardly confined to that country although it is the first to make it national policy. China remains the great enigma in these terms. Obviously the participation of working people in every phase of their work and in every phase of social life is enormous. A Chinese hospital with patients, technicians, doctors, orderlies and cooks all consulting together might seem like almost a caricature of worker management and workplace democracy carried too far—except for the fact that people visiting such hospitals are enormously impressed and even moved by the quality of life-giving, loving cooperation which as any patient in a dull, gray bureaucratic beehive of a hospital here can tell you, might sometimes be the difference between recovery and decline. Also, a community where the purpose of medical skill is to prevent illness and not just treat symptoms—and incidentally create a special skilled class—strikes many observers now as an absolute necessity and not just a Utopian dream. Whether China's many moves toward the decentralization of power and democratization of work can withstand a post-Mao power struggle, or the arguments of national security which distort freedom in China as sharply as anywhere else, is yet to be seen. But the vastness of the experiment so far suggests that its impact cannot simply be obliterated by a new mandarin class should one emerge and consolidate itself. Although discontent in the Soviet Union has so far been concentrated, at least for our ears, in very high literary and artistic circles, it seems to me impossible that the great differences between party bureaucrats and working people generally will not become, sooner rather than later, a matter of serious social contention, with demands for workplace democracy and local self-control and political freedom following inevitably.

In America it is most likely that the demands for local political freedoms will advance ahead of demands for democracy in the workplace. Capitalism has been as insistent, and even sometimes as violently so, as Communism that the means of production be managed by an elite and not by the workers themselves. Capitalists may shout all they wish against federal central planning but they themselves are the most committed advocates of central planning and central authority when it comes to their own affairs. Also, if one is looking for a philosophical attitude that is truly "collectivist" in the sense of saying that the collective (the institution) must be placed ahead of the people who serve under or in it, then you need look no further than the nearest big American corporation, where human consideration is rarely permitted to intrude on the imperious demands of the collective, the management, the Company. Democracy in the workplace flies in the face of absolutely every rule by which modern corporate management conducts itself.

Actually, what workplace democracy most threatens is the very notion of management as a superior skill, a notion used always to justify the amazing differences between the rewards of owners and managers and the rewards of the people who actually do the work, design the machines, invent the technology, and conceive the science.

It is my proposition, and there are concrete demonstrations of it in many parts of the world, including some small examples in this country, that people involved in a process—*all* the people involved in a process—could and should make the decisions regarding that process and that, further, people affected by the process also should be given a voice in deciding its operation. Life is far too short and could be far too pleasant to permit the dead hand of custom and conventional prerogatives to turn it into a drudge for the many in order to exalt the few, to make most people work willy-nilly in order that a precious few not have to work at all.

Workplace democracy will, of course, be stubbornly resisted. Even so, the difficulties of a successful resistance are already indicated in the emergence of potentially powerful forces which will not, I believe, be assuaged in the long run by anything *but* workplace democracy. Those forces include the successful revolt in the United Mine Workers. In that revolt, a rank-and-file group, which obviously does not consider workplace democracy the taboo that stuffier unions do, swept away a corrupt, murderous old leadership. It could happen in other unions. Already, young workers in the auto union are making life more and more difficult for those union leaders who seem to want only to mark time with customary contracts until sweet retirement to pensioned idleness. The conditions of work are being questioned. Inevitably that must lead to more and more concern for controlling the work and not being victimized by it.

There is another inexorable force at work. Assembly-line production is producing more failures and flaws these days than it produces anything else. Drug use is rampant on the deadly lines. Mechanical flaws are a proliferating sign of worker sabotage, a form of resistance that is like an anguished relief for people slowly going mad in their work. And generally, throughout American industry, the insistence of management in shoving working people further and further away from any say-so in what they do, in keeping them ever more in the dark about processes and purposes—to preserve the holy management prerogatives—is resulting in the death of craftsmanship. Why should workers care if they are treated simply as extensions of machines?

In the obvious decline of craftsmanship there is a portent of some significance for the system. It is going to fail. Even if it is vastly automated, the maintenance of the machines and even the manufacture of the machines is going to be flawed by the don't-give-a-damn attitude of working people who are simply and justly reflecting the don't-give-a-damn attitude of their employers. People who simply don't care about their work will not do it well. People who do not care about their products, except as items in a profit system (in which even junk can be sold for a while, if properly packaged and lied about) will not be able to inspire better work on. those or any other products.

The decline in craftsmanship is accompanied by an increase of administration. We are day by day approaching the point where more people will be making their living by watching people work—by supervising—than by actually doing concrete, productive work. (Productive work, of course, includes intellectual and creative work and even includes *some* administrative work, but only administrative work that directly supports—by keeping track of things, or coordinating them—productive work. Administrators who just manipulate financial systems, or personnel systems, or whose work is only "getting ahead" cannot be said to be productive of any real value supportive of community life or in a concrete sense of human life. Such people support only institutional life and advancement and would be of no use otherwise.)

As corporate capitalism nears the dominance of managers rather than workers (machine operators, engineers, scientists, laborers, technicians, craftspeople) the system itself becomes more and more delicate. With fewer people actually competent to design, repair and build tools, every managerial mistake has more lasting effects, waste becomes less tolerable, and real innovations less likely.

When I worked in industry, one of our corporation's consultants was the renowned Peter Drucker and he preached, in our offices, the new doctrine of management in which managers would not be involved in productive knowledge at all but would be solely social manipulators, able to "manage" anything and, incidentally, to manage whatever it might be for benevolent purposes. I recall that when Drucker consulted with me he discovered that I had "a craft bias." This meant that I was happier with the people in the mills than in the executive suites and that I felt the crucial factor in production was the skills of the people on the line and in the labs and not the blarney of the managers. He felt, of course, that the highest skills are those which manipulate people and that material skills are simply low-order matters which, presumably, can always be whistled up.

It's not true. Now we have a multitude of the superb managers Drucker and others have always wanted. We have fewer and fewer of the superb craftspeople, designers, and engineers needed actually to carry out tasks (or, to put it another way, those people have less and less reason to take their work seriously since the managers, committed to managerial rather than craft bias in every sense, also don't take products or people seriously, but only profits).

The vitality to sustain a truly productive and innovative system is draining away. And it is draining away at the most crucial time. It is draining away when all of the easy supports for production such as cheap fuel, unlimited access to raw materials and a totally dedicated work force are also draining away. To maintain productive facilities today there must be magnificent imagination and new purpose and a quick willingness to switch from institutional values to human values. It might be wise, for instance, to abandon the automobile as a long-distance mover altogether and substitute that most efficient and ecologically sound machine, the railroad, for long-distance moving, and concentrate on alternatively powered (hydrogen, electric, windup, who knows!), locally buildable devices for all local hauling. Communities can make such switches on the basis of self-interest. General Motors cannot—on the basis of *its* self-interest.

To sum it up: As the problems multiply, the institutions to deal with them shrink in number but spread vastly in scope, so that fewer rather than more people are "officially" involved in the solutions. Common sense, on the other hand, would surely suggest that with more problems you might need more and not fewer solvers, more and not less skill, and more not fewer willing hands.

There are moves in some supposedly enlightened companies to play around with ideas of "humanizing" if not democratizing working conditions. Teams of people working together, setting their own pace and schedule and work roles, are found to be "more efficient" than assembly lines—less sabotage, less absenteeism, less flawed production, happier people. Characteristically, however, the humanizations are permitted to go only so far, are confined to small units, and become encrusted with new red tape. If permitted to develop freely, with workers assuming more and more control over their work lives, there is no telling where it would all end. Or, rather, there is a good guess where it would all end: with democracy in the workplace and with a hardening determination by working people to become themselves fully human rather than just having their work "humanized." What that "fully human" would mean could change the face of America and eventually the world. People working in a process would insist on being human parts of that process—thoughtful, feeling parts and not just cog parts, supposedly devoid of imagination, spirit, or any feeling other than greed for a paycheck. The quality of work would become as important as the quantity of work. People would want to understand everything about the process, including its purpose and its impact on them and their neighbors, and would not be content just with following orders. Wherever working people have more responsibility they also have more self-respect. Where they have more self-respect they have more curiosity, more demands for decency and for purposes broader than brute existence. Few employers ever publicly say that this would happen. It is their contention that employees are somehow genetically lazy, dishonest, and dumb. Employees, they keep saying, could never manage their own affairs. They are quite correct. *Employees* probably can't. Why should they? They receive salaries in their own self-interest but the actual work they do is not in their own self-interest. It is just part of a subsistence process. And many employees go from job to job in that process without ever seriously considering what sort of work could really engage their interest. Their interests usually show up elsewhere, as in hobbies.

Yet even while managers constantly complain that working people have no initiative, no skill, no commitment, they strenuously resist any opportunity that might provide a test of that statement. Or, when tests are made, they withdraw from the test as soon as positive results are shown—fearful, presumably, that if their pessimism about working people were ever dispelled by a demonstration, doubt would be cast on all other conventional wisdom about the workplace. The final and crucial doubt would be about ownership and control itself and would have working people wondering if scraps of paper and government-supported titles really have any standing in morality or in material necessity. That is, is ownership of business and industry today the result of creative work on the part of the owners, or is it by and large just the result of financial and political manipulation, inheritance and, sometimes, sheer spin-of-the-wheel luck? I think that, by and large, the latter broadly describes the true situation. And I believe that most working people would agree—if given an opportunity to test for themselves how much responsibility they could assume, how much creativity they could apply to work, and how the meaning of work and the purpose of life (which surely must be more than drudgery) could be brought closer together without risking anything more than dispossessing a few people of power which they actually never earned but which simply accrued to them in a world where ledgers have conquered life itself.

Along with the sort of questioning and testing which might eventually collapse the conventional wisdom about working people not being able to manage themselves and their work, there are two other conventional wisdoms that must collapse before working people generally, but employees in particular, can break away from the patterns now being enforced by corporate capitalism. One is the assumption that American free private enterprise as it now exists guarantees more freedom of choice than any other system ever has or, more important, could; and the other is that, without this enterprise and its credo of growth, there would be no "progress."

First, about freedom of choice. Having written hundreds of speeches about it as a right winger, I should begin by pointing out that freedom of choice is an unexamined defense of corporate capitalism. It is not examined at all by those who flaunt it most. It is simply accepted and trumpeted. Never once, in my many discussions with corporate leaders and leading politicians about freedom of choice, was there ever any substantial discussion of what the choices are. There was only discussion of the fact that the choices existed.

So, for instance, in a speech which I wrote with Warren Nutter, then on leave from head of the department of economics at the University of Virginia, we discussed the freedom of choice offered by the automobile and described it as the world's greatest vehicle of liberation. It gives unlimited choice of where you go.

The cost of the going was not considered. Pollution control was not even a factor, just as under the Ford Administration it is less and less of a factor, after enjoying a brief vogue. Fiscal cost, saddling people with relatively enormous and ongoing debts, was not considered. Traffic jams were not assessed, nor was the impact of more and more land disappearing under more and more concrete. Finally, the automobile was accepted as a great tool of freedom in enabling people to work wherever they wanted. What nonsense. People work, by and large, where owners put places for them to work and, just as critically, they live where real estate developers or government housing programs put places for them to live. The banking arrangements and tax arrangements, not to mention real estate red tape which turns more and more people toward accepting whatever the speculators offer rather than trying to do it themselves, are well known to everyone who has even thought about a house lately. The increasing separation of workplace and living place also is well known. The automobile, far from liberating people, simply makes it possible for them to meet, as willing sheep, the clipping demands of the businessmen (moving to the low-rent suburbs, for instance) and the real estate developers.

How many times recently have *you* thought, even if fleetingly, of how much freer you would be, if you didn't have to drive everywhere, than you are now, suspended between distant work, scattered shopping, isolated housing? Or, how liberating have you felt the car to be when it became necessary to repair it?

Other freedom-of-choice assumptions which we would do well to question concern food. There has been a commercial on television, for instance, that shows a supermarket with crowded shelves. The commentator says that even though such supermarkets offer the world's widest selection of food (more freedom of choice here than anywhere!) it may be necessary to supplement regular food purchases with vitamins and minerals. The reason is straightforward enough. The nutritional quality of the packaged foods which today dominate supermarket shelves is dubious and declining. We do, indeed, have the choice of more foods than any other people on earth— but the value of the food is somewhat less, as food, every year. The cost of the packaging now makes the value of the nutrition a secondary consideration. Examples abound. The protein content of corn is falling steadily as growers demand faster yields, yields tailored to the demands of giant packaging companies, rather than demanding corn of better and better nutritional quality. The corn fed to pigs and cattle today is often supplemented with soy beans to make it useful. Probably the most commonly accepted example, however, is the hard, watery, tasteless, artificially-reddened tomato which, in its little plastic tray, has become the almost universal American substitute for the tasty tomatoes that our parents remember. Tomatoes, to be picked by machines, must be harvested unripe, made red with chemicals, and then, to absorb the cost of all that, sold at a packaged premium.

Freedom of choice in food is fast becoming a senseless illusion, in other words. There are more labels. But they don't mean much. We choose between more and more but the more and more is less and less different. A dull sameness, a franchise-store tinsel quality closes in on our basic need, food.

The same sort of case can be made everywhere in corporate enterprise. There are more and more television diversions but less and less to choose from them as they cluster around safe averages, seldom even trying for differences. Freedom of choice is the freedom to choose between versions of similar things.

Politicians, of course, reflect the same shallowness of what freedom of choice has come to mean.

In the larger matters of work, life-style, even companionship, freedom of choice is so harshly restricted by the other realities of corporate life (the boss's schedule, not yours, controls your household; the banker's schedule, not yours, controls most of your economic planning; and so forth). And, of course, about a third of most incomes is simply stripped away at the outset by the demands of various levels of government. At best, most Americans can exercise freedom of choice over only two-thirds of their income, virtually none over the nature, place, condition, or meaning of their work, hardly more over where they live and how they live (municipal and other planning now reaches into virtually every phase of domesticity).

But, it could be argued, no one has much freedom of choice. The independent farmer doesn't have much freedom of choice from the conditions imposed by the weather. Yet the farmer is able to meet the weather head on, knows why the job must be done, knows that in return for it, the farm family has a distinct life-style, and so forth. The suburban family is not in quite the same situation. Its confrontations with nature or the conditions of work are so intricately filtered through managerial red tape, customs, and regulations that, unlike the farmer facing the weather as a part of nature, the suburban family faces existence as part of something quite unnatural, the blueprints of the corporation. The difference may seem slight, to be faced with the harsh demands of the weather or the harsh demands of the boss. So, perhaps, rather than argue the merits of either, the proper case would be to argue for the freedom to choose between them—a freedom which, speaking of choices, is one of the most drastically curtailed of all in the land. Farming as a family way of life is being snuffed out as regularly as is the corner store as a way of family life, or the craft shop.

The characteristic of the vastness, the admitted vastness, of freedom of choice which Americans have is that they have unlimited freedom to choose among products and decisions made by fewer and fewer people. They can, to be sure, choose from literally hundreds of models of everything imaginable. But choosing to have a role in assessing the array of things on which time and resources will be spent at the outset falls into fewer and fewer hands.

There is an old free enterprise argument which I used to appreciate and repeat. It says that the mechanism of the marketplace enables everyone to vote, in effect, for how time and resources will be spent. It says, further, that the marketplace *responds* to popular demand. That is not true. Common sense tells us it is far from true. Corporate capitalism bases much of its advances today on creating, not responding to, demands. Products are designed to keep factories busy and to make money and then are promoted on the basis of envy, greed, fear, lust— just about everything except actual utilitarian value. It is so striking to observe, for instance, just how many of the products promoted on television night after night have anything to do with bettering the conditions of life, love, community, or human aspirations. Hardly any do—unless women are prepared to say that they are worthless without varnished hair and men are prepared to say their lives are meaningless without a new car, and unless children are to be seen as totally incapable of imaginative play without a Hollywood designer to set their stages for them.

The most terrible possible evaluation of corporate capitalism is, it seems to me, the fact that it spends billions of dollars annually to convince once proud and self-reliant Americans that, in fact, they are worthless without their shiny dishes and hair, insignificant without a new car, deprived without a cheap toy imitation of a breakfast-cereal hero.

The contempt that corporate capitalism displays for Americans is so enormous, so shoddy, and so insulting that I would venture to say even a classical despotism would be preferable. In a traditional oppression, at least, people are treated as potentially dangerous and capable of human reactions, and the police oppress them precisely because of that. Under corporate capitalism, people are treated as subhuman blobs devoted only to their material possessions, incapable of doing anything for themselves, incapable of defining themselves in any way other than through what they buy. They are sheep to be fleeced, not even worthy of being called people to be policed. Docile, dumb, and infinitely greedy is the way corporate capitalism defines Americans, and evidence of it glows from every advertisement they present.

What are Americans? They are consumers! That is corporate capitalism's ultimate message and that is the only way corporate capitalists want to think of them. To think of them as producers would open up some dangerous avenues. Better to think of them, in that sense, as consumers of profit. (Witness the constant statement by corporate leaders that working people "consume" the major portion of every sales dollar. The fact that they also *produce* the products in the first place is a minor matter to the corporate spokesmen, who always act as though they are doing the working people a favor by hiring them and that the working people have the gall to ask for something in return.)

Politicians have an exactly similar view of the citizen as merely consumer and in essence it is a view as contemptuous of Americans as that held by the corporate managers. An advertisement for a 1974 telethon for the Democratic Party sums it up nicely. People are urged to send money to the Party. This is described as "personal involvement" and is said to be the answer to an improvement of the political process. Imagine! To politicians, citizenship is defined as the act of giving money. But, of course that has long *been* the definition for all parties and for the state itself. Citizens pay. Politicians spend. And that is called participation! It is called involvement! It is, in fact, nothing more than saying that you are an active participant in, rather than victim of, a crime when you hand your wallet over to the robber.

Americans have always had the good sense to resent and hate foreign regimes that treat people like animals to be herded. Someday, I am sure, they will have the good sense to resent, and put an end to, any system which herds *them* like animals and even speaks to them the same way.

But this is not to say there is less freedom here than in other lands. There is more actual freedom *available* here than anywhere else.

Freedom of choice is not turned into a sham because of police regulations. It is turned into a sham because so many of us willingly cooperate in the system, and for what are seen as practical and down-to-earth reasons such as the apparent lack of an alternative. And it would be absurd to try to convince Americans that the proliferation of things they have, even if the quality is more and more doubtful, isn't better than having less. We see people who have less and few of us envy them—so far.

It is precisely *because* there is so much potential freedom in America that I am convinced the corporate system and the system of government bureaucracy will both show greater and greater and greater cracks and will eventually collapse.

I cannot believe that Americans will put up with the many abuses of the commercial system and the political bureaucracy indefinitely. Yet I know that the Declaration of Independence makes a sound point when it suggests that people endure familiar ills as long as they can rather than move toward change and its inevitable implications of insecurity and the unknown.

The combination that should permit great change in America is exactly the combination of so much freedom available—for those who seize it—and the mounting failures of the major system, the proliferation of products without meaning or quality, and the growing realization that politicians as leaders are not adequate to the tasks which must, ultimately, be accomplished by people as good neighbors and hard workers.

But to what end would change be made? What, in some new sense, would substitute for progress in the old sense?

Progress in the old sense means, only and absolutely, economic expansion. So long as there is more money there is said to be progress. So long as profits go up there is said to be prosperity. It is gross amounts that are considered the gauge of progress and not the direction, purpose, or even use of the wealth. How it is shared is of so trivial interest as to be without any significant role in American reality. The distribution of income in America has changed less than in practically any other country on earth. Economically we are vastly expansionist, but that's all. We are also almost absolutely stable in the sense of guaranteeing the perpetuation of an ownership elite whose population in relation to the population generally remains rather static, certainly far more static than the ruling class of Great Britain where, by new necessity, the people generally are simply beginning to feel that they cannot afford the idle rich.

Again, this is not to argue against the undeniable fact that we do have tremendous tangible results of that economic progress. More people have more things than ever before. Absolute fact. More people have access to things once considered luxuries of only a few.

But as in the case of universal public education, the concept of more and more, of sheer quantity, has begun at this particular point in our history to overwhelm, in newly painful and apparent ways, the quality of what we have. More people are educated in public schools than ever before. Yet those same schools are such failures in as basic a matter as the teaching of reading that we have also become the world's only country to be forced to install a vast remedial reading program. How foolishly alienated from even our schools have we become to permit the perpetuation of reading-teaching techniques which are colossal failures? The same is true in so many areas. More has not meant better. For a time the sheer quantity probably will content most of us. But with inflation in prices, slippage in craftsmanship, and absolute decline in the quality of cities and even the countryside, the question of quality is inevitable. Americans will raise it. And when they do, there will surely be change.

If the questions are raised mainly by the sort of alliance I have suggested—people with some urge to be self-responsible and self-reliant—rather than by opportunists seeking to exploit the new demands for old means—such as organizing minorities or the poor on the behalf of partisan politics—then there will inevitably be social change of a liberatory nature. There also will be the problem of co-optation and of outright suppression. Rank-and-file insurgency in the unions will surely be fought by both the union bureaucrats and the managers. Both have a vested interest in maintaining working people as either a constituency or a labor pool. The insurgents speak a different language. They at least threaten the possibility of working people organizing and moving on their own behalf specifically, and in their own long-term interests—rather than short-term obsession with contracts and rather than in accord with the growth plans of either the labor or management bureaucrats. Also, the various business-sponsored "humanization" programs will go so far, but no farther, in trying to quell worker unrest. In the long term, corporate capitalism cannot give to young workers what many young workers seem to want—work that is not dreary, and a sense of accomplishment and craft rather than just a sense of treadmill earning.

Some generation would have to question the conventional wisdom of work. This one is well situated to do it and, in large measure, that situation is made good by the existence of modern technology and the deep penetrations of scientific discovery into virtually every corner of the material world.

It might have been necessary to say at various times in history that there just wasn't enough to go around and that, therefore, endless toil was our lot and competition and struggle one against the other the only way to divide up scarce resources.

Actually, the scarce resource that kept the world so shackled to material necessity and to harsh hierarchical organization was the resource of knowledge. The rulers knew things, at least certain things, which were carefully kept from ordinary people. Therefore, they ruled.

Today knowledge is infinitely available. Books, computers, visual systems, scientific discovery and even language make it possible for anyone anywhere to seek out and understand all important material matters. Many material resources are, indeed, still scarce and always will be. But increased knowledge tells how to preserve them, re-use them, avoid depleting them, or substitute for them (solar energy, fuel cells, methanol, etc., as substitutes for fossil fuels, long-lived plastics as virtually permanent transformations of petrochemicals into usable building material, for instance).

In the availability of knowledge of how to do things, how to study things, how to evaluate human needs, there is a curious gap—the social impetus to use the knowledge to make life more pleasant, interesting, and even feasible for all of us. What now links most of us to the available new knowledge is not social self-interest at all. It is the same old links of institutional control and direction. The new knowledge, produced by millions of hardworking people, tells us that healthful food can be grown in small scale operations in and near cities, avoiding transportation and packaging costs. The old institutions tell us that farming is a corporate prerogative and that the goal of farming is not nutrition at all, but is first and foremost profits. The new knowledge tells us that disposable containers and tacky goods are technologically absurd and that more permanent, not wasteful things could be built and could even be built in organizations of rather small scale. The old institutions tell us, again, that profit is the goal, not general enhancement of life.

So long as progress is defined as doing the things that make the most sense to the bookkeepers there is simply no way to do the things that would make most sense to the citizens generally, and the designers, engineers, scientists, craftspeople, and health workers specifically.

And so the redefinition of progress is crucial. There are obvious signs of the disutilitarian nature of continuing to define progress as profits. Corporate profits already have soared to incredible levels but the quality of life and even the quantity of work available has shrunk observably. Mineral resources are known to be in a state of declining supply even while demand rises everywhere. Surely the solution in simple material terms cannot be to just plow ahead at the same old game, marking up the price of everything and considering the value of nothing.

As just one example: American industry today consumes roughly 60 percent of the entire annual mineral production of the entire earth. That ratio cannot continue indefinitely unless we are prepared to literally wage war against the 80-some percent of the people of the earth who do not live in America or the more than 99 percent of the people of the earth who do not share in the profits of the American businesses that consume the mineral resources. That figure, of course, includes most American citizens.

More and more, as a matter of fact, the giant international or multinational corporations, still heavily American despite the glittering new treasures of Arab rulers and Japanese monopolists, will make inevitable a clash between people generally and owners/rulers specifically. There are three billion people on this earth. Many of them are already fairly wise to a growing difference between what their knowledge of technology tells them and what the corporations deliver. Many of them are increasingly wise to the tolls in war, pollution, tension, unemployment, even starvation that corporate demands fasten on them. More of the three billion learn a little more each day. Or at least they have the potential to do this and therefore even if they don't raise questions today, surely they may tomorrow.

But while these three billion people face incredibly upsetting shifts in climate that have plunged great areas into massive famines, while they face upsetting possibilities in the pollution of the planet and in the destruction of its resources, while all this is going on, the actual fate of the world falls officially into fewer and fewer hands.

The multinational corporations make the old concentrations of corporate businesses inside single countries look pale. The power of the giant nation-states, such as the Soviet and the United States, and the kingly powers which great rulers now claim everywhere, inflate the scale of social organization to incredible new levels. Fewer people rule more today than ever before in history—actually rule their destinies, being able to decide their work, their products, their governments, their very lives.

Whereas the king of the old myth had to retreat into a temper tantrum when the sea refused to roll back from its shores on command, the kings, rulers of today, could at the virtual drop of a law command millions of people to build a breakwater that would roll the ocean back—perhaps just to enable the ruler to have a broader beach!

It is the ruling few that define progress today and it is the increase in their powers and profits that *is* the definition. Can the rest of us afford it? In a very real sense, above and beyond human preference, it does not seem to me that we can. The corporations waste too many resources and are too careless of the quality of ordinary life. The politicians waste lives as well and also gauge progress by the increase of their power. (Presidents who usurp more and more power are said to be activist Presidents. A President who might want to permit the people to rule themselves would be called, particularly in the liberal press, a do-nothing President.)

Looking around the world, then, it would seem that the lives of perhaps three *billion* people are in virtual hock to the ambitions, the greeds, the pomps, the ownerships of twenty to thirty *million* people, the major owners and politicians. (I simply grasp at that figure by taking internationally the sort of ratio of great owners and politicians to population as a whole that pertains in the United States—one to one hundred. Since there are countries in which power and ownership may be even more concentrated than that 1 percent, the figure does not seem at all improbable.)

Somewhere along the line, the idea of 1 percent of the earth's population controlling the other 99 percent is going to cease to make sense.

Then progress will have to be defined in new terms. It will have to be described, for instance, in terms of the most effective use of tools and technology for the purposes of many people and not just a few people. It will have to be described in terms of the enhancement of life everywhere and not just in terms of the conditions of the lawn around the White House, around the mansions, or at the country club.

If, today, the perhaps thirty million ruling people simply vanished from the earth, what would happen? What would happen if instead of the great owners and the big politicians, we all had to assume responsibility for our own lives and responsibility as well for cooperating with our neighbors, and with other neighborhoods, to accomplish tasks seen as desirable, to make things, to grow things?

The answer might surprise even the most dedicated believer in the superiority of rulers and the rich, if that person thought about it long enough and hard enough.

The great politicians spend most of their time dealing with

other great politicians. If the entire system of great politics declined, so would the need for such negotiations. People generally do not make war on one another or even construct the systems which threaten war. Specific rulers, leaders, do that. The problem of war is not a problem of human nature, it is a problem in human organization. So long as leaders have the power to command armies, they will. But how many of your neighbors do you really feel would spend all of their time plotting a war or plotting to gain power? Even if you think most of them would, *could they,* in a world in which political sovereignty was right there at home, where everyone can see and understand ambition, greed, and craftiness? When the town meetings dominated America, local matters were well served, but national ambitions were difficult. Is that so bad?

The great factories which seem so complicated and which, the managers say, require the special gifts of the great owners to organize, are also problems of organization and not necessities of technology. The thrust of all modern technology is toward miniaturization and cybernetic controls that make sophisticated production possible on a very small scale. Even the machinery of the steel industry is constantly reduced in scale as it increases in effectiveness. It is the demands of corporate power, and not of technology, that keep steel production as a concentrated blight in a few environments rather than letting it be more localized and lesser in environmental impact. (The most innovative plastics, as a matter of fact, are so obviously best used in small scale production settings that some giant corporations who have gone into plastics have got right out again because they simply couldn't compete with smaller, more technically innovative and flexible plants.)

The point is that among the ruling millions there simply are not enough working scientists, engineers, or designers, or materially creative people of any sort, to make much of a dent in actual, technical production matters should they all disappear or be thrown out.

The crucial people of our civilization are not the ruling people at all. The crucial people are the competent, creative working people. The most revolutionary question of course is when will they throw off the bosses? The following most revolutionary question is can they be resisted as a new class of rulers themselves? And the best hope for a decent answer to that, as I see it, is radical decentralization of all power, wider diffusion of scientific and technological information, and a growing sense among everyone—the young, the old, the most energetic and the least, the most creative and the least—that our shared interest as human beings is to live with one another and with nature in ways that do the least damage to either. To say that the goal of human progress is a few more lousy bucks in the bank for some billionaire is to make a pretty shabby thing of being human.

Eventually, it seems to me, most people on earth should respond to that. More immediately, it seems to me, the very special people of the new alliance which I have envisioned in America are the very ones to resent it, and to do something about it.

Is there a place in all this for regular liberals? Undoubtedly, although not as liberals. The liberal disposition to "do good" from as great a distance as possible, as from a legislative seat or a country club, rather than from a factory floor or a town meeting or a street corner is an obsolete luxury. It hasn't worked and it won't work. The assumption that the poor can only be helped by sending them social workers is so discredited as to require no more attack. What the liberals still control, however, is vast amounts of money. How they deploy it could be very important. One way would be to support financially, out of habit or stubborn resistance to the facts of failure, the outdated programs of welfarism and paternalism which they have legislatively supported in the past. As the government withdraws from such programs, the liberals might just move in and keep them going as private endowments, institutes, and other grant-based activities. The government, under such an arrangement, could attend full time to the business of policing the people, extending its national security and police powers (which so many conservatives *and* liberals still support as a legitimate federal function—the conservatives in order to control ideas, the liberals in order to control guns, to cite major objectives).

This division of labor would find such huge institutions as the Lilly Foundation, the various Rockefeller funds, and the Ford Foundation heavily subsidizing highly-bureaucratized welfare programs in the big cities. If past experience is any guide, this would mean that potential action for social change, rather than social comfort, would be splintered into hot competition for foundation-funded jobs and grants just as in the near past it was splintered by competition for government jobs and grants.

Actually, the pattern already has been set and is obvious. The foundations are stepping in to perpetuate failed government programs.

The alternative would be to fund actions which promise the broadest possible participation of people in solving their own problems, in creating new institutions for their social and productive life, and in innovating the applications of tools and technology to the purposes of liberation from habits of poverty, habits of dependence, or the grim erosion of life quality.

An example from personal experience involves the neighborhood in which I live and work. When some of us sought foundation and other help for a project to establish worker-managed, community-owned light industrial or building maintenance groups in the neighborhood, the established donors whom we approached turned us down flat for a reason which, in one way or another, they all expressed: We wanted to do something which poor people could not do (manage their own lives and tools as well). It was their assumption in common that black people, poor whites, and young people generally could only be helped by traditional welfare-type actions in which they would be given not the tools of production but the alms of simple sustenance and the diversions of singing and dancing. (Incidentally, the difference between singing and dancing as seen by the liberal foundations and as seen from a work-centered point of view is also revealing. In our neighborhood we have had a lot of singing and dancing as celebration of work accomplished, such as at the end of a neighborhood clean-up campaign. That, it seems to me, is when singing and dancing have their richest meaning: as celebration. To the liberal foundations, singing and dancing are separate parts of life, an opportunity for some poor people to get ahead by becoming professional entertainers; they are the sorts of activities to be supported to "get people out of the neighborhood and into the world." The liberals do not see singing and dancing as cultural, but as simply commercial; the same way they see work as only commercial.)

Another striking example is that liberal foundations have lately been giving millions of dollars in grants to "observers" to go and watch the funny people of the counter culture or of alternative technology as they do their quaint things, such as design solar energy systems, operate cooperative food systems, or establish community "banks." The observers then write long reports which may be racked up in the better university and foundation libraries. The foundations rarely, however, will help finance the work which the observers are observing! Again, the emphasis is on people who watch work being done rather than on people who do work.

Here and there a few foundations, but not the giants such as Lilly, Rockefeller, and Ford, show a spirit of adventure in supporting work rather than watching and a few young, rich people have joined working groups. The speed with which social alternatives develop will depend in part on how that trend advances or retreats. To expect the giant foundations to finance innovation, rather than reform, remains a fantasy.

The fact of social change, although wealth could speed it, will depend on the people who, in fact, have the most to gain from it and will be fought against by those who feel they have something to lose—the rich and the powerful and their most devoted servants.

The path of social change, regardless of speed, will be through all the familiar landscapes of politics, and beyond them. For, in fact, the new world is already shaping in the shell of the old.

9

THINKING SMALL

While the institutions of great scale fall apart around our ears, the proprietors of those institutions recognize that decentralization is urgently required—but they see and suggest the requirement only as a *function* of the Great Institutions.

They offer the failed institution itself as a solution to the failure.

An example. The federal government's Executive makes a crucial issue of executive power and privilege. The Executive demands, or takes, the power of an absolute monarch. And everything continues to go wrong. So—the Executive embarks, collaterally, upon a campaign to decentralize government.

What does it mean? That the Executive understands that *only* by delegating responsibilities can any social organization be innovative, resist rot and, as is today demanded, figure its way out of the disasters caused directly by the inevitable miscalculations and misperceptions of central power. Central power is preoccupied, in every known instance, with the preservation of privilege and not with innovation and creativity, things that inevitably challenge accreted and self-serving, noncreative authority.

But, even as the Executive understands the need to decentralize so that people may survive, it also has an institutional imperative that says the people must survive to serve the institution.

Another example. Industrial leaders begin, as though it is a difficult perception, to see that the assembly line has a diminishing utility because, over time, it drives people quite mad, causing them either to work badly because of sheer boredom or because of active hatred. Either way, the line becomes a target for industrial sabotage of an order previously known only in places being occupied by a tyrant enemy.

Finally, an example for a particular argument. The cities are falling apart. Nothing works in them. Crime goes up and so does the police budget. The police can't protect. Transportation declines and the highway budget goes up. The roads can't deliver, they can only congest. Kids seem to get dumber but the school budgets stay high. Schools can't educate—at best they candidly try to pacify.

Some cities, notably New York, try to decentralize with little town halls, police auxiliaries, elaborate traffic laws, and wild experimentation in the school system. But always the great institutional ooze pervades. It is all done within the reinforcing system of the city government itself.

A reaction. In some places, like the neighborhood in which I live, people understand the need to decentralize, but in a way that actually will detach them from the big institutions; that will permit them the space for their own survival, not just the "privilege" of being volunteer rather than coerced servants of institutional ambition. (An industrial version of this occurs when a management lets workers form production teams rather than work on the assembly line. Production, of course, goes up. The workers are a bit happier. But their relationship to the ruling institution remains unchanged. They have been made happier, not for humane reasons, but for the strictly businesslike one of getting more and better work out of them. It is like a sweet, secret wage cut in the final analysis.)

After understanding that the great institutions have failed, what?

In the Adams-Morgan section of Washington, D.C. (racially

and economically mixed but predominantly poor and black), the first step, taken out of desperate impatience with past "civic association" organizations, was to form a neighborhood assembly, based on the town meeting model but with an important innovation, open committees. In fact, the committees came first.

Neighborhood people, galled by the filth of the streets left untended by the city and admittedly spoiled by uncaring attitudes that flourish in neglect, decided to form a committee to get folks together for volunteer cleanup days. Since the first meetings to discuss an overall neighborhood assembly had been held, the committee to clean the streets identified itself with the larger group, but it worked independently and creatively. It got the streets, at least some of them, cleaned up. Neighbors began meeting neighbors while sweeping. Neighbors *became* neighbors. They became citizens of their neighborhood.

Other committees began working on housing (how to stop speculators from uprooting the neighborhood), rats (how to kill them), and recreation (in an area of 31,000 persons with only two tiny play areas).

The recreation committee built a ball park, bleachers, and playground equipment on a vacant lot which became Community Park despite the wails of the titular owner. It remains Community Park. The housing people galvanized enough community support to defeat an invading gas station (there are five already in the neighborhood) and to hold the line against a number of evictions from houses bought by speculators—and to begin accumulating the support and capital to start the local, hopefully cooperative purchase of vacant buildings.

Meantime, the town meeting went ahead. Membership has risen to more than 3,000 with more and more neighbors join-
ach month.

nother spontaneous committee began collecting clothes and discarded household equipment which is given free at the storefront office of the Adams-Morgan Organization (AMO).

Because of the regular town meetings, the established politicians in colonial Washington have begun to take notice of Adams-Morgan and even obsequiously seek it out. The people, bless them, have not been conned. At each meeting, the attitude of doing it ourselves seems to strengthen and fear of "downtown" to weaken. (At a recent ceremony, to count block-by-block votes for an operating council to carry out assembly decisions between meetings, a local judge was scheduled to preside. He was so obviously scornful of the local attitudes and informality that he was asked to leave; an act of *lèse majesté* with profoundly encouraging implications for a neighborhood that just two years ago was totally dominated by a hat-in-hand attitude toward government officials.)

Next on the neighborhood agenda are crime prevention actions (neighborhood patrols, youth programs run by and not for young people, and whatever else the apparently endless ingenuity of the neighbors can come up with). Also, a committee is forming to start a health-training and service center, and a co-op real estate office. There already is an exemplary co-op grocery store, record store, and a video center which uses portable tape machines as a way for people to engage in what amounts to an audiovisual debate about anything and everything that affects their lives.

Also, there is a highly regarded therapeutic community of recovered drug users; a credit union; a community assistance cooperative for Spanish-speaking people; two nonprofit weekly newspapers; a woodworking guild; a prisoner-release program and an "alternatives to prison" program; plans for a co-op pharmacy and for a co-op hardware store; a brilliantly innovative community studies program through Communitas College, also in the neighborhood; volunteer work by Antioch law school students, also in the neighborhood; and a growing feeling that when you say hello to someone on the streets the greeting has new and neighborly meaning.

My own particular interest, while regularly working on sev-

eral AMO committees, is in a project begun by Communitas
College and the Institute for Policy Studies. It is called Community Technology, is an incorporated, nonprofit group and
is made up of a mathematician and an engineer from the Johns
Hopkins Applied Physics Lab (who has just been fired for refusing, as a Quaker, to work on weapons), an engineer from the
Naval Research Lab, a consulting chemist, an organic farmer,
an auto mechanic, a theoretical physicist with a practical turn of
mind, a carpenter, two women with lab jobs or training, a
woman weaver, a welder (me) and the founder of Communitas.

Specific projects already under way are: high-density fish
culture to provide local protein from basement-sized "fish factories," hydroponic and high yield rooftop gardens for vege-
tables, solar power devices, wind power tests, nonwasting waste
disposal and utilization, junk reclamation and distribution, and
community cooperative production and transportation.

The scientific method itself, which is just common sense and
experimentation, is a denial of the failed, big-scale tragedies of
farm, factory and forum which now threaten to bury us in their
rubble. And, it seems to me, this same commonsense approach
now demands that we look to small victories in small places, to
creative community, to neighborliness, as the way to our grandest victory—the return to human scale, human purpose, and
human rather than institutional values.

The modern megalopolis and the corporate state that nur-
tures it are the exact opposite of everything that is local, humanistic, and human in scale.

As the big institutions break down or become repressive,
and as smaller, human-scale organizations reemerge, it becomes
obvious that one of the most important things we must heal in
the process is the currently great separation between the tools of
technology and the purposes of human life. Lately it seems that
the tools have a life of their own, superior even to human life.

I feel strongly about this; strongly enough to break into what has so far been a personal narrative to discuss the points more academically. The points are subtle and precise, like much of the technology, and warrant everyone's most serious, hard thinking and not just passing reactions.

In the modern, mass-scale corporate state and its cities and workplaces, human purposes are viewed as statutory and economic, rather than social. Personnel replace people. Real estate replaces the landscape. Human action, exerted as corporate action, is practiced as though bound *only* by organizational, political and institutional economic conventions. The physical and natural sciences are taken to be *solely* utilitarian. Ethics and philosophy derive, in this style, more from understanding or interpreting the conventions of organizational politics and institutional economics than from understanding the natural world.

It is a style which, in practice, divides human groups into those which do manipulate the natural world and those which, *like* the natural world, are merely manipulated.

A contrary opinion, leading to a different view of human life-styles, could hold that humans are a kind of natural life, still evolving, extraordinary but not separate, infinitely creative but not unbounded. Their life-styles, therefore, could be a style of life in nature, not apart from it, based upon relationships in and not the conquest of nature. Understanding nature, in such a style, would provide the ways to comprehend, as fully as possible, the consequences of human action and not simply the conveniences. It would seek to avoid the disasters of not knowing those consequences.

There is no regular system of accountability in the institutional life of the human race today which can even weigh the difference between consequence and convenience. All widely accepted human accounting systems today are based upon convenience—the immediate return of rewards. Consequences are accountable only as deficits in the convenience or delays in the reward. A vivid example, from the outstanding capitalist theorist Murray Rothbard, concerns developmental economic ventures which require the disruption of the marine ecosystem. Given such a situation, he writes, he would always choose "people over plankton," the specific economic development over the wider environment. Socialist economists take a similar position: political plans first, material environment second.

An assumption of the accounting system is that, regardless of the unhealthy impact upon the natural world of human action, further human action will remedy it. Thus, the plankton and the oceans could be killed, to serve a human purpose; then another human purpose would provide the artificial environments which might be needed, other human actions would provide the fuels and materials for those environments, further actions would armor them against a globe stripped of air cover and open to cosmic radiation, and so forth down to the ultimate deep shelter or up to the last escaping starship. This is plausible, but for those who favor such a life-style it can be suggested that prudence dictates the arrangement of the various salvations prior to, and not just haphazardly after, each disaster. Even for those convinced that the planet is simply a mine pit, the accounting system should be concerned with consequences and not merely convenience. This exercise would also provide an opportunity for people to understand that for each move called "progress" there is a price. It is never *just* humans or plankton. It is entire ways and systems of life that are involved.

The ability to predict the results of human action in the natural world (a large concern of science) is in itself a distinctive mark of a human style. Other life-forms seem more bound by the environment than aware of their impact upon it. Unlike us, they are not free to alter that impact virtually at will. That *human* ability involves the use of the human mind. The mind, like legs and arms, is simply there in the human arrangement. It can be belittled or adored, but it cannot be denied.

To suggest that human life should only involve arms and

legs (natural action) without the human mind would be as unnatural as to suggest that human life involve only human minds (natural reflection or intellectualization). One view says there are no individuated humans to have a life-style, there is only Life. Another says that life-styles are *simply* rational, that humans are unlike other life, rising above nature by sheer mental power to live in a realm of desires bound only by rational conventions. Another states that human life is at best simply muscular and emotional (an animal like any other animal).

My view is different. It is a view of humans living in nature *and able to understand it.* It is of human life-styles that include awareness of the consequences of actions and people fully responsible or accountable for those actions. And, finally, it is a life-style which is above all just that: a LIFE-style, a style of behavior which emphasizes life as supremely important, as necessary for the derivation of all *human* values, and as morally, ethically, and culturally different from ways of behavior which hold death as the most significant factor in human action, and the most worthy preoccupation of human "life-styles."

It is my contention, further, that the culture of death is a significant characteristic of the large-scale social organization and the modern corporate state. War has been the principal historic renown of both. Political immortality, not human mortality, has been their preoccupation. Inanimate objects are used as the measure of their efficacy. Uniforms are saluted, not people. Even the structure of every large-scale social organization and every corporate institution—hierarchy—is the structure of a culture of tombs—the pyramid.

An alternative to the pyramidal determinants of life-style would be small-scale social organization and nonhierarchical human actions. An alternative to simply using nature, and being prepared to destroy and then synthesize every one of its processes, would be to live at greater peace with it. The alternatives require more, not less, understanding of the fields of natural and physical science.

Scientific investigation has developed fundamental informa-tion regarding virtually every natural process and relationship; not just terrestrially but even, to a beginning extent, galactically. Technology is the human activity which is said to apply that information to concrete action in the material world.

Today's ordinary technology is corporate technology. It in-volves the application of scientifically derived information to projects evaluated mainly in terms of cash profitability in the so-called private sector or national military security in the so-called public sector. It also involves the restriction of that in-formation to persons and projects committed to those standards of evaluation and the development of widespread legal, edu-cational, and cultural programs to support the restriction.

An alternative technology could be evaluated in terms of its long-term support of individual human lives and assimila-tion by discrete, self-aware, and self-controlled human com-munities.

The major characteristics of such an alternative technology would be:

(1) It would not increase the incidence of death, disease, or nervousness.

(2) It would conform to, rather than attempt to defy, the widest possible array of physical principles, and would not be evaluated just in terms of its own operation. It would, in other words, exist in nature and not in isolation from it.

(3) Its application would be organized by those who would operate the tool or process in consultative conjunction with anyone affected by the tool or process. They would be account-able for their work because they could be absolutely identified with it. There would be no right of ownership which would pre-vent the use of the tool or process by anyone else capable of operating it and willing to be accountable for it.

(4) It would mainly use resources that could be renewed, re-placed, or recycled. If such virtually irreplaceable resources as fossil hydrocarbons (petroleum, coal) were used, they should

be used in ways with the least possible impact on the environment.

(5) It would be appropriate for widespread community participation and understanding. It could be operated nonhierarchically, would encourage productive involvement and discourage consideration of itself solely in terms of consumption.

(6) Its availability to small human communities would be an important measure of its effectiveness. This contrasts with the current technological standard of effective support of large institutions.

(7) It would foster a culture in which the *applications* of scientific principles would always be guided by such tests as these:

> Is the application such that if everyone in the world were individually availed of its use, or involved in its operation, no human life would be threatened by it, no community destroyed by it, no future threatened by it?
>
> Or,
>
> The application of any scientific principle should do unto others as we would wish to have done to ourselves by others applying the same principle.

A strong reinforcement of an alternative technology's limiting principle would be the absence of restrictions on information regarding any scientific principle and the rejection of any restrictive rights of ownership in regard to the application of any scientific principle.

This does not negate all forms of ownership. There are natural rights of ownership that may be derived along the following lines: There should be no right of ownership in the design of a piano; anyone who can build the piano should be free to build it. On the other hand, in the playing of that piano there is a natural ownership right pertaining to the person who plays it this way or that way—the ownership being of the technique and style of playing which inheres in the person, not in the machine. The machine (the piano) involves the application of scientific principles. The playing involves also the application of human skill. One (the principle) is informational and should not be restricted. The other (the playing) is an interior ability and cannot be *other* than owned by the performer, even though many may share in the listening.

Nuclear technology is a challenge to this notion and there are these points regarding it:

The only aggressive use of nuclear technology has been during periods of maximum ownership; i.e., the monopoly period. On the other hand, today's widespread distribution of fissile materials, through the programs of *peaceful* use, makes perfectly possible the criminal use of nuclear technology by a small group of people, a discrete human community, if you will. That community, however, would not have been involved in the other parts of the process of an alternative technology. They would have merely stolen the wherewithal for their crime from a corporate technological enterprise such as the state or a giant power company, or they would *be* a state or a giant power company.

The pertinent facet of an alternative technology here is that, in such a technology, the prior necessities of the technology, such as the refinement of the uranium, also would have had to be the responsibility of a discrete human community.

The power requirements of uranium refinement today are such that not even all the existing nuclear power generators are said to be capable of producing enough energy to have created their own uranium feed stocks. Discrete communities, in order to refine uranium, would have to undergo massive energy deficits or charges against their environment and society. If the charge could not be passed along, if it had to be borne locally, might not there be the best chance of avoiding the process at the outset? Might not nuclear technology, then, be restricted, in the nature of things, to such small scale, and seemingly benign applications as research tracer isotopes and medical materials? Against this hope must be contrasted the so-far failed hope of simply controlling the technology by agreements not among communities but among institutions.

Or take the final dilemma of the position of control versus the position of decentralization: What force on earth or beyond it could control an agency given the absolute power to stamp out nuclear technology? Wouldn't such a force have to be armed *with* it, to enforce against any adversary who might gain it? Wouldn't such an agency have to keep the technology alive even if just to identify its reappearance elsewhere? And even if the members of such an agency could be psycho-controlled to resist all temptations to aggression or even be robots incapable of aggression, wouldn't either technology suggest the ability of the "controllers of the controllers" to use their power in exactly opposite, or aggressive fashion?

Finally, where is the best repository of human freedom? In free humans? In a restrictive institution? Obviously this is a central concern for us all. But even considering the question open and debatable, should we not press ahead with thinking about the alternative technology?

The ultimate point of departure between a world of technological terror and tyranny and a world of humane tools for human purposes might be a culture in which the scientific principle is applied only for and by human communities—communities of individuals responsible for the resources and operation of the process.

In the growth of such a culture there is an absolute requirement for the understanding of natural (scientific) principles by people. Just as the mystification of social principles in religion (molding society to heavenly designs—i.e., lordly power —rather than society growing organically from participatory

life) produces the mystified nation-state and the corporate society, so does a mystified science—a science excluding common
understanding—produce corporate technology.

The democratization of ordinary life, the establishment of
participatory citizenship, is not possible without general understanding of its principles such as the arduous necessity of participation, the responsibility for actions, the social contract as
process and agreed procedure rather than as privileged power.

The humane use of technology is not possible, either, without
such understanding. Just as with social citizenship, scientific or
technological citizenship cannot be delegated in a permanent
institutional manner without being lost.

To control one's part in social life or technological life (actions involving work other than artistic or familial creativity or
relationships) it is essential to be an operator of technology or
at least to understand fully the principles of the operation so as
to prevent caste or priestly hierarchical decisions from being
passed down, rather than shared.

Paul and Percival Goodman, in their book *Communitas,* elaborate on this point:

> Technology is a sacred cow left strictly to (unknown)
> experts, as if the form of the industrial machine did not
> profoundly affect every person; and people are remarkably
> superstitious about it. They think it is more efficient to
> centralize, whereas it is usually more inefficient. . . .
> They imagine as an article of faith that big factories must
> be more efficient than smaller ones; it does not occur to
> them, for instance, that it is cheaper to haul machine parts
> than to transport workmen.
>
> Indeed, they are outraged by good humored demon-
> strations of Borsodi that, in hours and minutes of labor,
> it is probably cheaper to grow and can your own tomatoes
> than to buy them at the supermarket, not to speak of the
> quality. Here once again we have the inevitable irony of

history; industry, invention, scientific method, have opened new opportunities, but just at the moment of opportunity, people have become ignorant of specialization and superstitious of science and technology, so that they no longer know what they want, nor do they dare to command it. The facts are exactly like the world of Kafka: a person has every kind of electrical appliance in his home, but he is balked, cold-fed, and even plunged into darkness because he no longer knows how to fix a faulty connection.

That irony persists. While communities break down under the onslaught of large-scale development, technological advances have reached the point where one can speak with some confidence of the immediate possibility of neighborhood, or municipal, self-sufficiency. We are involved in what John Blair has called "The New Industrial Revolution," the revolution of new techniques, new tools, and new materials which allow for decentralized technology that is relatively simple to use and inexpensive to operate. As Dr. Blair states: "These new materials are neither labor intensive, nor capital intensive. They are knowledge intensive."

But, although the technology and knowledge are available, people seem to be becoming even more unknowledgeable and insecure—and even superstitious—about technological factors. The current discussions of food prices, energy shortages, and housing scarcity almost always revolve around national and international factors. They are seen as solely economic problems on a grand scale, not as material problems on a natural scale.

The purpose of many experiments and experiences is to seek, in practical terms, more knowledge of the possibilities of democratized science, nonhierarchical and small-scale organization and technology. Here and abroad, the development of "village technology" occupies many groups. "Intermediate technology" or "low impact technology" is used to describe the work of others. "Community technology" is used to describe some of the experiments in an urban setting, such as the one described earlier with which I am involved.

The potential of our project even as it gets off the ground suggests the breadth of possibilities. To repeat, and expand somewhat, we have developed a satisfactory technology for the high-intensity production of food fish in urban basements, on a scale sufficient for neighborhood self-sufficiency. Solar heating, cooking, cooling, and power generating devices are being tested. Fuels such as hydrogen and methanol will be studied for local production. Windmills suited to urban conditions will be tested. Hydroponic gardens, in rooftop greenhouses, as well as traditional gardens in unused urban land spaces, are part of the project. There is a major study already outlined to understand the ways in which, for an urban neighborhood, the entire food-waste cycle could be closed, thus turning human and household waste from a problem to a resource, and losing the often dangerous distance between where food is grown and where it is eaten.

The possibilities and meaning of small-scale industrial or even mineral production, with a community base, and the redesign of transportation and construction systems are also being explored. Throughout the project we remain aware of the many interactions among, as well as within, neighborhoods and regions.

But, overall, it is contended by our actions that in any consideration of new life-styles there must be serious consideration also of the material base of that life-style. It is that consideration which occupies me these days. And it is from that consideration that I derive the most optimistic sense of possibility for a life-style that is human in scale, pacific in its impact upon the natural world generally, fully aware of the consequences of human action and actively seeking knowledge of those consequences.

In such a life-style, technologies would be applied not simply because they were known but only because they were prudently needed. It would be a world of diversity, not frantic conformity. Physicists undoubtedly would pursue the deeper meanings of material particles, but perhaps with accelerators made by themselves, rather than in remote factories by government grant. Medical researchers undoubtedly would chase the virus into its molecular lair, but health care might be more a matter of everyday community activity than an exotic performance in a marble hall. Gravity might be conquered for some purposes, and yet the horse might serve perfectly well to carry a person for other purposes. And food, of course, would be a matter of nutrition, rather than packaging.

In this life-style of human scale, based upon a technology of a similarly suitable scale, society could emerge from the collapsing structure of the state, democracy could reach out from the fallen hierarchies, communities of individual responsibility and group purpose could replace the corporate structures of anonymous, unaccountable decision and private purpose fueled by public servitude.

And then there might be a life-style that is distinctly human. We even suspect that, behind the histories of the kings and the wars, there always has been a reality in which many humans, through most time, behaved *as* humans; helping, caring, creating, and loving. Having human styles of life.

10

COMING HOME

At two of the first seminars I ever attended at the Institute for Policy Studies I heard two points made which I have never forgotten and which stand for me as actual beacons in finding my way through complicated matters to simple truths.

At one, Milton Kotler remarked that every person preaching on behalf of social change should be willing to, should be able to, and should be required to state clearly, "What's in it for me?" People who preach social change to help "the masses," to aid "the poor," to succor "the suffering," and who say they have no other motive might be saints but more regularly turn out to be social sinners, masking ambition behind nobility.

Marc Raskin, at another seminar, listened patiently while a colleague delivered a ponderous and pompous ultimatum on behalf of some then-current "cause" and then asked, "Would it be possible for you to speak as just a human being and not as a force of history?" People who preach social change as though they are mere messengers of fate, or fury, or history, or a messiah do not often seem content to remain mere messengers. They move to mastery as fast as they can.

Sometime later, one of our colleagues, a remnant of the old left and thus at constant odds with the generally libertarian spirit of the rest of the Institute, made an impassioned defense of concentrating power in the hands of a few to benefit the future of the many. Recalling the Kotler-Raskin formulations I asked if the person would be willing to assume such power and to exercise it. Of course, was the reply. Why you? I asked. "Because I have studied and know what needs to be done." For everyone in the entire world? I asked. "Of course," was the reply. "Marxism-Leninism shows the correct way for everyone."

There is nothing more healthy to a spirit of resistance than to see a monarch close up; to understand that under all the noble rhetoric of history and destiny there is a human brow itching for a crown. At that particular meeting I saw a brow itching on its left side. Previously I had seen so many itching on the right side. Briefly I had thought there might be a preference. I don't think that any more.

No person is so grand or wise or perfect as to be the master of another person. Teacher, perhaps. Setter of good examples, perhaps. Genius, perhaps. But master, no. There are times when a doctor or a carpenter, a musician or an artist, might lead you in a certain undertaking because of energy, skill, or information that you might not have. But that is temporary and special. It is, or should be, merely commonsense expedience and, of course, it should be possible because of your agreement, also in common sense. It is not mastery. The carpenter does not retain leadership when the planks are all laid and the enterprise shifts to painting. The doctor is not a master to be consulted when a song is to be sung, or a plant plucked. Commonplace leadership can be by virtue of skill, energy, or information which, although universally accessible, might not be universally sought. Mastery is by conferred or inherited power, by accumulation of privilege, by institutional support, by the holding of information which is deliberately restricted in order to gain or hold power.

The difference is clear in our everyday lives. When it becomes clear that the same differences pertain in all human affairs, acts of liberation might truly be the most lasting and significant ever. Liberation would not mean to move from one set of masters to another, as is urged by the spirit of party (whether masked as Marxism-Leninism, Republicanism, Capitalism, Communism, Socialism, or orthodoxy of any sort). Liberation in its grandest meaning should be liberation from imposed authority and institutionalized hierarchy itself. Liberation merely from a tyrant is a temporary thing, as it has turned out. Liberation from tyranny is a more decent, more substantial goal.

There is a special variant of this concern which I must mention although it is happily of declining importance. For some time during the sixties and early seventies there were people who were regarded as both left wingers and as counter-cultural who said that the only way to liberate oneself was to be liberated *from* self altogether and to reject all authority, whether imposed or not. Thus, it was said that when a person's sense of self disappeared, the person could be one with the universe. Thus, it was said that *any* knowledge was essentially elitist and essentially either trivial or evil. Such people even resented language since it implied an intellectual activity. They wanted activity of "the whole person" and in some bizarre way seemed to exempt the human mind from that whole. They wanted to obliterate the sense of self which, beyond any other feeling, seems to me to be the feeling which is most human, which is, I feel, the only sensible definition for "human nature."

Such people drifted to farms where they listened for inner voices rather than paying attention to sun and frost and rain. They wanted so to be a part of the universe that they forgot the nature of Earth. Many drifted even further, into eternally drugged somnolence, assuring with chemistry the incoherence they had sought spiritually. More grew through and out of it, retaining the gentle reverence for inexplicable "spirit," but also decently in tune with the spirit of material skills and the material world, including the world of other human beings with whom they finally learned to communicate as human beings, with words, with music, with shared work, with love, rather than as they once tried, with cross-legged, ultimately detached and isolated "vibes."

Such people are strong forces for social change today, diligently going about homely tasks in familiar settings. So are most people who, having held some strong position which they subjected to critical analysis, and then changed, have moved from fanaticism to determination. People who have never really cared, who have served only whatever master was most near or convenient, are least likely to change or to support change. They will change masters easily enough, as in the way so many conservatives changed to liberal-like groupies for Presidential power. They will change little else because they have little else to change, little to give but their loyalty. The same is true of partisan leftists who lose their minds to slogans and their actions first to demagogues, then to commissars, and finally to police sergeants.

Change will be made around such people, a swirling process which, although it may never move many people from the center at any particular time, will always be unsettling them around the edges of their existence, finally eroding away their protective shells and, in the best of circumstances, showing the possibility of change rather than commanding it.

But what *is* in it for me? And can I work for change without posing as or seeming to be a force of history? Can I do it as a person among many people, a self among many selves, a neighbor among neighbors, in a neighborhood among neighborhoods, in a world which is a real and particular point in a real and at least recognizable universe?

When I was very young, I most wanted to be a scientist, isolated and brilliant, probing and illuminating mysteries, a pure soul floating in a laboratory universe, detached, cool, exalted. Then I wanted to be famous and a bit rich, noted for having political power without the mess of political responsibility, a speech-writing ghost but still a sort of pure soul floating in a marble-halled universe, detached, cool, and celebrated. What I want now is so different. It requires nothing but space and time and work. It does not float, it walks in the neighborhood. It is not detached, it is a mosaic of meetings, friendships, tasks, celebrations (without celebrity). It still includes science but it knows science as the most social of human actions, a shared heritage, an age-long persistence of reason, something that floats beautifully in the head, not in outer space, an occasion for the pleasures of creativity more than the proddings of pride. For honor it substitutes, simply, honesty and for loyalty it certainly substitutes friendship.

What I want from social change is freedom from all those institutional chains which in the past have bound us to the purposes and projects of others, without consent, without real recourse. I want the freedom to be responsible for my own actions, and I want my actions to be judged by those whom those actions affect. I want my citizenship in a community to be a nondelegatable aspect of my life, reflecting my place in the community and respecting yours. I want to live in a community where people are so sure of themselves, as human beings, that they can respect differences in others without being deferential to difference, or frightened by it, or cowed by it. I want to join in the applause for a neighbor's task superbly done but I do not want to be enlisted in a fan club. I want to live in a community where, no matter any other skills, decent human beings all will practice those skills which all may possess in common, truthfulness, consideration of others, a sense of proportion in undertakings and in ambitions, and the various human traits associated with deep love of another and an abiding respectful sense of self.

In practical terms, as it turns out, it means living very much as I live today. For me and for many people I know, social change has been made, even though we know it has been made within institutional spaces which could close at a moment's notice. Changes have been made. They have not been secured.

To secure such change does not mean that everybody in the world must act the same way or agree to the same cultures, to the same work, to the same patterns of community or social life or civic interaction. But it does mean, so far as I can see, that practices which permit a few to lord it over many would have to be resisted, and eventually abolished. So long as the purposes of power are placed ahead of the purposes of people generally, free communities and self-reliant people will never be secured or general. The purposes of power are to control most people by the decisions of a few people. The general language is that it is done for "their own good." The reality is that people who are controlled, even if by the most benevolent prince, lord, or god, are mere puppets. They dangle on strings held by others, never to dance their own steps or to hold another hand except by permission of the strings on their own hands.

Perhaps this is the area in which, ultimately, even as passionate a lover of reason as I am, I must admit that mere belief rules. I simply believe that freedom is a better and more desirable condition for human beings. If pressed to prove it, I could go no further than to say that humans have the tool to conceive and to live in freedom: the human mind. That mind, that tool of thought and conception and even idealization, would seem to have no function of importance if it did not urge and press people toward that freedom. If freedom were not a desirable human condition, then why has the urge to it persisted through the millennial attempts to supplant it with mystery, mysticism, despotism, authority, legality, regimentation, and regulation?

Freedom is functionally appropriate to human beings. Freedom is a persistent idea among human beings even though it has never been a globally dominant fact, even when the earliest humans roamed in what might seem freedom, they were of course bound to harsh necessity and could exercise only fairly feeble choices, choosing rarely, even if brilliantly, to decorate a cave; choosing painfully to make a tool a bit better than the one made before it, and so forth.

But beyond that, again, I will admit that the idea must ultimately be defended as a belief; a belief that it is better to live self-realized and self-responsible than to live dominated, to live with a sense of self only as defined by others, and to live on the end of strings which, called destiny, history, or national politics, are actually pulled or cut by other human beings wearing the masks of power.

It is also my belief, bolstered by but certainly not proven by travel, study, and experience over more than a half century, that most people on earth have a deep-seated feeling that free communities would be the best communities and the free life the best life. Most people with whom I discuss this agree that, preferentially, it is correct. They only disagree with whether it is practical. Fair enough.

Having come to the point where practicality is the question facing us, we can take alternative courses. We can assume that it is impractical. Conventional wisdom says this. Leaders say this. The powerful say this. History says it. To accept the assumption would be to accept the power that flows from the assumption. Science, dialectics, critical judgment, curiosity, call it what you will, urges another course. It urges that we do not assume the teaching of the past without at least measuring it against the knowledge of the present.

First we have relatively new social knowledge to test it all against. Rather than the customary histories of the past, histories which were recitals of the actions of rulers (King Glotz waged war against the Prince of Putz) we now have histories based on the most painstaking archeology and reading of everyday records of commerce and culture rather than just regal records. From this social knowledge it becomes very clear that beyond the realm of rulers there always have been societies and cultures which have thrived on principles of mutual aid rather than on principles of authority and competition. While the rulers waged their wars, many people went about their day-to-day affairs distant from both the fighting and the institutional power that made it possible. (There have been *no* popular wars, organized by people generally. Wars require institutions of power. Raiding parties can be organized out of self-reliant communities, to be sure. But no matter how brutal, such raids are at least localized and even more feasible to defend against than the rampaging of armies organized under institutional power.)

In short, there exists by demonstration a social capacity of people to live by mutual aid, rather than competition, and in communities. Even cities, which are often these days said to be the "proof" that small scale social organization is impractical, are nothing more than just agglomerations of little communities, gobbled up in the annexations of a powerful administrative unit. The size and scale of city administrations are not a natural but a wholly administrative phenomenon.

Most importantly there is new material knowledge having to do with the use of scientific principles and the use of technology or technics and tools. The more that knowledge of this sort expands, the more apparent it becomes that old-fashioned scales of application are no longer essential. The new technology, it has been exactly said, is neither labor intensive nor capital intensive. It is knowledge intensive. The storage and retrieval of information, so essential to a free society in which information is not hoarded but is disseminated, now give the capability of containing the information of the world's largest library in tiny microfiche dots which require less than a small roomful of file cabinets. Mathematical testing of plans or projects which once might have required armies of technicians or costly years of experimentation now is done in days with machines that could fit in a kitchen, be shared by a neighborhood, and operated by people with skills easily and feasibly acquired. Semiconductors, replacing old vacuum tubes, make electronics a possibility for neighborhood-sized operations rather than just for vast industrial plants. Plastics, perhaps the least wasteful way, among other things, of using fossil hydrocarbons and even vegetable wastes, are handily susceptible to very moderate scales of operation and, since many can replace steel and iron altogether, may show the way to the most extreme reduction of the scale of basic building materials. But even steel, that once most gigantic gobbler of space, fuel, and labor, moves to smaller and smaller production units such as continuous slab casters. Smaller and smaller, and better and better, is an obvious possibility of modern technology. If it is not realized it is not because of physical practicality but because of administrative practicality.

The production of food is the same. Knowing nature, through science, botanists can speak of the technical feasibility of growing food always close to where it is eaten, not wasting so much on transport and packaging and processing. Botanists may say that. Corporate executives do not.

Transportation itself must be viewed not on old assumptions, but afresh. The railroad, virtually abandoned in favor of the highway system, meets with amazing effectiveness many of the most demanding criteria of the environment, of resource conservation, and even social humanism and esthetics. It is not a system with as much inherent slaughter connected with it as the highways. It does not disrupt environments but almost literally disappears into them.

But this does not mean to assume that the notion of highways is obsolete. Maybe what is obsolete is just our notion of what highways *are*. Wooded paths might be highways for air-glide cars, or for horses. The point is not to be taken lightly. There is enough knowledge of the physical world and the use of resources and energy to enable us now to use appropriate rather than merely convenient technologies. The horse is most appropriate to some ways of life. The Amish find the horse perfectly appropriate even though they live in industrial states. A helicopter might be more appropriate as an ambulance in a city, or as a transport vehicle for a factory necessarily far from a population center.

There are myriad possibilities of appropriate ways of doing things. Certainly the rigid, confined monocultures of corporate capitalism and state socialism are denials of this. They are obsolete ways of organizing resources in the sense that resources can be organized in so many more different and more appropriate ways than the singleminded ways of corporate capitalism and state socialism.

All forms of factory production which seem to call for giant, centralized facilities, can alternatively be imagined as small, localized operations using, for instance, direct numerical control (cybernated) machinery. A small plant of this sort in Roanoke, Virginia, for instance, turns out a stunning array of machine parts, required a relatively small capital investment, and is operated by local people who trained easily for the job. The giant plant may be appropriate for a giant corporation and its small owning clique. The small, local plant might be far more appropriate for the interests of a small town and all of the people in it. The environmental impact of small plants, also, might be far more appropriate to a clean and long-lived living space than a giant factory.

Hospitals, now moving right along the path to giantism and even absorption by big corporations, could be imagined alternatively as smaller, more localized facilities for most patient-care problems (and, also, using patients as part of the team rather than as mere bodies to be shunted from pillar to post) with perhaps regional facilities for more complex treatments requiring machines costly to duplicate. But, of course, jurisdictional jealousies would have to be replaced by broad cooperation. The point is that big, competitive hospitals are appropriate to a world of high-profit medicine, freewheeling pharmaceutical firms, and jurisdictional exclusivity. Local facilities might be far more appropriate to the actual needs of local people.

Franchise food chains are appropriate to a world in which power at all levels concentrates into fewer and fewer hands. Also, the products they usually peddle are appropriate to a "game plan" in which chrome gimmickry and heavy advertising replace actual nourishment as the product being peddled. Provision of food, on the other hand, could be imagined in a much more old-fashioned way as simply a matter for local initiative and the resources of local people. The franchise, among other things, deliberately attempts to convince people that they cannot, on their own, do anything. They must seek the help of all-knowing outsiders. Federal laws, and some state ones as well, may play into the hands of this approach, of course, by seriously harassing the efforts of local enterprises and requiring a host of legal advice even to get started. Franchises thrive, in part, by being able to deal with such legal red tape. The franchises, then, might also be said to be appropriate to a system in which red tape does, in fact, strangle creativity and initiative at every turn. Local enterprise would be appropriate to a free society where such harassment did not exist.

The list of alternatives and the analysis of appropriateness are endless. You can probably think of more and better examples. And you should. To expect from a book such as this very detailed answers as to how things should be done is to misunderstand the very spirit of the book and of the freedom I have been talking about.

The freedom I envision is the freedom for you and your neighbors to decide how things should be done, constrained only by consideration that in a free society there is no handy way (as through government programs or absentee property ownership) to force that way on others or to demand that they subsidize it or suffer for it. In short, freedom lives in self-responsibility and is inspired by self-determination. Additionally, in the sort of freedom I cherish, self is always seen as part of community since I have no disposition to live as a hermit and since I see living with and working with other people as one of the truly human delights of life. For those who feel otherwise and who are convinced that they live best when they live without reference to other people, it should be clear that freedom affords them every opportunity to do that—but to do it solely by their own effort. Heroic hermits who say they live by their own lights alone, but then exhibit inherited wealth or stock dividends, do not, to me, make a very good case. There is a particularly odd breed of theoretical loners who, for instance, claim that they will not be bound by anyone else's wishes. They flourish their unbridled egos like battle banners, and tell us that they stand, walk, and, apparently, talk alone, proud, mighty and unchecked. I sigh. Most of them that I have met are sad, dependent people who grow no food, build nothing, seem singularly inept overall and, when asked how they support their grand and unbridled egos, blazingly reveal that they deal in the commodities market or in foreign exchange or some such nonsense. They are like gamblers, dependent upon the operators of the casino. They claim independence but they are totally dependent upon complex structures of finance which they have not built, which they do not control, which they do not operate. They merely nibble, like mice, at the edges of corporate capitalism and delude themselves that they are free. There are dangers for all of us in misperceiving the meaning of freedom. It surely doesn't sensibly include freedom from hunger if you are removed from food. It doesn't include freedom from cold if you are removed from warmth. Freedom is not freedom *from,* in any case. It is freedom *to*—to be responsible, to be a person, not a cog, to be creative, affectionate, or, on the other hand, to withdraw, but to withdraw without mistaking that withdrawal for freedom. The withdrawn person does not become free. Those who withdraw usually become dependents of some sort. (And, to repeat what may be obvious but which never should be forgotten, none of this implies that people who are withdrawn from work because of natural causes—infirmity, age, lack of mind—are to be abandoned because they cannot be self-responsible. They need to be cared for, of course. It is my notion here that they need to be cared for by the people closest to them.)

My vision of freedom, then, is formed around the rights of natural association, of people coming together in community for perhaps varied reasons, even for accidental geographic reasons. It is formed from the observed ability of people to decide for themselves, in such a natural association, how best to get along together, how to work, how to play, how to make divisions between those things which are wanted to be done alone and those wanted to be done together, and so forth.

The vision emphasizes being a person and doing things in a specific time and place. This is an important point. Alternative visions (particularly those we usually think of as liberal) reject the notion of time and place and substitute instead the notion of cosmopolitanism and eternity. The central value of such alternative visions is cultural and physical mobility, moving around. Such visions are never work-centered or very keen about science, knowledge, or cooperative efforts since they see people as pretty much isolated social units bouncing around on the rungs of mobility ladders, and not working so much as being employed.

The perpetrators of these visions apparently feel that, for instance, the resource waste and pollution of giant jets are quite justified by making it possible for "anybody" to have lunch in London and dinner in New York. The fact that there is only enough magnesium and petroleum in the entire world to permit just a tiny fraction of people to enjoy such a luxury does not bother them because they always mean just a few when they say everybody, anyway.

Such people argue against any idea of localism for similar special reasons. Local communities (as opposed, for example, to a global village) might, they dither, be culturally exclusive, might even exclude certain people (as many white communities used to and as some black communities do now). No matter that they and their friends may live in those most exclusive of all communities—the communities of affluence—they worry about local freedom. Every community, they feel, should be just like every other community. They hate differences and probably fear them. From difference comes change.

They justify it all theoretically by talking endlessly about eternity, about future generations. Local freedom is to be avoided because, in local settings, people might become too interested in current affairs and not spend enough time dwelling on future generations. I personally think that is nonsense. People who are involved in constant travel, as a matter of fact, might be far more careless about resources and the future than people who might have to face that future directly, themselves, and where they are.

Not to make a virtue out of never moving. I suggest simply that most work and most living is done by most people, for very practical reasons, in one or a few places and not in little jumps and hops around the globe.

Further, the sort of community that requires day-to-day human cooperation most is a community with a real location, a place where people do live and where they would be best advised to live together in mutual aid.

Again, it is not the function of a vision, it seems to me, to tell you what your community should be like. People are different. They do and should form different communities. The freedom to do it is the crucial point.

Prophetic visions of freedom, I believe, should be visions of the possibility that freedom *is possible* and not visions of the exact shape of the things to come.

Let me suggest a test of visions. If the vision is of fairly exact, universally prescriptive, systems which will *serve* people, which do not require that the people actually make and operate the system, which see people as consumers rather than producers, then the vision constitutes a concrete mold for an abstract notion of sameness.

If, on the other hand, the vision may not be of an exact system, but of a way of life in which systems arise by consent and cooperation and, most of all, by participation, with the process being precious and the results being local, special, and *not* universalized, then the vision is an abstract mold for concrete, socially open-ended diversity.

Neither vision can be realized in a stroke. The visions of sameness do emphasize, usually, great strokes which are given great importance, such as "the revolution," or as in the inordinate importance attached to the elevation of particular leaders, but the fact of the matter is that human events like human habitations are put together a board here, a footing there, a shingle there.

Many of the small works (the sidings, the doorknobs, you might say) toward the sort of society I cherish have been made. There are people around the world who are experimenting with, or even settling down to live with, very cooperative forms of community, large and small, and with very cooperative forms of work as well. These people are not giving up anything; they are gaining much. They would not concede that forsaking a fourteen-hour-a-day grind to get a Cadillac is a sacrifice. They would prefer as a positive virtue the ability to create alternative transportation for themselves—as well as an alternative to the fourteen-hour days which (what with transportation and other demands) is far more characteristic of corporate capitalism than the old-fashioned eight-hour day. (Just how many hours a day do you spend getting to and from, recovering, and worrying about or suffering the results of your job or keeping up with the social demands that it generates?)

Experimentation is at the heart of change and social health, it seems to me. But it should not, certainly, be a heartless experimentation of the liberal sort in which the subjects are other people. A good experimenter should be part of the experiment as well as an observer and a mover. In fact, to stretch the point as far as it will go, modern physics is a constant reminder that the observer cannot be extracted from the experiment at any rate. The very light that enables you to see an experiment has an effect on the experiment itself. The observer's observation is part of and not detachable from the experiment.

But of course there are steps to be taken in many areas and many ways. I do not even discount for a moment the importance of steps taken in the most familiar places, even those places most hostile to local freedom and to the concepts of cooperation, as opposed to competition, and the concepts of participatory freedom as opposed to institutional power.

For instance, there is the matter of the withholding tax, both at state and national levels. It is this particular device which, in this day and age, actually makes vast government power possible in this country. I believe that it goes without saying that if the various government levels could not take money from people before they even get their hands on it, people would simply be unwilling and unable to support government of the size that now dominates us.

There is a point of very important principle here. It seems difficult today to say that America is governed by the consent of the governed. The withholding tax, passed as a wartime measure to support the Second World War, has surely not been the subject of continuing popular consent. Rather than having a chance to consent to this most crucial foundation of government power, people have been simply subjected to it. It is possible to say, of course, that the governed consent at least tacitly, by supporting Congressmen who will not repeal the withholding tax. Therefore, in order to truly test whether we are being governed by consent, or coercion, it would seem to me that there is no more crucial venture than to subject the withholding tax to constant voter review, wherever it exists. This is a law unlike most laws. It is not some detail of government power which need not concern us except on rare occasions. It is the very financial foundation of government power and it needs to concern us every day. It would seem to me that a high order of legislative priority, then, would be to seek referenda on the withholding tax in the states where it exists and, finally, to subject the national withholding tax to constant review through court challenges where possible and through Congressional action and even through constitutional amendment, as many conservatives, in one of their most truly radical gestures, have desired. (I wonder how many so-called conservatives, today, would want to, literally, undermine their beloved government by abolishing the financial foundation of that government?)

Since it is sensible to suggest what might happen subsequent to such an abolition, this might be said: First, the size of government would be subjected to the most serious discipline by citizen action which, in effect, withdrew the government's power to write checks without regard for income. Second, while a sense of national projects exists there undoubtedly will be need for national taxes. How to suggest an alternative? Marcus Raskin, of the Institute for Policy Studies, has long advocated a system in which individuals could earmark some amount of money for specific federal projects, even within the context of an overall budget suggested by Congressional action. It might work this way: Congressional action would specify a budget of so many dollars, to cover all envisioned federal activities. An individual share of this (perhaps on a flat-rate, no-loopholes basis) would come to so many dollars. Taxpayers, however, could assign their share to whatever purpose they deemed most useful, withholding it from any other purpose. Congress and the government, after that annual tax vote had been taken, would then have to re-jigger programs to fit funds. For the supercautious, who might fear that nobody would support certain federal activities, there might be a proportional method in which part of the tax share would be for general use of the government, with only another part assignable by the taxpayer.

Of course none of that is part of what I hope the world eventually will be like. I am personally convinced that a society of mutual aid, without coercive institutions, could exist and thrive. Cooperation would replace enforced taxation, for instance. To those who say that people would not cooperate in supporting government such as we now have, I say, "Exactly!" They would not.

But, admitting that my view is extreme, there are nevertheless many alternatives to the present way of governing that certainly would be improvements. They are mentioned to indicate that between here and hope, there are a lot of possible way stations and it would not be prudent at all to simply waive judgment as to which might be preferable even if, in the long run, none is needed and, as I hope, could all be replaced by day-to-day cooperation.

The national defense function, which seems to preoccupy people who might be willing to see freedom spread in every other area, might also be seen in a way that would make at least some sense to defense fanatics *and* disarmament fanatics.

Such a system as that of the ocean-roving Polaris submarines seems as close as anything to a real deterrent against anyone else's use of nuclear weapons. So even if defense preoccupies you, why should it preoccupy you past the Polaris system? Other than nuclear weapons, what else *are* we guarding against? Is it really a possibility that we require a vast air force and ground force to guard against an actual Russian invasion? Incredible! With Polaris submarines roaming the oceans? Besides, who in the world would maintain control in Russia if the Red Army moved to America? And even if it did, can you do anything but weep at the prospect of Russian soldiers—probably no better or no worse or even much different from our own soldiers—grappling with the resistance movements of Alabama, Texas, and the lower East Side of Manhattan?

No, the government of the United States, common sense tells us, maintains vast air armadas and divisions of foot soldiers in order to wage conventional warfare: a sort of warfare that no nation on the face of the earth actually is prepared to wage against us! Would Canada invade? Would Mexico? Wouldn't the ultimate threat that we could pose against anyone and, in fact, everyone on the face of the earth with the Polaris system deter crazy adventures? Wouldn't a volunteer militia at home simply round off the defense? Our maintenance of a huge defense establishment, beyond the Polaris system, can only be justified by a plan to wage war ourselves (as in Vietnam) or by a plan to serve as the police force for the entire world. Both plans, it seems to me, have over the years been rejected by Americans generally. Only the government persists with them.

Again, I do not mention this matter of defense because I feel it of basic and ongoing importance to a free society. Hardly. I feel that a free society with free people in free communities would both inspire peace everywhere and make clear the folly of attempts at conquest. What would a conqueror win? Total resistance! Who wants or needs that?

I would hope that, if political power could be withdrawn from great governments and passed back to people where they live, the entire obsessive psychology of big arms to empower big nations would subside and soften. For those who think that a disarmed world is as hopeless a vision as a free world, I can only say that big arms and big nations are even more hopeless; they keep us all on the brink of disaster. It may be called visionary to seek an alternative. It also could be called purely practical.

The defense matter is raised as an example, only an example, of ways in which, even while much of the old system remains, we could ease our way into a better future.

Other possibilities, quickly mentioned, are:

—Laws requiring full personal accountability of bureaucrats, so long as bureaucrats exist. This would enable citizens to bring suit against individual bureaucrats for exceeding authority, misfeasance, and other malperformances of duty. Such legislation has been suggested and deserves wide support even from those who, with me, also are working earnestly for a system in which bureaucracy would be abandoned altogether.

—Laws restricting, absolutely, the ability of rich corporations, individuals, and labor unions to dump large amounts of money into political campaigns. With Milton Kotler of the Institute for Policy Studies, I have been working for some time on a plan which would be almost a modernized poll tax in which people wishing to vote would buy a certain amount of "electoral scrip" which they could give to the candidates of their choice. Candidates could pay for major campaign expenses such as travel and media *only* with this scrip. Cash payments for any such thing would be a crime. This would mean that candidates, from the outset, even at primary time, would have to have the support of citizens at large and not just a few fat cats.

—Any and all actions which transfer power to neighborhoods and away from larger political jurisdictions. Mark Hatfield, the exemplary Senator from Oregon, has made interesting proposals along these lines. His legislation would enable neighborhoods to be identified and then to move toward actual political identity and power, taking over more and more functions now exercised by other levels of government.

Neighborhoods actually are towns. All of them started as towns, before annexation into the city. Many still have town characteristics, although they are a distinct part of the city. Beyond that, however, the actual towns exist, thousands of them, all across America, places where the potential for a life of human scale and freedom have always been obvious. (Liberals, of course, shy from the towns as they do from the neighborhoods, fearing that they will be—as some are—small minded, mean, even vicious. But, since nations are meaner and more vicious by a thousandfold, freedom's chances in small places seem at least a good bet, certainly worthy of a chance.)

For the towns of America, particularly, I would urge the following checklist of immediate possibilities:

(1) To know what you're up against, you've got to know exactly where you stand. Here are some steps that could be taken:

—A community survey of the patterns of ownership in your town. Who owns the property? Local people? Out-of-towners? Financial institutions? It makes a difference, but few towns have ever bothered to study it closely.

—A tax study. Where does the tax money go? What is the full flow of public money into the community and out of the community? Many a town has been astonished to discover that more goes out than ever comes in, in terms of public money actually locatable in the town.

—A study of the real economy of the town. What jobs are there? What jobs *were* there? What is produced, by which people, on what machines or from what resources, and, most importantly, for whose profit and security?

—The material base of the community. Where does the food come from? The energy? Building materials, other raw materials? In short, what is the material situation of the town, overall, not just in terms of isolated businesses, interests, or instances?

(2) With a clear picture of the town, you and your neighbors may be able to share a clear vision of a better future, of how to change things. Here are some areas of possibility:

—The threatened closing of a key business or industry is a

crucial, even fatal, time for many a town. Does the town have to accept the closing and suffer the consequences or can it act in its own best interest, legally, to do something about it? The subject is wide open for imaginative study. The right of eminent domain, used so often to acquire property for traditional public use, could be explored as a possibility to acquire actual productive facilities whose loss would cripple the town.

—Community ownership of productive facilities can be considered. This process is familiar when it comes to such things as recreation areas, water supply, even some power companies. Could and should the community expand that concept to other areas to sustain its survival?

—Community development of new productive facilities to enhance the self-reliance and the survivability of the town can be considered. Many communities are familiar with the process of a tax-supported industrial site being offered to an outside business to bring them in. Might the town be better served by going one important step beyond the traditional process and studying the possibility of a publicly-owned production *facility* as well as a publicly-supported *site?*

—Community federations of self-support and assistance can be formed. This is a possibility that might grow out of the steps already mentioned. If one community chooses to support its own survivability by community-owned and -operated productive facilities, it might be reasonable to assume that others will follow suit—and that trade between those self-supporting community enterprises would be a natural development which could lead to actual regional federations of such community work.

(3) The material building blocks of community survival and self-reliance are energy, food, housing, and transportation. Here are some possibilities:

—Traditional energy sources such as electricity and gas are often too slow in responding to community needs. Frankly and honestly, they are committed first to the needs of owners whose interests may lie elsewhere. Many towns have taken over power and light facilities for community ownership as a step to bring the interests of the enterprise and the community closer together. By all reports, it is a perfectly workable system.

—Traditional energy sources are not the only sources that a town should study. Solar power is a highly developed technology that can economically supply certain energy needs today. In some towns, even water and wind power could be studied. In virtually all towns, the problems of waste disposal and power are closely related—with unused, and often polluting, sewage being a major problem rather than being treated as a resource from which major amounts, for instance, of methane fuel can be economically produced for community sale and use as well as the by-product production of high-quality, safe fertilizers. Alternate energy studies should have an important place in your town in these days of energy crisis.

—There may also be alternate sources of food. Traditional food sources are often distant farming areas whose produce is shipped expensively to your town, through large chains, while local produce is shipped elsewhere in an extravaganza of patchwork marketing. Food system planning for your town, taking advantage of the latest high technology growing processes—which are carefully nonpolluting and consciously nutritious—could be an important step toward survival and self-reliance. Tremendous amounts of food, and at low cost, can be raised right in the center of a town, even the smallest town, using these technologies (such as those described briefly elsewhere in this book—basement trout "farms" and rooftop hydroponic gardens). Cooperative, community-controlled marketing systems also have yielded cost and community benefits. Your town's food system is a crucial element in your town's survival.

—And new and better ways to build. Traditional housing codes and techniques have led to waves of so-called urban renewal or, in many cases, urban dislocation. But many townspeople have begun to wonder if just tearing down part of a town is real progress after all. Making better use of existing housing is an alternative. A community study could be made to show how. And would the community be better served by a system of community-controlled, perhaps individual neighborhood housing plans than by large-scale plans often drawn by outsiders? What good or bad effects would there be to the use of innovative rather than traditional building techniques? Would community-controlled real estate firms help ease the problems of runaway speculation?

—Do unused properties, held for speculation, present a clear and present danger to town survival and stability? If they do, if space is wasted for the profit of people who may not even live in the town, or if the future of the many is balanced dangerously on the speculation of a few, the community might want to consider, for example, new programs of urban homesteading, with unused properties being returned to productive and locally needed use by people in the actual neighborhoods involved.

—Is your town being buried by a road? With a good part of every town already paved over, with superhighways lacing the land for purposes which no longer seem quite so important compared to the problems of everyday survival, many towns may want to start doing something about transportation rather than just accepting everything that the highway interests throw at them. Some of the possibilities might involve the reshaping of certain town areas exclusively for bus, bike, or electric cart travel; the use of small-vehicle "jitneys" for community transportation, operated by community people; the use of equipment that is often idle (school buses, official cars) for new community purposes; the closing of certain streets; and restrictions of certain types of high pollution vehicles to certain areas. As with everything else in a time of really pressing problems, the needs of the community should be carefully studied without being inhibited by those who advise against any change simply because "we've never done it that way before."

The main point is this: Towns must look to their own survival today. The whims and fancies of traditional ownership patterns are clearly too flighty and too shallow for the deep needs of most communities today. The people in the towns do not need slogans and ideological promises. They need real substance and substantial community enterprises for sustained community self-reliance.

Actually, the steps outlined that your town *could* take are not very radical if viewed in the American tradition. That tradition, I like to think, has always preached self-reliance, creativity, and community enterprise. Americans have always been described as the people who reject doing everything "by the book." Today, the book is being rewritten anyway.

Hopefully, no American town will perish just because it wouldn't turn the next page of its own history.

Of overall importance in even thinking about the immediate steps that can be taken toward the future, there is an attitude which I would say is crucial. It involves resistance to any extensions of government power even for the most benevolent reasons, along with resistance to the extension of corporate powers, even for the most plaintive reasons of efficiency. In neither case, experience tells us, can we expect the claimed good to endure. What endures is the power, and power—concentrated social power—is the foremost enemy of freedom.

Most Americans have a healthy distrust of nationalization already. Unfortunately, it is difficult to see the true extent of it in the United States. It is not in official and overt policies that the central government has nationalized so much of our lives (although for the poor, the policies *are* overt and quite complete, enrolling low-income families into almost complete government ownership and control). Nor is it the action of the central government alone that has nationalized so much of our lives. Yet much is nationalized.

Business and industry in the country are being nationalized—but big corporations are doing it, instead of big government. Big government helps, of course, by applying laws and regulations which seriously restrict small businessmen but give the green light to just about anything the big boys want to do.

But how can free private enterprise nationalize our business industry? Isn't that some sort of contradiction in terms? Well, it all depends on how you look at it. One of the most significant aspects of nationalization is that the control of business and industry is put into the hands of a relatively small number of bureaucrats. If the bureaucrats are government bureaucrats, of course, they have the crucial added power of being able to use the police and the military directly to enforce their decisions.

But what if the bureaucrats are actually businessmen themselves? In the most important sense, the effect is the same. Control passes from wherever it used to be into the hands of a relatively small number of bureaucrats. And, even if they can't call on the police and the military directly, we all know that big businessmen can *use* the police and the military (as when they break strikes with soldiers) without much trouble.

The way it has happened in America is evident all around us. Big businesses are gobbling up small business every day. Look around your own hometown. How many businesses are actually owned by people who live in the town? Even the hamburger stands are part of giant corporations these days. The truth is that American business and industry are being nationalized right before our eyes without much opposition at all. Big business is gobbling up control of *all* business just as surely as government gobbles it up in other countries. The differences may look big on paper—but in actual practice, I wonder if they really are. Distant bureaucrats, whether businessmen or politicians, still end up controlling your lives while affairs that once were strictly local become strictly national. They become nationalized.

People who really care about freedom won't care about the labels that are put on this sort of process. They'll look beneath the labels. When they do they will see just what Americans always have feared—the heavy, cold hands of nationalization squeezing the life from our freedom.

Liberals and the old left, generally, still favor the solution of nationalization. The right wing, meantime, will and does argue just the opposite. They want every restriction taken off business and industry. They say profits are never high enough, that all profits are fair and are essential to expansion (expansion in the quantity of business, of course, not enlargement of the quality of life). The difference between the right and the left, when it is all boiled down, is just that the liberals and the old left want all business and industry run by government bureaucrats while the right wing wants it all run by business bureaucrats. Both sides want it done by big, powerful groups, big business or big government.

There is an alternative. It is an alternative that harks back to the original ideas of freedom in America even while it looks ahead to the most technologically advanced demands of the future. The alternative is to *de*centralize rather than centralize business and industrial control. Instead of nationalizing business and industry, such an alternative would call for consideration of turning basic industries and businesses over to the people either of the regions where they operate or to the people who actually work in those businesses or industries.

The alternative of decentralization takes special notice of the role that science and technology should play in our lives as opposed to the role they have played. In the past they have been used primarily to promote profits. The alternative would be to put them into service for people in their hometowns and in their own businesses and industries. Instead of serving rich boards of directors, science and technology could be used primarily to upgrade the quality of life, to make work better and more meaningful, to make our towns and cities more liveable, and to make sure that natural-resource disasters do not overtake us just because of greed.

But most of all, the alternative of decentralization takes into account the overpowering fact that the very problems which plague us today, which make every American vaguely or sharply aware of things not being right, that these very problems have been brought to peril points at a time when big business and big government both have more power than ever before in history. If big central planning and control systems are causing problems everywhere on the globe why should enlarging the power of big central planning be a solution? Wouldn't it be just more of the same old bad news? Decentralization would be an actual alternative, one that would put our future back into our own hands—for better or for worse.

For the sort of life which I want to live and which I see as most fitting to human capabilities, there are no easy or universal answers. What I can do, and have tried to do here, is say what I have done and hope to do. There may be useful information in it. There is, of course, an invitation in it, an invitation to join in the broad process of change that is under way in the world, a change away from authoritarianism, mystification, and institutions, a change toward self-reliance, community, and creative diversity, a change away from massive plans and even cities, a change toward scales of enterprise that are more human in size and humanistic in hope.

There is a fervent personal hope in it: that you will be as critical of the life you now lead as you may well be of the life which I suggest you could lead. You should owe allegiance to no crown, to no guru, to no savior. We are not just senseless atoms in this universe. You are, we are, human; you have, we have, those unique abilities which can set us free—intuition which can inspire discovery and creativity, and reason which can make it whole and meaningful in the natural world.

There can be, therefore, no end to a book like this or to the process of being human. There are only beginnings, endless, dawning, wonderful beginnings. And the good work of being people, friends, lovers—and good neighbors.